To Grandpa —

Happy 83rd. Birthday.

Love

Joyce & Heather

MY OWN YEARS

MY OWN YEARS

BARRY BROADFOOT

1983
Doubleday Canada Limited, Toronto, Ontario
Doubleday & Company, Inc., Garden City, New York

Library of Congress Catalog Card Number 78-68345
ISBN 0-385-14319-2

Typeset by ART-U Graphics Ltd.
Printed and bound in Canada by T. H. Best Printing Company Ltd.
Jacket design by Matthew Berger

Canadian Cataloguing in Publication Data

Broadfoot, Barry, 1926-
  My own years

ISBN 0-385-14319-2

1. Broadfoot, Barry, 1926-   2. Authors, Canadian
(English) — 20th century — Biography.   3. Canada —
Civilization. I. Title.

FC601.B76A35   971.06′092′4   C83-098581-6
F1034.3.B76A35

Song excerpt on page 47 printed by permission of the copyright owner, Jerry Vogel Music
Co., Inc. (successor in interest to F. B. Haviland Pub. Co.)

PREFACE

My editor, Betty Corson, told me I had to write a preface. I replied, "Why does this book, or any book, have to have a preface?" "Because," she said, "readers want to know why the author has written the book."

I'm not sure that was the answer I was looking for, but it made sense. Recalling the thousands of books I have read, it does seem that most if not all nonfiction books do have a preface.

As far as I'm concerned, a preface, or introduction if you will, serves to inform the reader who this presumptuous fellow is who would take his money and his time and leave him materially poorer—but I hope intellectually, philosophically, or even spiritually enriched.

The point of this preface is to pique the interest of anyone who happens to be browsing through the "new book" shelves and who might open this book to this page and read this far and chuckle, "Hey, hey, not bad," and buy it, thus ensuring me a happy and rich old age. I'm not against being rich, or even not poor, and I'm sure it's better to be happy than unhappy. However, at the age of fifty-seven I am not convinced of the advantages of the biblical "threescore and ten."

So, here goes. I was born at an early age in Winnipeg and seem to have mastered the necessary skills to deal with this conundrum called living. Our home was modest but loving; I lived on a quiet, pleasant street and did most of the things my playmates did—except for reading, and there I was the champ. My younger sister and I hated each other through childhood until we discovered that we were nice people and we have been wonderful friends ever since. I was the only kid in Lord Roberts Secondary School with two prominent gold teeth, thanks to a hockey puck I did not see. I was small for my age, but fairly tough and cocky. I rode imaginary horses on the muddy trails along the Red River and dreamed of being an explorer. I got good grades and my old-maid teachers kept saying I could do better.

I enjoyed my childhood. I can still taste those charred wienies roasted over a fire, and I remember fishing endlessly without ever catching more than three-inch bullheads. But what I recall most vividly is my love of reading. As my tastes and appetite broadened, I devoured books on every subject you can think of, and by the time I joined the army at seventeen my eyes were burned out, and I have worn glasses ever since. My knowledge today should be staggering, but I think somehow it all just washed over me. Oh, enough stayed, but I'm not a pedant. I like the way Oscar Levant put it: "a smattering of ignorance"—that's what I have.

You might say—and I wouldn't disagree with you—that I've been in the writing game for a long time. My first job was as a copy boy on the dear, dead-and-gone Winnipeg Tribune in the summer after I graduated from high school, and because there was a war on I quickly became a junior reporter, at twelve dollars a week. The die was cast then, I guess. I went off to war myself and worked on camp newspapers, after which I endured four years of university—the best part of which were my efforts on behalf of the campus newspaper.

In 1949 I headed west in the first snowstorm of the year and landed in Vancouver in the middle of a three-day rainstorm. When the sky cleared and I saw the morning sun polishing the snowy slopes of the North Shore mountains I said, "You can't buy that view for a ten-dollar bill!" With a happy crew of underpaid and overworked lads and lasses I toiled on the now defunct News Herald and in time moved on to Edmonton. When the Bulletin there folded, I joined the British United Press in Montreal and that was another experience, let me tell you! After that I was in Toronto and spent a year in Calgary as manager of the one-man BUP office. Eventually I wound up back in wonderful Vancouver, first on the News Herald again and finally on the Vancouver Sun, a wacky sheet whose frivolities were more imaginary than real. Today, when oldtimers gather around a bottle of whisky, it all makes good telling, listening, and laughing.

During my twenty-six years of newspapering I covered every imagi-

nable kind of story, from hangings to forest fires, to temperamental actresses, and a lot of zany folks and screwy situations too numerous to count. I did just about every job there is to do on newspapers, including two stints as columnist, and traveled a great deal on assignments in Canada and overseas.

Finally one morning in March 1972 I decided that if I was going to be a serious writer I had better get started, and I quit then and there. On five minutes' notice I walked out of the city room and never returned. All I carried was a shoebox half full of mementoes of those happy, often tumultuous, sometimes grim years—but I had a treasury of great memories and friendships with some of the finest people I have ever met.

I had already written four books, all of them about B.C. and of no consequence. When Ten Lost Years *was published by Doubleday in 1973 its success was astounding. Before, I had just been a fun-loving, hard-drinking, and fairly talented character known only to other Canadian newspapermen. Now, I was a celebrity and the pressure was enormous. Everybody wanted a piece of me, something from me. It took me a while to catch on to what was happening.*

I survived the ordeal and went on to write Six War Years, The Pioneer Years, *and* Years of Sorrow, Years of Shame, *all of them best-sellers. My secret is that I write for my fellow human beings, while so many Canadian writers today write for other writers. I'm in love, and my big romance is with my readers so when I write for myself I am writing for their enjoyment too.*

People and offers were zooming in at me from every point on the compass and life was great. Wasn't it? I won't say my personal life did not suffer because it did, and it was my fault alone. Too much booze and then pills, taken innocently at first, caught up with me. I beat them more than two years ago simply by throwing the whole lot down the sink. In the meantime I had retired to a home on Bowen Island and later I moved to a lovely waterfront home in Nanaimo, within view of Bowen and the city of Vancouver. A perfect spot to get down to more "serious writing," I said.

People kept asking me "What's your next book about?" I didn't answer them. For several years I had been banging away at my typewriter, more or less keeping my mind in gear and my fingers supple; and when I finally read over what I had written, I knew I had just been doodling. Then I got to thinking about how my life had been so enriched by my experiences and friendships, and I decided to write a book about them. I set to work in a creative frenzy, combining recent encounters and adventures on the road with more youthful memories. Over eight months the manuscript took shape—and when it was finished, I liked it and so did Doubleday.

Whoever said "I am a part of all that I have met" sure knew what he was talking about; these recollections of people, places, and peregrinations have proved that. Essentially, I write this book for myself, but I hope that others will enjoy it too. I have not tried to be philosophical or tell the world how it should be run; I simply want to share some parts of my own years of living. With luck, "the best is yet to be."

Barry Broadfoot,
Nanaimo, 1983

CONTENTS

MY OWN YEARS

1

N.F.A.—No Fixed Abode

In my day I've met quite a few people with no fixed abode, and each one has a different story to tell. They don't seem to have much in common—except N.F.A.—and I've never been able to figure out exactly what makes them tick. Take the three people in this chapter, for instance...

The young French Canadian farm hand bumming around British Columbia said he felt it was the only way to become a true Canadian. I ask myself if he will ever settle down or will he always be looking for another intriguing name on the map to explore. And I wonder if he ever picked up a few ounces of gold from a long-stripped streambed in Likely...

The hustler in Vancouver told just good enough a story to hold my interest, but what was a high-rolling gambler doing in a cheap room in a small family-run hotel? And was there really a manuscript to show me or was that part of his conning me? I'll never know...

Gordon—no last name—like so many rodeo cowboys was looking for a good ride, some winnings, a few drinks, a soft bed, and a woman. Some make it big and wear expensive boots and marry the daughters of rich oilmen. But many just hit the circuit year after year, like the weary ranch hand lugging his saddle and hobbling down the road to Grand Forks. Did he ever make it or did he just turn into dust and become a part of a burned-out, rocky landscape? Ride 'em, cowboy...

"Have You Ever Been to Likely?"

He was going south on Highway 95 from Prince George when I picked him up. He had been walking resolutely under his large pack and leaving a disreputable band of hitchhikers behind, lying semi-prone against their packs, their transistor radios blaring and at the end of a languid arm raised to each vehicle was a thumb. When they see you are not stopping, the thumb becomes a finger, an obscene gesture.

I slowed down passing him, shot him a quick look, decided, and pulled over. I will only pick up a single hitchhiker. Never a girl or woman with a child. That way lies madness. I had a long way to drive and wanted company and besides, writing is my business and they say that in every person there is a story.

He jogged up, opened the rear door, slung in his pack, got in the front, and said, "Good morning. Thank you." By his accent I knew he was French Canadian.

In the manner of strangers meeting who know they will never meet again, our talk moved back and forth with an easy sway. He did most of the talking because, as he put it, "This is the best way to know my English. Books take you a way along, but talking is now the way for me and if I say something wrong I would please you to show me."

I told him my first name and he said, almost ritually, "My first name is Jacques. My last name is Thieverge. I am twenty-three years old. I come from Quebec and I work when I can to make money so I don't have to look for work when there is no work. I am a survivor."

I asked him about the hitchhikers we had left behind and he said, "Those people are no good. Some of them are bad. I was in the hostel in Prince George with some of them and they would talk about how they would rob an old man who came out of the beer parlor and take his money or how they would steal food in a grocery store and all these kinds of things. The manager at the hostel told them if they didn't behave he would have the Mounties move them. He also told them to take a bath. Lots of hot water and towels and those guys won't take a bath. They got kicked out last night for drinking. They'll sit on the road until some guy with a truck comes along and lets them ride behind. Others weren't in the hostel but when I go by, they call me names and think I'm crazy. Walking. I show them, don't I? I walk because people will know I am walking because I have to get some-where to do something. *Comprenez vous?*"

I said yes, I understood, and he said he did not speak French at all anymore because he had to learn English well. I was relieved that he did not say 'learn English good' the way so many English-speaking Canadians do.

Jacques was eager to tell all. He had been born in Quebec City and his mother had died when he was ten, leaving behind four other sons, three daughters, and a drunken husband, all living in a slum house in Lower Town.

"I had the nuns for a few years in school and then our priest said he thought I had some brains, so they sent me to the Jesuits. If the nuns were cruel but sometimes kind, the black crows were cruel and never kind. It was work, work, work with figures and things I do not care about right now. All I wanted to do was look at books about farms and fields and animals and making the sugar in the spring. I knew that if I was good at what I was studying, the Jesuits would make me join them. So, yes, I did not study hard. Hardly at all. I would say, goofed off. I would run away and get a job on a farm across the river and work very hard and the farmer would pay me some money. Always the provincials would find me and take me back to the Jesuits until they said, 'Jacques, we don't want you here. You are no good and you will be worthless. Go 'way. Don't come back.'

"Then I felt good. I took my clothes from the house and said bye-bye to my little sisters and brothers and told the housekeeper I would send some money for the kids. I got a job on a big farm and they asked me what I wanted to do. No, they asked me what I could do. I said I was good at haying and I liked animals. I could chop wood and currycomb horses and I worked at that big farm for three whole years, and then I went to Monsieur Beauharnois and I told him I was going to British Columbia to see *les montaignes*. He said, 'Are you crazy, kid?' I could have said sure, I was a crazy kid, for working for him for three years and doing so much work. Him, he is paying this guy, me, two hundred dollars a month when guys on farms around are making four dollars an hour. Twenty-five dollars a day. I know, they did not get a bed and food and they used the big machinery and I would not touch machinery on the farm. I did not like it.

"Mr. Beauharnois said he would raise my wages and I said no thank

you, I like you and your family but I am going to the West and see what
there is there. He said I was crazy and even if I am okay, he said I did
not speak a word of English and everybody there does, and if I did not
speak it, they would get me, cheat me, let me make a fool of me."

I asked, "And did they, Jacques?"

"No, not at first. No, not really any time. I thanked Mr. Beauharnois
and I packed my bag and Mrs. Beauharnois gave me a big box of food
and, after he drove me to the train in Quebec City, he thanked me and
gave me two twenty dollars. I got on the train and about three days
later I got off the train at Prince George. I had been told there was
work there, but two days I couldn't find any. The hotel was twelve a
night and I wouldn't have much money soon, so I went to a phone and
looked for French names. The first four I called, they couldn't understand me. A lady was home each time. Maybe she didn't want to
understand.

"The next time I got a man and he spoke French to me. I told him
who I was and he said to wait by the phone and he would pick me up.
He was a nice man and he had a nice family and they had come from
the Saguenay. They let me sleep in their trailer that night and next day
Mr. Leblanc took me to a place and talked to the boss and I got a job. I
didn't like it because it was all machinery and I had to shovel cement
into corners of a building they were building. It was hard work. The
cement was so heavy. I sweated and worked hard, and the boss at the
time we quit, he patted me on the shoulder and smiled. He meant I was
a good worker. I know now it was a job nobody else would want, but I
got seven dollars an hour, and I saved, and in two weeks I had five
hundred dollars. I couldn't believe it. I then had seven hundred and I
gave Mrs. Leblanc one hundred for her meals I had eaten, and told
them I was quitting the job because I had to learn English.

"Mr. Leblanc said that was a good idea and he said I could use the
trailer and I said I would feed myself now, you see, and I went to a
store that sold old books. A secondhand store. I bought an Agatha
Christie book for ten cents and an English-French dictionary for fifty
cents. I had read all the Agatha Christie books I could find; they were
in French, and I figured if I knew the stories it would be easier to learn
English that way. The first book—and I had to work very hard—I
finished in six days, but that was studying twelve hours a day. Then I
bought more of the books and the second I did in four days. Then the

next one in three and in about three weeks I could read a book in two days."

I remarked that not too many people read a book every two days and he smiled and said, "Oh yes, but I was still reading twelve hours a day."

He then bought other books, and he said the Mickey Spillane books taught him about killing and how bad people were, as he put it. He was incredibly naive about the world around him. After Spillane—he bought by author—he read Erle Stanley Gardner and was intelligent enough to know that this was not how the Canadian legal system worked. He fell afoul of Louis L'Amour and that famous Western writer taught him "how to be a good and tough man and build railroads and fight Indians and find a goldmine." John D. MacDonald came next, the Travis McGee series, and he said, "He taught me philosophy of a smart man and how to talk with white women" he corrected himself and said 'English women'—"and how to beat up on big men."

Beat up on big men?

It is time to describe my passenger. He was about five foot eight, slim, about 135 pounds. He had a straggly goatee and freely admitted that it took him six months to grow it and he rarely shaved, which indicated he had a strong strain of Indian blood. His face was long, long in chin, nose, dark from the sun or because of race. It was the face of an ascetic, the face of a nomadic Arab one sees in the *National Geographic*. His hair was black and his eyes a very deep brown. His fingers were long, artistic and well cared for. Despite the life he led he did not smell. His clothes? Well, a hat not unlike that of an Australian infantryman lay in his lap. His shirt was a heavy wool, with a black and orange-red design. His denims were clean and patched and had seen better days, and his workman's boots definitely were ready for a decent burial, gaping apart at the seams. He told me how he gets his clothes.

"On a sunny morning I will go into the Salvation Army thrift shop in Victoria and the place will have only a few customers. I smile at the two ladies who are working there and they smile back because everybody smiles on a nice, sunny morning.

"I walk around and see what I want and then I go over to the shelf of paperback books and, after I have looked at the books for a while, I walk over to the counter and I ask them that if I washed their front windows inside and out would they give me a few pieces of clothing and some books. They know I am not asking for money; I am asking for some of their things they got for free anyway. They politely turn their backs on me and whisper and I knew nobody has asked them this before. I do not say it would cost them twenty-five dollars to have windows cleaned. They know that. Maybe it would cost more. They know that too. I hear one speaking softly and I can't hear the words, but I see the other lady nodding the head, and I smile inside me; I know they will say yes.

"One lady asks what I meant by some clothing and I tell them I would like a pair of pants and two shirts and some socks and underwear, and maybe a dozen books. I can see the wheels turning in their heads. They know it will come to eight dollars or so, and getting the windows cleaned would cost three times as much. Besides they still might not be able to sell the things I want.

"So the lady who is asking says I can do it, and I get their bucket and fill it with hot water and get some soap and rags off them. I wash their windows and I polish them and I hum a little tune and in two hours I am finished and those windows look very good. Very good.

"When I am finished cleaning up I go around the counters and I pick carefully a pair of pants that fit and look good and are two dollars, and the shirts, three of them for seventy-five cents each, the underwear and socks and six pocketbooks at twenty cents each, and it comes to about eight dollars. I take them to the counter and they count up the prices and smile at each other. Eight dollars. Then they smile at me and one lady asks if I am foreign. I don't say no. I say I was born in Quebec City.

"The lady says, 'Oh well, you've got a nice accent anyway.'

"I smile and she says, 'Now, you come back here any time we can help you,' and she means come back so we can get twenty-five dollars of work for eight dollars. I say I will and thank them and I leave. They think they have beat me, how you say it? They are happy. I am happy, too, because I have got eight dollars of stuff for two hours' work—that is four dollars an hour and that is above the minimum wage—and I am not really working. So we all are happy, not so?

"And that is how I survive.

"I am here and there and everywhere, but always in British Columbia. Right now the front seat of your automobile is my home and in my pack in the back seat are my possessions and I am riding to somewhere else and there are the mountains"—he always pronounced them '*les montaignes*,' just as he gave the French for other words that were similar in English—"and they make me happy and the sun makes me happy and I don't know where I am going."

I told him there was a road map in the glove compartment if he wanted to know where he was going, and he took it out, opened it, and studied for a while. Then, like even the most seasoned traveler, he had a hell of a time getting it folded correctly.

Under my gentle questioning he said he did not drink, not even wine. He refused the cigarette I offered him, looking at the package with such distaste that I felt I should throw it out the window. He ate meat only once a week, and laughed and admitted that on the train to B.C. he had eaten meat three times a day for three days. Mrs. Beauharnois had filled the picnic box with a dozen hefty pork and beef pies and some fruit and raw vegetables and hard-boiled eggs, so he had little choice. He didn't drink tea or coffee.

I didn't ask but he said, "I don't have a girl, but I like girls. I am not the way you might think, you know. I am twenty-three but there is still a lot of time. Girls can come when I am ready."

Offhandedly, I asked him if he was religious and in his high-pitched voice, almost a whine, he said, "When you have been to the nuns' school for six years, eh? The mother superior was, how you say it, a monster, and she made the nuns be monsters too. Even the young ones, teachers for the little children. After five years with the Jesuits then, how can you be religious? If I would swear, I would swear at those people." His view was the same as that of others I have known who have taken part in the Quebec religious school system. "For a while you think you might want to be a priest, but then you say, 'If I am to be a priest then I must be like those people.' When you leave, after a year you know you never wanted to be a priest."

He opened up the road map again, studied it for minutes, and said, "Have you ever been to Likely?"

"Yes," I said. "It's a little place, not even a village. It has a store and a filling station. Some lodges and cabins. There's good fishing around. A lot of Americans go there to fish. It's on a gravel road that goes off this road over toward the mountains. It's a nice place in the summer. Why?"

"I think I will go there. I have finished the cherry picking at Osoyoos, the place I went for two years. The man who has the orchards likes me, but this year it was bad. The rain split the cherries just when they were nearly ripe and I only made five hundred dollars in three weeks and I worked very hard, hard. I should have made about twelve hundred. I did last year."

I asked him if he had just been in the Okanagan Valley, then what was he doing in Prince George where I picked him up?

"I go to see my friends who helped me when I was such a dumb kid. Mr. Leblanc says there is no work for anybody there, and I do not have cards so I cannot get the insurance, but maybe the welfare—but I do not want the welfare." He thought a few moments and added, "But maybe the welfare. This winter in Victoria, maybe it will be bad, but I don't think so. Maybe some people will remember Jacques the window-washer man? You think? I do not want to bother my friends a long time, so I leave when my free week is up and now I am with you, driving in your nice, green car. So, I think I will go to Likely. You say it is good."

I told him I liked the place—peace and tranquility, nice people. Jacques interjected, "Are there bears there? In this place, Likely?" This was the third time he had mentioned bears and I wondered why.

He said, "You know, English is a funny language. It is easy to learn to read and then you can write because the alphabet is the same, but words in English are funny. Bear means an animal. Bear means you carry something. Bear, same b-e-a-r, means you have something that worries you, you can't bear it, so you are more unhappy. B-a-r-e means you take off your clothes. It means, too, you are naked. A funny language. It is hard. I am afraid of bears. The animals."

Yes, I said, there would be bears around Likely, but they do not bother anyone. Just don't bother them, I warned.

"Yes, I will go to Likely. It is a nice name. Into the bush. I will stay there two months and then go to a man's orchard in the Okanagan when the McIntosh apple is ready. If it is a good season I will work hard until it is dark. Every day for a month. Not Sunday. That day I wash clothes, fix them, go to town, and buy food. The family will give you meals for ten dollars each day you eat, but for two dollars I can eat better by myself. We live in sheds with a electric light and beds. You call them cots. A table and chairs, and they have a little stove and dishes. If you want to eat there you use the stove.

"There will be Indians. From over there," and he waved his arm to the right where the dark blue hills bracketing the Chilcotin Country to the east loomed up. "They are good people, work hard, but when they get their money, they get drunk and come back and yell, 'Frenchie, come here. Have some wine.' I say no, my father drank very much and it is no good. They think I have Indian in me and they laugh and go to sleep and wake up and go away and come back three days later.

"Boys who go to college work there. They are just kids. They think work in the orchard is fun. The second day they know it is no fun. Some stay. Some older guys sit and talk about girls, jobs, their kids, the war. A lot about war. They are old men and they don't make much money. High school kids are good pickers. They haven't studied how to work hard to make it easy, so they work hard and sweat. I am the best picker I have seen. I like this orchard. It has pygmy trees, so the apples are down there. Not those ladders—up, down, up, down. This year is tough times, so I think there will be a lot of people just looking for work. They think it is easy, eh? The owner knows me, so I get a good job, the best trees. In a month and a half I make two thousand dollars. That and cherry picking, that is my best wages for the year. I work, other things, but it doesn't count. Apples and cherries."

"So you're going to Likely, into the bush. Two months?" I asked. "What about money? Food?"

Jacques flicked a hand to the back seat and said, "There's my food. My house. Tools. Everything I need," and he described the pack, which he said weighed about forty-five pounds. "In there I have seven pounds of cheddar cheese. Cheese cost me sixteen dollars in the market at Prince George. I buy flour in the natural food store. Beans, three kinds. Four pounds of rice. Molasses. Some spices I always carry. Carob. Makes a good hot drink, like chocolate. Four pounds of peanuts. A bag of wheat germ. Dried spaghetti. Dried Chinese mushrooms. Skippy Peanut Butter. I will make jam from berries. At this store at Likely I will get a big bag of potatoes and some tins of Carnation. Inside, too, there is a knife, fork, and two spoons, my big cutting knife, tin plate, cup, frying pan to do bean sprouts. I have them too. A small shovel, like soldiers use. My hatchet and sharpening stone. Soap. Matches. A tiny oil lantern. Lots of candles. My radio. Three pots that go inside each other. Clothes, socks, underwear. My first-aid box. Scissors. A big area of plastic. She's my tent. I've got a good sleeping bag. You should air it out every day…"

I cut in, saying, "You seem to have it down to a science. I guess you have done it before?"

"Two years ago, when I came out, I looked like a fool. Last year I knew what to do and I threw away the little book I had about it. I know what berries I can pick and I know about roots and things, and if there is a fish in the water I can catch him. Are there fish? Is there gold? I sleep about eight hours. I get up. Exercise. Eat. Clean my camp. Walk around. Go swimming. Look for roots. Walk around. Fish. Maybe a nice fish for supper. Read. I have thirty books with me. Paperbacks, bought cheap. I don't read mystery, or cowboys now. Philosophy, psychology, archeology, paleontology, science. Even poetry. The Russian and French and English and American writers. You see, some of those big words I said I can't pronounce much good. Every book I read twice. That's the way I learn to be educated in English.

"If there is gold I will go around and maybe pick a few ounces. Maybe two. Gold it was three hundred and eighty on the London market Friday. Yes, a few ounces of gold, I think."

"Jacques, listen," I said. "If you find gold, let me know. That used to be gold country, but five thousand miners from a dozen nations went over it a hundred years ago and then the Chinese came through later, and if there was gold left those Chinese fellows would find it. There's none left."

With the supreme confidence of the young, he said, "If there was gold before, there will be gold now. Gold does not grow out of ground. It comes from somewhere. Water brings it from somewhere else. Yes, I'll pick some gold."

"So what happens after you've picked the gold and read the books and eaten your cheese and escaped being eaten by a bear?"

"I go to Kelowna and work very hard and make money. I dry apples until I have sixty pounds and then I go to Victoria. And before I leave, a week, I send a letter to the paper and I ask them to put in an advertisement that I want a nice, quiet, warm room cheap and I will help around the house, like work in the yard or help with the garden, and when I get to Victoria there will be letters waiting for me. The first year I got a nice room with a nice lady for sixty-five dollars each month, you see. I helped her with the garden and shined the car and polished her windows and did things for her. Soon, every night, I would have dinner with her and her mother.

"The next year the nice lady, her mother had died, so she moved to an apartment, but I found another house. It cost one hundred dollars and I helped the family. If they went away for Christmas or something I looked after the dog Exeter. Funny name for a dog. The cats. My room was big. A stove. A small fridge. The Rutlands gave me a television. I cleaned the basement up and I could sell the things they didn't need. I sold a good girl's bicycle for twenty dollars and Mr. Rutland said, 'Jacques, you are a lad who should be in business.' They would feed me too. Is it 'also'?

"Okay, either. I would sleep ten hours, have a shower. The bathroom was next to my room. I would ask Mrs. Rutland if there was anything and if she said yes, I would do it. I'd have my lunch and that would be breakfast too. My dried apples and two glasses of powdered milk. Much cheaper. Some yogurt. A slice of bread I make and a cupful of raisins and nuts. Herbal tea, which is good, and with the tea I'd have a small raw potato, my dessert. So walk downtown and maybe go to the park and look at *les montaignes.* I had my money, but if there was a free concert in the afternoon I'd go and not to a motion picture. I looked funny at those concerts, just two hundred schoolchildren and their teachers and me. I got funny looks.

"I'd go to the library once a week, and the girls liked me and one was from Quebec and we'd talk. She'd start to talk in French, and I'd tell her not to. 'Don't talk French,' I'd tell her. 'They don't know if we're talking about them and it is very wrong to do it.' The librarian would give me books and when I brought them back she'd say, 'Jacques, how did you like this one?' and I'd say I did or I didn't. She'd say be more, how was it, specific? She asked me to write a little bit about it, if it was a new book, and I'd put it down and she'd read it and say, 'Good, Jacques. You could be a critic. You write simplistically.' No, that is wrong. I wrote with simplicity, she would say. I don't know what happened to those little pieces.

"Okay, Barry. I'd walk around. One day I would go to the golf course and follow men playing. I'd help them find lost balls or if one wanted to walk maybe, I'd run his little wagon for him. Once a man I'd helped before said, 'Hey kid. You want a trip to Calgary? Somebody's got to deliver my car there. You drive it, expenses like money to eat and sleep and buy fuel, you understand, and a hundred bucks on top.' I said I was sorry but I didn't drive and he said, 'Okay, Frenchie, learn though.' Once four of them took me to a huge, big Chinese meal that cost an awful lot of money, but it was the best food I've eaten. That day I ate a lot of meat.

"Another day I would walk to Sidney, which is about seventeen miles. Sit down on the pier and eat my yogurt and potato and the peanut butter sandwich and watch the sea. Then I'd buy a paper and catch the bus and go home."

He said that anything that was free, or cheap entertainment, he went to and I asked him if he had become a familiar figure around downtown Victoria and he said yes. People, he said, used to nod and smile at him as if they knew him. A newsstand owner would give him a paper that was ripped or tear off the cover of a news magazine and give him the magazine. If a refuse box was overflowing, he said he would stuff the waste in and pack it hard and shopkeepers would thank him. Once, after his good deed, a merchant gave him an overcoat and a raincoat and he said, "Take them. I took them in on a trade. They're no good to me." He kept the raincoat and sold the overcoat for sixteen dollars and felt that was a good day.

He did the Salvation Army windows for the second time, and he could have had steady work just washing and polishing glass for other stores because his rate was cheap, and often in barter, and the merchants knew the deal they were getting. His hair was cut regularly by a barber whose windows and mirrors he worked over.

Food and clothing and books piled up, and every month or so he would sell off the extras for a few dollars.

Mrs. Rutland's friends constantly needed a handyman, and if she had had her way she could have had him working full time at good pay. Any friend who tried to take advantage of Jacques would have to reckon with her wrath. It was too much, and did not fit into his philosophy of life. A warm room, good food, long walks, entertainment, reading, some work here and there, and talks with strangers and he was happy.

"There were guys from Quebec hanging around downtown. They

thought it was a dumb place and the girls didn't like them. It was warm, not like Quebec. I'd walk by them and they'd see I was from Quebec when I answered them, and they'd laugh at me. After a while I stopped talking to them. They were against everything and always talking how they were going to beat up whitey. That's you to those guys. They're so dumb they think only Quebec is Canada. I don't speak much French now. Quebec is not Canada. They will find out soon someday. Those guys are bad and I think they robbed stores some nights."

As the second winter came to a close Jacques counted his money and found he was far ahead of the game, so he sent five hundred dollars to his elder sister and told her to buy something nice for the kids, his sisters and brothers. He didn't know if the family was living together any more, or about his father. He had not written them in two years.

In the spring, as he had done the year before, he rode out to Saanich and its daffodil farms and got a job as an assistant gardener at four dollars an hour. He could have phoned his former employer, but he said, "It is better to look straight in the eye the man who will be paying you your money."

He thanked the Rutlands, took back his library books, stored in bags and boxes the things he would not need in the Rutlands' basement, and moved out to a cottage on the farm at Saanichtown. The job lasted five weeks and then it was well into spring and he returned to Victoria. He put a thousand in the bank, took the Rutland family to Chinatown, and slept in a hotel. The next morning he took the ferry to Tswwassen and a bus to Mission and then began his hitchhiking again, his nomadic rounds, his own caravan to distant places. He went where the car he was in was going, and for six weeks he roamed, sleeping in barns or in culverts and smelling the flowers. Two weeks of haying added to his dwindling poke and he beelined for Osoyoos and the cherry crop failure. Now he was heading for Likely, an unknown which he had picked from a road map because he liked the name. I liked him for that.

A dozen miles from the Likely turn-off, Jacques said a startling thing. He asked if I had been in the army. Yes. When? During the war. Did I like it? I said it had been the most miserable time of my life, but I looked back on it all now with affection. A great adventure.

"I think I should go into the army," he said after a long pause.

"For God's sakes, why?"

"My soul, I think, needs some discipline."

"Jacques, forget your bloody soul. Don't you associate the army with killing? You're against killing. I can tell that. You don't even want to eat meat. Suppose you were in the army and the fellows you grew up with, suppose they were rioting in Quebec City and your platoon had to go in and bash a few heads? Would you do that?"

He was silent.

At the turn-off he slapped the old Aussie digger's hat on his head, shook my hand with considerable strength, and easily swung out the heavy pack, removing it through the front door. It was only then that I realized how strong my guest of two hours was.

He hunched over to look in and said, "Okay, soldier, no army."

I said, "If you find gold, look me up. Tell me where it is."

Earnestly he said, "When I pick the gold I'll tell you where it is."

He crossed the highway, walked thirty feet, and was slinging on his pack with the sleeping bag jauntily on top when a battered, Cariboo-style, ill-bred pickup stopped. He dropped the packsack in the box, waved to me, and climbed in.

Pure, pure luck. A lonely road, and an immediate ride. Maybe he will find gold.

"I Told You. I'm A Hustler"

Alone in the city. Nothing to do. All day to do it. Wandering round town not spending a dime. Nine-thirty. A zingingly perfect April morning, and no better place to be than leaning against the waist-high concrete wall at Granville Place with the bountiful harbor spread before me. The two Seabuses are skittering between the Vancouver terminal and the North Shore, purposeful large orange bugs. Fishboats, seemingly aimless, but each steered by an intent and serious man, laze along toward First Narrows and the open sea. Two of Cates Towing's small, butting tugs hustle a wallowing rustbucket of a freighter, probably Liberian registry, to a wharf up by Second Narrows. Seven bottoms gracefully swing around into a freshening southeast breeze, a convoy to nowhere, a convoy in the sun.

Nothing to do, and I hummed a line from a bawdy wartime sailor's song.

A voice spoke: "Got a light?"

I passed a book of matches to the man who had come up and was standing a couple of feet away and he said, "Thanks. Left mine in there," and he gestured to the Tyndall stone mammoth of the Canadian Pacific Railway Station, the kind one sees in every large Canadian city as a reminder to the citizenry that the railroads of the nation are still the biggest, most important, and richest corporations in their lives. The Vancouver gargantua had a quiet, hardly patronized, high-domed Victorian restaurant tucked in at its west end, and it was where I often ate breakfast.

"Saw you in the restaurant," the man said, and I indeed recognized him as having been the only other customer.

He pointed to a Seabus slowing to enter the berth below us and said, "Took that thing back a bit. Curious. There and back. There was this woman. Saw me and I saw her. Darned if it wasn't a little girl I'd gone to school with. Northern Saskatchewan. The bush. Last stop on the railroad, first to get frost. That says it. Recognized her. Girl called Mary. She knew me. I'd changed but she hadn't. Least, thought I'd changed. Came over and said, 'John?' I said no, my name was Horace. Asked her if I looked like a John. Little joke. She didn't get it. Said I looked like the spitting image, a guy she'd known in high school. Named the town. She was right. It was Mary, all right. Said hoped she'd find her John. Still didn't get it. Didn't think she believed me. Went back to her seat. Kept eyeing me. Too close for comfort. Just didn't want to be known to be here."

I was getting a little annoyed at his staccato manner of speech. No 'I's' in his conversation. It was disconcerting—if you started to look for the personal pronoun 'I,' you lost the gist of what he was saying.

"Saw you in restaurant. Like the place. Food same as anywhere, but that waitress. Been there twenty years, she says. Friendly old thing. Go there once, get that friendly morning sunshine smile, you're hooked."

I said I went there for breakfast often because I had always wanted to eat in Westminster Abbey.

He flipped his glowing cigarette out on the C.P.R. property and said, "Burn this place down. Torch it. Man's body begins to die when he's born. Same with a big company. Railroads the same. Used to be all passengers. Great company then. Now, the C.P.R., all freight trains, planes, mines, real estate, office towers, and where's the passengers? Don't give much of a damn for us now. Was in Calgary. Walking to airline office. Saw sign in travel agency—Ride the train. See the Rockies. Dine in splendor. Sleep the sleep of the just—that got me. Went over to station, train leaving at 10:00 A.M. Bought ticket, magazines, candy bars, morning papers. Got on. Gave porter five bucks. Last I saw of him. Who cares? Tough making a living when you're black.

"Breakfast over when we pulled out. Great morning. Mountains, Rockies great. Can't buy them for a hundred-dollar bill. Lunch good, but not much of it. Too expensive. Six people in diner, three waiters. Went to observation car, read, sipped whiskey, read. Nobody seemed like talking. Great scenery. Where were the girls? Were in travel poster, but where were they? Up there, thirty-five thousand feet up. Flying west in one hour, sipping a drink at six hundred mph.

"In parlor car, talked with old railroader. Retired. A conductor. Lifetime pass. Just travels. Said he liked it. Travels for fun. Said railroads don't want passengers. We're a nuisance. Cost the C.P.R. one helluva lot of money.

"I ask, why have them? People take cars, buses, planes. He says trains are Canada. Trains are people. People are Canada. Throw out passenger trains, you're throwing out people. Then people would throw out the politicians. So, politicians fight passenger-train cuts. So, politicians fighting for people. So, then people vote politicians back in again. Simple, way he put it.

"Dinner. About six people eating. Small plates, smaller portions. Train rocking, wheezing, groaning, bucketing along like an old whore. Yelling in the galley! Steward came out looking upset. Peasant revolt? Went to parlor car. Four people sitting, drinking, mostly beer, looking at nothing out the window. Outside blacker than fifty feet down a well. Talked to big, redheaded bartender. A porter, doubling as bartender. Said he'd bet anyone there would be no passenger service like this in ten years. C.P.R. waiting, ready to strike. Said was looking for better job. Played crib with him. Loser pays. At ten nobody left in car, and he said, 'Closing time.' Asked if I wanted to buy half a dozen mini-bottles. He'd lock up but leave pitcher of water for me. Thanked him, said no. He said, 'Better piss here.' Said in couple hours I'd have to go, have to get out, lift up bed, go wee-wee, put back bed, and try to sleep after that. Did. Pissed. Went to bed. Read *Time, Newsweek*. Wished the world well on its road to hell. Went to sleep.

"In here at seven. No breakfast. None of those famous C.P.R. Winnipeg Goldeyes. Thanked porter I hadn't seen since Calgary for excellent service. Walked around. Pretty jumpy today. Always am after a trip." He flipped another glowing cigarette onto C.P.R. property. His third.

"Care for a beer?" he asked. "Early, I know, but I feel like talking. The Anchor opened at nine. See the sailormen, pockets full of dough. The fishermen, even more dough. See the stevedores goofing off the job. See the bums from Gastown and Skid Road. See the hookers. See the world."

I said what the hell and he reached down and picked up a large and expensive but worn businessman's overnight case and I got a better chance to look him over. He might have been thirty-five years old. Very well dressed. Fine Scotch tweed jacket, brown woolen turtleneck, and, naturally, tailored slacks. His designer loafers looked as if they had had a shine that morning. Where can a man get a high shine in this town any time of day? Certainly not from the porter on the train. They didn't do that sort of thing anymore.

We strolled down Cordova, past small garment factories full of Philippine girls working at slave labor, past warehouses, greasy spoons, cut-rate clothing stores, and beer parlors still shuttered, the debris of the night before lying in front of their doors. He stopped at Harkley and Haywood and admired a sporting rifle for a minute and said, "A beautiful rifle is like a melody."

Gastown at ten-fifteen was awakening for a new day. Sidewalks were being scrubbed. Street hucksters were setting up their pushcarts of cheap leatherwork and necklaces of tiny pink shells imported all the way from Hawaii. The first come-on-in-and-buy music was blaring. Slicky-picky boutiques had their doors open and antique shops of junque also beckoned. Delivery trucks stood outside restaurants unloading the lunchtime fare. They would compete with frowsy Mother Earth restaurants, their menus heavy on the bean curd and alfalfa sprouts. There were no tourists. Converting old buildings into stores and shops had been a good idea, but the whole plan had degenerated into jimcrackery and dross. The area's *raison d'être* was now based on the supposition that every person who walked by was the natural prey of these new-type businessmen.

The Anchor is one of the oldest pubs on the waterfront. Cool and quiet. A few hangovers were being carefully nursed on the poor remains in the patrons' wallets. The bookies hadn't begun to circulate and the whores were still abed.

We sat in the farthest corner and he ordered four drafts and said, "Call me Horace." I told him my name was Barry and asked, "Thought you told me that woman on the Seabus called you John?" He said yes, John was his name, but he usually answered to Horace. He laughed, for the first time, and said he couldn't think of any mother naming her son Horace.

I asked him what he did for a living, figuring that the expensive clothes and hand luggage pegged him as a lawyer, albeit a very strange one. He said no, he wasn't a lawyer. He said he'd been a teacher but wasn't one now. He'd taken his Arts degree in Edmonton and a teaching degree in Vancouver and he had taught for five years.

"I'm thirty-seven and I've been a hustler for eight years. Pool, poker, dice, people. If I stayed here until lunchtime half the people coming in would know me."

I said there was nothing about me that he could hustle and he nodded. Affirmatively? Negatively?

"Your next question will be why I quit teaching. Too many kids who want to be dumb forever. Too many vicious parents. Too many inspectors. Too much administration. Inspectors and administrators are those who didn't have the ability to teach. Too many teachers who don't care, don't give a sweet tinker's damn. Just the pay check, just the union protection, just the pension. Just sit on their asses and wait out their time. Not for me. My own road, I'll walk that alone."

A sharp "whsssst!" sounded, the way one summons a waiter in a Spanish restaurant. My newfound friend looked at the door where a tiny, wizened Indian woman stood waving at him. He quickly walked over and I saw her put something in the pocket of her faded blue sweater. They spoke briefly and he came back, sat down and patted the handkerchief pocket of his jacket. "I keep my quick-draw money here.

This is my office every morning for an hour. Julie, gave her five bucks. Keeps her in a bit of beer money. One of my spies. The best one because she's a smart little lady and keeps on the move. She drifts around the hotels. Ones I don't want to be seen in, in duds like this. She says, 'The West. Dresses good. Broken nose. Talks dirty,' or 'Tall. Red hair. Drinks wine. Balmoral.' That tells me somebody new in town, hustling, is taking up a chair and a pool cue at the West Hotel or the Balmoral. I may drop by at noon tomorrow and see if the boys still have money to lose."

My opinion of Horace certainly was changing. "Back to teaching," I said. "I'm really interested."

"Sure. Big hassle. Good teachers, some. They're disgusted with a system gone wrong and the young ones, the dedicated ones with stars in their eyes, they learn quickly. They don't let the system break them. They learn the bullshit fast. Go along with the system and get good recommendations every June. That's what education is all about. Not to teach kids. To keep the kids out of the principal's hair. Good recommendations mean better jobs.

"Sure, there are lots of good kids, bright kids. But bullies, knotheads, mama's boys, they ruin it. Kid mucks up, the old days, teacher could swing the big strap. Principal could expel them. Not now. Big lout was goofing up my class, talking dirty to the girls, cursing me. You can't do a thing now. Last school was in the Okanagan. Real nice place to teach. Big kid was screwing up, other kids and me. Finally got principal to send registered letter to his parents. Said the kid had to smarten up or he was out. Father had his lawyer send letter to principal and me. Gist of it was, my client's kid don't have to take no crap from you. That did it. Wiped me right out of the school system. When term ended, I packed my car. So long, Okanagan, and so long, teaching. Drive to coast. Goodbye, Arts degree. Goodbye, teaching degree. So long, summer extension courses. Seven years down the drain. Anyhoo, who wants to be a principal at forty-five in a four-room school at Moose Swamp, British Columbia? I'm not a quitter. No, I'm the smart one."

What does he do now?

"Told you, I'm a hustler. I hustle. Everything but women. When I hustle medium- and big-time, I dress like this to impress. A successful salesman passing through, until it is too late and I've got their loot. For lousy places, I put on my welfare-case disguise. Old shirt and jacket, old pants, old shoes, all from the Sally Ann. A day's beard. A dumb old wool cap. Where else would you get a dumb old wool hat except the Sally Ann? Act a bit shaky. They think you're on welfare, desperate. Willing to take your last farthing. How wrong," and he laughed gleefully and slapped his hands together hard. I noticed he was wearing a very good watch.

He said he knew early in life that he was a very good pool player. As he spoke, his hand motions appeared to be caressing a nonexistent pool cue. He said he didn't think about shots. He just made them. At twelve in the dingy pool hall and barbershop in his home town he was champion of the municipality and constituency. At fifteen he was beating the best the province had to offer. He could be beaten by someone lucky, but that player had to be very lucky. He practiced constantly and on his pool winnings he learned the honorable and ancient game of poker, and there wasn't a big dice game for miles around that he didn't wangle into. For a while he lost his pool earnings at pocker and dice, but he felt he was merely paying for an education. All at fifteen, sixteen, seventeen.

"I made my tuition and board, my walking-around money at university playing in half a dozen pool palaces in Edmonton. Those oil workers and the farm boys, they were pretty good. Sometimes I would get my clock cleaned, but that was an off-night for me and an on-night for them. I didn't drink and half those guys had a mickey tucked inside their shirts. That's no way. You want to live up to your nickname of 'The Kid' with these hotshots, you make like you're a kid. People said I should turn professional. In Canada? Don't make me laugh. Be a professional and starve. A guy like that, he gets known, walks into any pool hall and somebody knows him. Sure, he'll get a few games, right? Just like there's always some guy wants to slug it out with Muhammed Ali. Says he could beat a pro. Never happens, not in the haul over ten games. Never."

He ordered over two more beers and when I went to pay he touched my arm and said, "No way. Calgary was good.

"Anyway, there really was no big money hustling in Edmonton and I had always wanted to teach kids, so I took my suitcase and my Arts degree and piled into my car and went to Vancouver and I picked up another degree, teaching. You could find me on Friday nights and

Saturdays usually up the Fraser Valley or Vancouver Island. Shooting for ten, twenty, forty. I did well. I stayed out of Vancouver. If I had only known then just how easy the pickings are. Just reach out and take the stuff out of their pockets.

"When I got my first job it was in the Cariboo, and there was no action there. Just poker, the mayor, the implement dealer, a couple of ranchers, the bulk oil dealer, Saturday nights and Sunday. If I could have got into that game I wouldn't have survived two weeks because in British Columbia a teacher has to set an example. Not only to the students but to the town. They expect you to go to church on Sunday. So I'd drive fifty miles down the road on a late Saturday night and I'd rent the town's pool hall for Saturday midnight to Sunday midnight. Twenty-five bucks. I'd take milk and chocolate bars, sausage rolls, and peanuts and cigarettes and I'd play, practicing, about twenty hours. Just me and the mice. When I went to the Okanagan I did the same. Practice, practice, and more practice. Every game. I was a wreck for school Monday at nine, but maybe I saw the handwriting on the wall for me."

I was feeding him questions—although he didn't need them because I've rarely seen a more hyped-up fellow.

"Where do I live? You better believe it. Not in any apartment in the West End. I live in a small hotel only a quarter of a mile from here. Run by a Yugoslav family. A nice hotel. Big, warm room and two changes of linen a week. Bath and shower down the hall. Got basin in room. Bought hot plate for four bucks, pots and pans and dishes. Cutlery. Small fridge, fifteen. Keep bacon, ham, eggs, fruit, coffee cream, that kind of thing, in fridge. Cupboard drawer has the rest, peanuts, canned goods, sardines, tea, coffee, cocoa, everything I need, all in that cupboard. Clothes, cigarettes, radio, record player, long-plays. No television. That I can do without.

"The room cost $160 a month, not bad, and I work four overnight shifts a month at the desk and that knocks rent down to $80, and that's fine with me."

I put up my hand, stopping-onrushing-train fashion, and asked, "I gather you make damn good money and you're working overnight four times a month to cut your room rent down to eighty dollars? How come? It doesn't add up."

"That suits me right down to a T, pardner. I like it that way. So that's one home. Other one, right here," and he picked up his case. "On the road. Second home," and he opened it and ticked off the contents. "Two shirts, Arrow. Underwear, three changes. Two turtlenecks, my trade mark, brown and rust. Socks, three changes. Slacks, one pair. Hankies. Shaving kit. Cologne, Grey Flannel. Three paperbacks. Pint of whiskey, Dewar's. Manicure kit. Lowney's chocolate bars. Instamatic camera. Two packs of Bicycles. Pocket calculator. Bedside alarm clock. Shoe polish, brush. Pens. Manuscript. All there, and ready to go in five minutes."

I casually asked about the manuscript, saying I knew a bit about writing. What was it about and how far along was he with it?

"Working on it for two years. Some parts good, I think. Some so-so, so I guess so-so is bad. It is about war. Never in any war, far too young," and for the first time in this bizarre encounter he was not on the defensive. His cool was gone. So was the icy confidence. He seemed apprehensive. His nervousness was still there but he was using the pronoun 'I' more. I felt that with all of his successes against less able fellow men, he was now up against something he was unable to handle. Writing.

"It's about the war my father fought. I don't really remember him going to war in '39 and I never saw him come back. I was old enough in '45 and reading all that shit in the papers that I wanted to see him come back as a hero. One of those kid things. My mother didn't tell me he was not coming back until everybody else had come back. He was killed in 1944. I'm not sure I can write this, but I want to."

I said, "Look, don't worry. Stephen Crane wrote *The Red Badge of Courage*, which is a classic about an infantryman in the American Civil War, and he never heard a shot fired in anger. Books galore have been written about Alexander the Great conquering the mighty Persian Empire two thousand years ago and, hell, they can't even find the ruins of some of the cities he conquered. How many books have been written about Shakespeare? Hundreds. Yet today there are some scholars who will bet good money there never was a Shakespeare. Forget it. You'll do it. Write it your way."

"I guess so," he said, "but how do I know what my old man did? He never mentioned anything in his letters. Damn few letters. He was training. He went on leave to London. Things like that. As far as I know he never even got to Dieppe. I'll just have to work him into his regiment's history. I've got that. Christ, he's not even mentioned in that except to say he was killed. But I'll make a hero of my old man if it is the last thing I do. Anyway, every writer copies from all the others."

It was time to change the subject and I asked him again: "You said you make a good living hustling, so why would you live in one room in a small hotel and work four nights a month?"

He looked at me and lifted his empty and I said no, no more beer for me, and he said okay, none for him either. He might decide to go out and test the action that afternoon.

"There's many an advantage. A nice room, warm. Four shifts at the hotel when nobody bothers me. That's when I write. I don't have to spend money to be content. You see, everything is there, and if I want to take a girl to my room nobody is going to get upset. It is the perfect setup and besides, I like the family. Nice old man and lady. Hardworking, and so are the kids.

"I can walk out like a toff, dressed to the nines, if I'm going out hunting on one of my traplines, Edmonton, Calgary, Winnipeg, Seattle. If I walk out dressed in my old pants and my dumb wool cap, nobody wonders because I'm going out as the welfare case. A few old timers live at the hotel regularly. Like me. They're always sitting around the lobby. Each has his own chair. I've always wondered what they talk about. Anything, I guess. One buys a *Province* and I guess one buys the *Sun* later, and they pass the sections around and talk about the world. Or maybe they're talking about how rich they used to be, or how they lost the farm in the Depression. Nobody asks me anything, but I am doubly-damned sure they do a lot of wondering. I say, 'Hi, George' to one and 'Hi, Jake' to another. That's about it."

It was getting on, the place was filling up, and I asked, "You seemed pretty jumpy when you asked for a light back there. What was the matter?"

He laughed and said, "Sure I was jumpy. I still am. Sure, I'll tell you. I said I just got off the train from Calgary. Okay, last Sunday I caught a plane to Prince George, a town that thinks it's the big city. Let me laugh for five minutes. I figure I make more than two big ones a month. I can put a thousand into one of my bank accounts every month, or bonds. I'm saving it for something but I'm really damned if I know for what. Maybe to buy a big white Mercedes. A condominium. A wife. Who knows?

"So I go to Prince George and the dumbbells from the bush are in and I make $250 without trying. Next morning I fly to Kamloops, book into a downtown motel, and go around and sure, there is action. Guys with big paychecks and think they know how to shoot any kind of game and play any kind of poker. In one afternoon in two palaces I make $300. Again, it is easy as taking candy away from a baby. That night there is one of these backroom games of poker. Draw, stud, five and seven cards…they didn't peg me for Big City right off, and anyway it takes about an hour to get a table warmed up with those guys. Who's the new guy, they're asking? I win $430 in that game, but there's another guy in this seven-hand game and he must have taken $1,000 out of the pot, so nobody is really giving me the long and hard look. About one in the morning I say thanks, fellows, and fade. Back to my motel and eat a few candy bars, first food I've eaten in hours. I have to have food to keep me going and Lowney's is the best.

"Next morning there's a P.W.A. out to Calgary and I get a hotel room and drift down to Centre Street and in a hotel there I see a guy in the bar I know. Calgary is not such a hot-shot town, as they say. He shills me into an afternoon of shooting. He's maybe taking a chance doing that, but I make another $450 for four hours' work and I give him a hundred, and he's so happy I ask him if he knows where there's a game. This guy, Phil, he phones. Just one call and up he comes with a nice little game in some biggie's suite in a hotel on the Macleod Trail. I give him fifty and he gives me the hotel and the room and the time. At six o'clock I pick up my gear at the downtown hotel and taxi out to this other motel. The slip of paper says the fifth floor and I ask the desk clerk for a room on the fourth floor. No problem. April, so the hotel's half empty. At seven I knock on the door and I'm let in. I play the salesman from Vancouver, like my friend said I was.

"Well, it looks like heaven. There's six guys there already and there are three big glasses of rye or scotch on the table. That's great, just perfect. Three guys on their way to getting sloshed. That practically gives me an extra card in any hand. What's better is that one of the guys there is a fellow I know. His name is Gary. I've played in games with him. He's a hustler too. He wins at the table and loses next day to the bookies. He passes me the sign and damn it all, more luck, we're both in seats at that table where we can do each other the most good.

"There's a lot of bull going back and forth among the other guys.

They know each other. The talk is about oil and equipment and leases and then we get down to business. I buy in for $500. There's Gary and myself against five others and three of them are half-cut and the two others start on that route too. In four hours, eleven o'clock, I'm ahead $1,500 and Gary is doing just fine, too. A couple of those guys would bluff with two sixes when they're beat right on the table.

"I'm pushing my luck and so I say I've got a heavy date at the International and a big day tomorrow and I cash out. Gary does the same and we do it fast. We're out the door before they catch on, and thank God they're playing with the Queen's real money otherwise they might stop their checks next morning. But no checks.

"As we're closing the door I hear one guy saying, 'Christ, we been had,' and we run for the elevator and luckily catch one just going down. My luck had been good for three days. We punch off at four, go to my room and I yard a bottle out of this bag here and we kill a bottle of Dewar's. Always drink Dewar's. You can't go wrong.

"I suppose there is a hullabaloo about it, but we won fair and square. Those hot-shot oil types just lost dumb and round. Gary leaves about 1:00 A.M. and I sleep, check out at 7:00, go downtown and eat, and that's when I saw the poster saying what a big deal it is traveling through the Rockies on a train."

"What was your take in those three days?"

"Taking off expenses, just over $2,000. That's what I figure to clear free in a month. It's only April the sixth now, so I guess I could coast for a month. I won't, of course."

I probed: "Any other vices, apart from cleaning out dumb pool players and drunk Calgary citizens of high renown?"

"I drink very little. I've never taken dope, not even a joint. I leave the ponies for the jerks. How the hell can you tell what nine horses over six furlongs are thinking? I don't carry a gun. Those things have a habit of going off at the funniest times, like when it might be pointed at someone.

"And one other vice. Picking up authors outside railway stations."

I didn't blink, but all the time I had known there was something more than his asking for a light. Something more than just this outpouring of his background and his life and his trade. Something much more, but I couldn't put a finger on it.

"The manuscript?" I asked. "Your father's story?"

"Yeah, the waitress—the one where you ate, the one with the big smile—you must go in there too because she told me you were a writer. I always carry the manuscript with me, working on it a bit. Correcting. Things like that. I decided, 'What the hell,' and tried you out. So...."

"So, you want me to look at your manuscript?"

"I would appreciate it. Really would."

Okay, I said, I couldn't take it then but if he'd give me his hotel I'd phone in a week or so and arrange to pick it up and give him an evaluation. Maybe, I said, he had the best-seller of the year, although I told him books on war weren't all that popular any more. After all, it happened a long time ago.

Perfectly philosophical, he said that was fine with him and we shook hands. I thanked him for the beer and the conversation and we walked out. I went west on Water Street and he went east.

Things got in the way and it was two weeks before I phoned the hotel and asked for him. A woman with a heavy foreign voice said he had checked out the week before and all he left was some things in storage. He hadn't said where he was going or when he'd be back. They had rented out his room.

"If" Is Part of Rodeo

The big dude at the next table with whom I had struck up a casual conversation was a rodeo performer, and he drawled—yes, he drawled—that he had been struck out of competition earlier in the afternoon and had wandered over to the wide covered concourse at the Calgary Stampede to have a few beers. He said his name was Gordon. Gordon what? Just Gordon.

"Don't like drinking out of these big, waxy paper cups," he said. "Shows no class—but if there was class, then I wouldn't be here.

"Just a poor cowboy," he added. "Not like that honcho," and he pointed to a man tall and lean whose smoothness and elegance and style might have marked him as a national racquetball champion.

"Now that fellow has class but he ain't no cowboy like I know 'em. Those boots he's wearing are Luchesses and if you got 'em in lizardskin like he has, why, they'd put you back $1,300. Probably got 'em for less because the manufacturer gives those kind of boots to them kind of performers just so they can walk around and show 'em off. That shirt, she's cashmere for sure, and maybe $350. Them fancy pants, the darlings, are a good $250 on the shanks, and you go to buy that Stetson, you better have another $300 in your kick.

"Know where he's goin'? He's just strolling through on his way upstairs where the rich people are eating their caesar salads and their big steaks and drinking their French wine.

"You know where that fellow's been? He's been out there with me. He made the finals but he lost out in the first event, calf-ropin', so he high-tailed it back to the cowboys' quarters and showered like hell after dumping his working duds. Now he's all gussied up and he's going up there to the rich people. And you know what? He's gonna try and get a society woman and he probably will.

"Tomorrow bright and early he's gonna be out at the airport and one or another of his friends in the association, they're gonna get a fancy jet airplane and fly back to the States. And a couple of days from now they're gonna fly to another big rodeo and go for the top money. He's a real good rider—I can't take that away from him—and he makes a lot of money—and I don't begrudge him that—but still, he ain't what you call a cowboy. He's a rodeo cowboy looking for the quickest buck there is and they come to see him ride. They don't come to see me."

As he lifted two more beers off the tray of a passing waitress I asked, "So what are you going to do when they play 'The Last Post' here, so to speak?"

"You're talking about where I'm goin'. I'm thinking about where I should be now. I should be about two hours down the road heading for the border crossing at Milk River. I'm late now, but I moseyed over here to kind of relax. Well, when I finish these beers I'm going to have a shower and put on clean Levis and a clean shirt, and pull off these old boots and throw my saddle and duffel in the back of the truck. I'll drive for about four hours until I get hungry, then start going again and go until I hit Colorado."

"What about your horse? None?"

"Naw, not many guys on the circuit haul a trailer around now. Oh, some do, but only if they're in the calf-ropin' and that's not too important. They just borrow or rent a horse from a local cowboy. All I carry is my saddle," and he began to sing:

> *Oh, I started up the trail to punch me some cattle*
> *On a ten-buck horse and a forty-buck saddle.*

"That's from "The Old Chisholm Trail," which cowboys is supposed to sing around a campfire, but I can't remember the last time I saw a campfire. Most of the guys competin' today wouldn't know how to make one.

"You know, a lot of the fellows out there today, they can't ride a horse, not like that Marlboro Man in the smoke ads is s'posed to. Sure, they can ride forty, fifty feet if they're a calf-roper, but no *real* riding. The other ones, all they have to do is know how to get on in that chute-o-reno and get ahold and give the nod and then stay on for eight seconds. That ain't called horse riding. No way. Still, we got to be in awful good shape, us all, and most is, despite the drinking and whoring and cheeseburgers and french fries."

Two young fellows swaggered past and one called, "Hey, Gord, going home or hanging round this neck of the woods?"

"Going home, entering two shows next Friday and Saturday," and he turned back to me. "Couple of young fellows just starting out. Won't win much for awhile, but they look pretty good."

"Where's home for you, Gord?"

"Well, home, you might say, is where you try and make a living. I hit two shows on the way up from Cheyenne and come to Calgary because it is so damn big and big money and I just might get lucky. Now I'll do two more shows in Colorado this week and just head back to Wyoming and think about it all. Drink a Coors or two and watch the sunset."

What did he think of the Calgary Stampede?

He said it was fine, great, but just a big factory producing a stampede, not a rodeo. He said a rodeo was for people, and he thought the Calgary effort was more of a plaything for a lot of people who wanted to be associated with the town's largest annual event. Big prize money and the best stock, horses and bulls, and the best public-address system and a good announcer and good pickup men. Everything good, he said, but he'd take a good old boy of a rodeo any time over it.

The whole thing began in 1882 when William F. Cody, the Buffalo Bill of story and song, staged an 'Old Glory Blow-out' at North Platte, Nebraska. About a thousand turned out to watch this latest aberration of an inventive mind. A year later Cody's now-famous 'Wild West Show' opened and cowboys, horses, and bulls have never been the same since.

Today many a city, town, and village in western Canada has a rodeo jammed between late May and mid-September, and not just in cattle country. The Okanagan Valley—very big in fruit, logging, tourism, and ugly subdivisions—has several. The Fraser Valley, long on crops and cattle, has six. Vancouver tried one once, a real three-rocket affair, and it fell like a lead balloon. The village of Falkland, deep in the logging area of B.C.—about four hundred people grouped around a store, a hotel, a garage, and a restaurant—can pull in more than five thousand on a sunny Saturday in June, plus good riders and good stock. Vancouver Island has four, and it is about as far from ranching country as the earth is from the moon.

Williams Lake has a good one, a three-day affair located in a cowtown in the heart of the Cariboo Country. Top cowboys go there, a reprieve from the heavy-duty, rough trail these men ride. A lot of Indians, working cowboys off the vast Chilcotin Plateau, show up, and if they can climb up and swing onto the beast, they stand a chance of picking up some money. Their loose way of riding out the jumps and fishtails is aided by the amount of liquor they've drunk that day. I once told Clive Stengoe, editor of the *Williams Lake Tribune* years ago, that when they put parking meters on the dusty streets they sure ruined a nice little town. Not a hitching post in sight.

The strangest rodeo is at the Red River Exposition at the town of Morris, forty miles south of Winnipeg, a quiet farming community with a large percentage of Mennonites. It is second biggest show in the West; big promotion and big purses draw the best on the circuit and hence the city slickers.

On the prairies, every widening-of-the-road has its show and, like all small ones, is combined with some type of local fair, with livestock, vegetable, cooking and baking exhibits, a ball tournament, and a couple of farm-equipment displays. Everybody for miles around has one hell of a time.

The prize money for the rodeo performers is very low, giving the winners little more than beer money and a carton of Sportsman cigarettes for all the aches and pains they get out of it. The money doesn't come easy for the cowboys, but they don't expect it anyway. It's the good riders—not anywhere near the top but better than the locals—who drift in and pick up the top money, but that is expected too.

Rodeo is a time for cowboys to sit, hunkered, behind the chutes and exchange stories with other riders. They'll meet old friends, friends who may live only fifteen miles away but whom they only see once a year, and they may meet the lady at the dance that night who will turn out to be the girl of their dreams. They'll compare notes, as pitchers do on opposing hitters, and one will say, "That Peppercorn is here. Y'know, the big bay out of Guthro's string. Still the same. Bucks to the right. His bag of tricks is just that. Stay for five jumps and you've got him. Remember, he broke Sonny's leg and some ribs up at Williams Lake two years ago."

Wherever you go, on the prairies or in British Columbia, the cowboys often are such in name only. Competitors can be lads from the city who know nothing about riding, let alone cowboying. As long as they can see lightning and hear thunder and aren't too drunk and can put up the twenty-five or fifty-dollar entry fee, they can have a go-round. They can be young farmers with not a rooster on the place, let alone a horse, who will take a run at it. Many are men who drift across the West and compete in rodeos between spring planting and fall harvest. They can also be truck drivers, athletes, loggers, mechanics, and accountants—and more than a few girls have been known to dress up as men and go for it. Usually the girls follow the regular cowboys, much the same as groupies follow a rock band, and their other moments of glory are in the barrel races. Many of the barrel-racing gals also come from wealthy families or off large ranches where trick riding just comes naturally.

Excellence doesn't always count. A rider can be the best, but if he draws a rank horse—one that won't buck or on any particular day doesn't feel like doing his eight-second stint—then the rider might as well have stayed in bed. A rider gets fifty points on his performance, and the meanness his entry puts out is worth another fifty points.

Mel Hyland, the World and Canadian Saddle-Bronc Riding

Champion in 1972—the only man to have won both prestigious titles the same year—has an old nag and in the off-season he keeps in shape practicing on her. That old mare just loves to buck, and he says, "There are days in practice that I could have won rodeos on her."

When Hyland joined the Canadian Professional Rodeo Association in 1962 he made $6,200, and it was better than packing a lunch bucket. Besides, he was doing what he wanted. In 1982 the top Canadian cowboy might make $25,000 and Hyland wonders if the winner is much farther ahead than he was in 1962 in the value of winnings. Likely not.

About fifty Canadians are on the North American pro circuit and compete in all the top shows. Only a very small percentage of all 5,300 members of the Professional Rodeo Cowboy Association made enough to buy those thousand-dollar, show-off boots. There is now more than $12,000,000 in prize money, and the ones who break $100,000 in a season can afford planes and Mercedes and marry the beautiful daughters of wealthy Texas ranchers, whose real money, incidently, comes from oil holdings.

In North America, more than 630 rodeos were sanctioned by the all-powerful PRCA in 1981 and 1982, with many, many more hundreds staged by towns, associations, or even a rancher or farmer who wanted to give the folks some fun and a show. In Canada, of those sanctioned rodeos, only 65 were professional. Still, attendance in 1982 at the 630 sanctioned rodeos topped 12,000,000 and the figure for all rodeos, including the barnyard variety, must top 20,000,000.

The big rodeos are planned two years in advance, always with a western theme, prize money up in the hundreds of thousands, an extravagant agricultural exhibition—in order to snare government grants—raucous midway barkers and garish honkytonk, and a two-mile parade with forty marching bands, costumed Indians, local celebrities, servicemen, and riding clubs.

But let us concentrate on the small-fry rodeo, where the best action is, and where the sun always shines on the big day. Keremeos, 200 miles east of Vancouver on Highway 3, is a typical town with one wide street, which is also the highway, and all the usual businesses. For miles you follow the bubbling Similkameen River through a long, quiet valley bordered by towering cliffs. Here and there are small white and Indian ranches, and the sun in late June has burned brown the grass on the slopes. A large fruit-growing area opens up to the east on the highway, and there is the lure of fresh fruit stands and the finest honey in the world. But few tourists stop there except for ice cream cones all-round before the haul into Penticton, where the good restaurants and motels are. Oldtimers like to see the cavalcade of vehicles pass on, saying, "Too trafficky here as it be now."

It may take fifteen committees and 250 volunteers, in addition to paid staff, to get the Calgary Stampede underway, but in Keremeos it's just the regulars getting together in the town hall or at the Elks or the Legion or somebody's house and deciding the date and how they're going to collect the donation money and whether the gate price should be jumped up. The chairman looks around the room and says, "Now Jeff, you take the events again and Helen, you can be in charge of the ladies and the concession for another year. Harry, you told me last week you'd handle the grounds and I hope you get more cooperation this year. I'd say, Wilf, that you should do the public address this time around again, but for God's sakes, go easy on those corny jokes of yours."

Mike agrees to work on the parking and he'll get in a cat to smooth out some of the humps, and the weekly editor will round up some kids to stick up posters around the countryside. The chairman figures he can handle the stock contractor again because he's got to know him well, and you've got to b.s. those Americans who provide the four-footed necessities.

Somebody says the price of admission is too damned high and should stay at two bucks fifty and after discussion Mr. Chairman settles the matter: "Every other damn thing has gone up. The contractor's price is going up, so let's split the difference and make it three bucks." Nobody had mentioned three-fifty. One of the silent woman members of the committee pipes up and says that something just has to be done about those outdoor toilets. A shame. A disgrace. Why do they always run out of paper? They steal it, another townsman adds. What can we do about the drinking? Nothing, unless the Mounties want to. A dance this year? Hell, we forgot that. Forgot to write it down. You go ahead, Millie, and that silent one gasps, and before she can squeak out a protest the party has moved on to the quality of the hamburgers. Groans. "So greasy I couldn't eat them last year," a councilor rumbles. Okay, better hamburgers and hotdogs, Helen. She protests that good lean beef is about $6.50 a kilo now and buns have gone up too, so they'll have to increase the price. More discussion. Agreed, raise the price ten cents. It won't kill anyone. How about firecrackers at dusk? A chorus of nays.

"Mr. Chairman, a question," spoken quietly. "The queen contest. We've always had one, you know. The girls look forward to it." Instant agreement, and the chairman adds a proviso. There should be an Indian girl entered this year. None last year. Hell, half the country is smoky. Got to have an Indian.

The condition of the grandstand, only a set of bleachers, is discussed and a couple of voices say a few buckets of paint splashed around might not hurt. Harry is ordered to make a thorough inspection of the corral and chutes and if that's all, ladies and gentlemen, this meeting stands adjourned. Ride 'em, cowboy! Let 'er buck!

That is the way things are done.

They don't expect hordes of visitors from the coast, and for all I know they don't want 'em. This is a local show.

Keremeos has a special place in Canadian rodeo history, for it was here, under those high and indifferent skies years ago, that Kenny McLean, then seventeen, an Indian kid off his father's small *rancherio* at Okanagan Falls, entered his first event.

"Us kids used to have nothin' to do, so we used to ride calves like every other kid, and when we got a bit bigger we'd have a try at the steers and they usually sent us flying," he remembered. "But I guess I got the bug on my dad's place and Keremeos was my first rodeo."

He didn't do well first time out, and no better as he moved around the interior of B.C. to the small rodeos. For McLean, a slim, wiry, black-eyed, black-haired, and soft-spoken Indian kid who wanted to turn pro, it wasn't just paying the fee, getting up on the chute, easing into the saddle, taking a firm grip, and, when the gate opened, hanging on. It was practice and more practice. He and a few other guys in an old car or pickup with their saddles and a kit bag hit the circuit, picking up on a suggestion or two from the "oldtimers," guys only five years McLean's senior. So McLean, all things considered, got better—he was a natural—and soon he had a new life to lead.

As time went by, there was a Canadian rookie-of-the-year award. He moved up and into the big time. Finally, he won the world championship in saddle-bronc riding. The newspapers were ho-hum.

So what? So he's a world champion. An Indian bronc rider. But his fellow pros knew they were watching the real thing, and he got far more applause at the big shows south of the border than he got back home in Vernon. In fact nobody in the town knew him, so quietly did he live with his wife, two kids, and two horses. There was a room chock-a-block full of beautiful carved saddles for winning, hand-tooled bridles, an array of coveted silver belt buckles that are prized by every cowboy, and cups and trophies galore.

On the road months at a time. Texas, Oklahoma, Montana, Colorado, Alberta, British Columbia, Washington, Oregon, wherever there were horses bucking and money to be made. The grind went on. He mainly preferred taking his own horse with him for the calf-roping events, and his heavy camper with trailer swaying behind traveled untold thousands of miles, hitting two, and sometimes three rodeos, large and small, in one week. To make money you have to compete and you can't compete if you're not there. Simple as that. Years went by.

He established a school in off-season for youngsters wanting to learn the rodeo trade, and today there are other like schools all over the continent, and more and more of the top men are their graduates. The trick was, these kids started off without any bad habits, so they were ahead from the first day.

Time passed and one morning a friend phoned me and said he wanted to nominate this quiet, shy man for the Order of Canada. Would I write the recommendation? Sure, glad to. I listed all his accomplishments, but something more was needed. I'd long felt that in the eyes of Canadians a rodeo professional was nothing more than an entertainer, no more than a man who juggles five balls, or a baton thrower who can do astonishing tricks. Someone who shows extraordinary dexterity but little more.

I emphasized that McLean was an athlete, a superb one, dedicated to keeping his mind and body in shape and dedicated to his job, and he had done what few Canadians had ever done—brought a world championship home. A skater or a skier or a weightlifter or a skeet shooter or a swimmer who had done the same thing would receive twenty times more applause and adulation than this self-taught, quiet man from Okanagan Falls.

I sent the form off and forgot about it. Weeks later I opened the *Vancouver Sun* and there was a front-page story showing Kenny

McLean, recipient of the Order of Canada. The only other British Columbian who had been honored in that short list was the former Social Credit premier, William Andrew Cecil Bennett, who had ruled the province for more than twenty years.

So there I am in Keremeos on a lovely morning, the village filled with folks from miles around, small farmers, fruit growers, Indians from up in the hills, ranchers—people passing through and people who liked small-town rodeos—and the parade is about to begin. The red-coated Mountie, self-conscious as hell and wondering what he has done to deserve to be leading this bedraggled little caravan. Official cars. Decorated cars. The queen and her princesses. A few bands, spaced so that they drown each other in blare. Floats worse from the wear because they have been in many parades the year before.

The parking lot at the fairgrounds begins to fill up. The best seats in the bleachers are gone. People are joshing and hi-ki-yiing to each other. Kids of every color and age and dress are everywhere. Picnic lunches are opened up and that old Canadian custom has begun: the passing of the bottle. Some have been passing it for a couple of hours. Lovers are already drifting off toward the river. The Canadian, provincial, and American flags snap in the wind from off the mountain to the north. The loudspeaker blares the music of rodeo, and then silence falls. Everybody rises. They've all been here before. "God Save the Queen" and perhaps "O Canada." One thing about rodeos and stampedes: no fooling around. At 1:00 P.M. it is all business.

The announcer calls, "Welcome, one and all, welcome to Keremeos and our rodeo and a special thanks to the boys, the organizers, all those dedicated men and women who made this happen again, and a special thanks to all those sponsors who also made it possible. Now, saddle-bronc. Eight of the best cowboys and eight of the meanest horses anywhere. The boys have all paid their entry fees, and one is gonna be top man, so there's some girl who's gonna get a special treat tonight. Maybe a Cadillac." Laughter from the crowd of about five hundred.

Cowboys don't seem to have wives; they only have girls.

"And now, chute two, on Blackie, Billy Weaver from Kelowna. A good boy. Watch Billy, he's a real comer."

Cowboys never seem to be men; they're always boys in rodeo.

The chute opens and Billy, left arm swinging wildly, loses his hat on the second jump and spills off on the fourth.

Billy picks himself up, dusts himself off as though to hold front and center for a few seconds more, limps over, picks up his hat, and slaps it against his thigh in disgust, as if to say he'd have done better if. "If" is part of rodeo. His slow pace toward the fence is like a pitcher's, having let two runs score, walked two and nobody out, being sent to the showers. "If" again.

A roman-nosed gelding comes out just-a-going. He's a plow-horse thing, but cowboys, top pro and poor amateur, fear this type. They usually have dumb names like Cremona or Babe's Pride and are just plain mean when that belly cinch is on and they hear the roar of the crowd. They are usually as sweet as pussycats at all other times. The buzzer sounds three seconds after the cowboy has been sent flying. A five-second ride. Tough. It won't win anything.

The events go by, clickety click. Most survive the rides, but scores like 72 and 68 wouldn't get them last place in some big shows.

Saddle-bronc over. Bareback-bronc done. Calf-roping, explosive and fast. Fearsome Brahma bulls, but the crazy clowns move in to distract and the flashing hooves never find their target.

Intermission. I've been sitting beside a couple from Edmonton, the Morgans, man and wife. Retired. They spend their summers traveling the circuit, picking their shows. It might be Cloverdale one weekend and Lethbridge the next. Keremeos is a favorite because a front-row seat is ringside and the dust, the snorting half-ton beasts, the sweat, the yells, and the excitement are but an arm's-length away. Real rodeo. They invite me to their trailer for a drink and a sandwich. Thank God. No hamburger and five ounces of crushed ice and two ounces of Coke in an eight-ounce cup for me this time. I'm sure the ladies manning the booth have the very best of intentions and could bake one hell of a cherry pie, but there must be a better way of cooking *cuisine à la rodeo.*

The trailer is cool, the scotch is Johnny Walker, the sandwiches are tuna, lettuce, and mayonnaise, and the cookies, chocolate chip. Morgan tells me they figure to make the long haul into Alberta, but first he wants to look at "these kids."

I find out what he means after we take new seats, ours having been usurped by three drunken slugs who can louse up a three-man race to a two-holer biffy. We aren't about to argue. Anyway, first come, first served.

"These kids" is a special event for thirteen-year-old boys and under, with smaller and gentler horses imported from across the line. Somebody has goofed, however, and instead of the Little Britches kind of horse, ordinary ones have been trailered up from Omak, Washington. The crowd groans when it is announced. No event. Then the announcer, showman to the end, calls, "But the kids want to ride. They've been looking forward to this day for a long time. So they're willing, and let's give 'em all a hand, eh, folks. Remember, they're just little fellows."

Morgan says "This is going to be murder. Putting 80- and 90-pound kids on those things," and I recall how several have charged the barrier in front of us, thundering, snorting, wild of eye. He adds, "That stock will think they've got a bug on their backs. Watch out. Catch them as they fly past."

For the next fifteen minutes it is mad. The gate opens and, bang, what's this irritant on top of me, and that 1,000 pounds of muscle puts on a show better than any that afternoon. Two, three seconds, not much more, and there's a body taking off at some angle. Not sliding off the withers or bumping off, but literally flying. The crowd is ecstatic. One kid, bigger, an Indian, manages to last about six jumps and though he loses he wins. To hell with the eight-second stay-on to the buzzer. The prize money is his.

Despite all, the only casualty is one broken arm; a badge of pride in the weeks to come, for his bravery—if not for his skill—is there for all to see.

"All their training was probably on steers," says Morgan. "Not much use today."

The day is about over. As far as I'm concerned, the barrel-racing and the wild-cow-milking are not rodeo. The wind from the west down the valley grows stiffer, and the crowd is getting tanked. As I leave to beat the rush, it is announced that a guy from Omak is all-round cowboy. Everyone has figured he would be. Not good enough for the big time, but good enough to pick up several hundred bucks for a day's work. There seems to be a limit to what a man can take of searing sun, blowing dust, and continual chatter from the p.a. Sometimes even the best rodeo's last just that much too long.

I drop in at the local beer parlor, full of drunks dressed as cowboys and women gussied up with white stetsons, well-filled blouses, tight jeans, and pink and blue feathers everywhere—folks who planned to go to the rodeo but didn't quite make it.

One fellow at the table next to me asks: "All over?"

"Yeah, just finished."

"Any good?"

"Not bad."

"Then that means it was no good. That stock should be hauling wagons and those boys should be milking cows. Ah, what the hell, Let 'em have their fun. Just a stupid game anyway."

On the highway east a mile down the road a figure is walking on the gravel, off the blacktop. You can see he has a saddle in a gunny sack slung over his back. Not hitching. Just walking. I stop and he tosses the sack in the back and gets in, saying nothing. I ask where he's going and he says Grand Forks and I tell him I'll drop him off part way, at Osoyoos, but a long way from home.

"Win anything back there?" A stupid question.

"Naw. Tried saddle-bronc. Never do. Never will. I just go. Save two months for entry and lose it in eight seconds."

I think of it all, Kenny McLean and the Order of Canada, kids cartwheeling into space, the smell of fried onions and burned grease, the dust and the flags, the sober Indians and the drunken whites, and I think I'll give a lift anytime to a broken-down cowboy.

2

In the Good Old Summertime

Oh, to be a running, laughing, shouting, carefree boy again. I can remember me always being first through the gate at Union Station in Winnipeg and racing to lay claim to four seats on the "Moonlight Special" going north to Grand Beach. I was first aboard the old Colonist car while my mother and father and sister trailed behind with the luggage. Every year our two-week summer holiday began that way. I always chose the seat that gave me a view to the north and west so I could see the vast expanse of Lake Winnipeg stretching away to the horizon. I could hardly wait to get there and do all the things I didn't do last year—and then before I had time to do them it was time to pack up and go home again...

Then there was one particular summer when I made a long and arduous trip—all of 200 miles—to my uncle's farm. I'll never forget that dusty old bus humping from dreary town to town, and the lady who smoked constantly and engaged the driver in silly conversation every mile of the way. At the time I was shocked—nice women did not speak to strange men, even bus drivers, and never, never smoked in public.

Grand Beach, the playground for thousands of low-income Protestant Winnipeg families is gone now—only the mile of sand beach, the wind-rumpled blue water, and the great trees remain. The farm will always be there, but large and powerful machines long ago replaced the sixteen docile but powerful horses. I sometimes think "change" is not always synonymous with "progress"...

Grand Beach, Then and Now

Oh, show me the way to go home
I'm tired and I wanna go to bed
I had a glass of beer about an hour ago
And it's gone right to my head.
(The word "head" was sung as 'he-e-e-ed!')

A song from my childhood, a song from the past, brings back the good old days when a family was closely knit and the Great Depression was a very tight belt around us all, and yet for two wonderful weeks every summer there was happiness in a small cottage among the pines. We spent long days on a mile-long beach of the finest sand, and at night we paraded along the boardwalk at Grand Beach as if it were a promenade in the south of France. Life was good.

I remember that song well. In that year, 1936, everyone was singing it as, in family groups, they strolled home to their cottages in the deepening dusk, each little house throwing out a warm rectangle of golden orange from the kerosene lamp, welcoming those who were coming home.

There we were, my father, my mother, my sister, seven, and myself, ten, strolling home, two by two. Each of us held a small cardboard box of chips, mine always awash in brown vinegar. We ate those long and slender chips slowly, savoring every one and hoping they would last until we got home. They never did. We didn't cast the boxes aside because people just did not litter in those days.

The price of the chips was five cents, and while it may seem extremely low compared to today's side of fries for eighty cents, many a canny mother thought them expensive, considering a hundred-pound sack of spuds could be bought for less than a dollar. It was said that the man who had won high bid on the chip concession stand from the Canadian National Railway, which owned Grand Beach resort, made enough in those two months of summer to own a fine house in Winnipeg, take a long luxury trip to Florida every winter, and—oh horrors!—play the ponies. That meant he was a gambling man, a person of sinister character, but he just looked like a man in a frenzy as he stood throwing panfuls of raw potatoes into his two huge kettles, tossing the heavy wire baskets to free the chips of the boiling grease, and dumping them into trays presided over by his two daughters. At the end of each day his white apron was splattered with grease and his chef's hat drooped to starboard. There was a joke made endlessly by those waiting in the two lineups—chips, five cents, on the left, and fish and chips, ten cents, on the right. Every time a nickel or dime dropped into the cups that served as cash register, someone would say, "Another two cents for Mr. Reynold's Florida holiday," and someone else would add, "While we're freezing."

Mr. Reynolds never smiled at these brilliant sallies. Nobody laughed at two cents. It was a lot of money in the Dirty Thirties. Five cents would buy a bottle of Coca-Cola or a bottle of Stone Ginger Beer, and if anyone had had the wit or wisdom then to save those Stone bottles, they would fetch fifteen or twenty dollars today on the collectables market.

On the long boardwalk leading to the lagoon more than a mile away, a concessionaire sold a hamburger—known in Winnipeg as a nip—for five cents; an ice-cream cone was also a nickel, and a juicy hotdog was another nickel. Even at these prices, he made a profit.

At the large grocery, where everybody said prices were exorbitant and shook their fists to the sky cursing the C.N.R. for grinding the faces of the poor in the dust, one could buy a one-quart bottle of orange or cola Kik for eight cents and hamburger meat for eight cents a pound. (Goddam the C.N.R.—in Winnipeg it was seven cents.) Buns were ten cents a dozen and Dad's cookies five cents a dozen.

One by one, the families would turn off to their cottages, but before that mothers would say, as they passed the large public toilets scattered throughout the campsite, "Anyone want to go? If you do, go now. I won't have any of you tykes stumbling around out here in the middle of the night," adding ominously, "when you never know what might happen." I always wondered what might happen. I know now. It would happen now, but it was unthinkable then and no one would ever know anyway because the newspapers did not print details of crimes like that. In those days even the most vicious gang rape was called "an assault." Today, an assault can be hitting a neighbor with a spitball.

The cottages were small and square, following the guidelines laid down by the C.N.R.'s management department. Any resident could go into someone else's cottage blindfolded and move around quite easily, even to finding the kindling and firewood supplied by the company. None of the 312 cottages—the twenty-six letters of the alphabet multiplied by twelve cottages to a block—were exactly the same, but essentially they were alike. If you met a friend on the boardwalk you would say you lived in R-9 and not Raspberry Rendezvous, which was the cottage we rented for years at twelve dollars a week. Each cottage had two or three bedrooms, but they were part of one large area because the walls were only seven feet high and the doors were heavy cloths hanging from crossbars. Each bedroom contained a Winnipeg couch, which folded out to double-size, and each had a chest of drawers. The main area was living-room-dining-room-kitchen-fighting-loving-card-playing-room, and it had a large table, several chairs, some old calendars on the walls, linoleum on the floor, and that was about it.

The part that served as kitchen had a big, black McCleery stove with four holes and a five-gallon heating reservoir. Dishes, pots, and pans went into cupboards as well as the groceries you lugged from Winnipeg or bought at that store with The! Exorbitant! Prices! Oh yes, there was the necessary icebox. The ice came in twenty-five-pound blocks, and they cost nothing because the C.N.R. provided each cottage with a book of ice tickets to last the summer—and woebetide the cottage tenant who could not come up with that book. Every cottage had a cart, a box fixed with tiny wheels and a handle to pull, and the ice was collected from a big barn that was filled every winter with two hundred-pound blocks, which the local Indians harvested from Lake Winnipeg. Many an Indian family of the Grand Marais Reserve could thank the C.N.R. and not the Department of Indian Affairs for their livelihood because of the ice-harvesting and maintenance work they did in the winter and spring.

During the summer months I never saw an Indian working for the C.N.R. The work was done by dozens of college students, and most must have come from families of some wealth who had influence. The jobs were never given to the thousands of destitute youths who found it impossible to get any kind of job, summer or winter. These coveted but low-paying jobs were passed on, down the years, from brother to brother, or friend to friend. It was believed that once a youth got an armlock on a job, his recommendation of a successor was always accepted. A recommendation, therefore, could mean money. Not much, perhaps, but a little went a very long way.

So we'd file into the room and my mother would light up another of the oil lamps and my father would settle down at the table with his copy of the *Winnipeg Free Press* that had come in on the "Moonlight Special", which had arrived from the city that evening. The paper was only five cents, but you got five dollars' worth of news in it. No one had a portable radio—which was as big as an apple box in those days—and besides, who could afford batteries? Why, only the rich folk who had eleven-room cottages called "summer places" at Lake of the Woods and who would never think of renting a twelve-dollar-a-week cottage with the public toilet four hundred yards away.

My father would read out the headlines, making dry wit of the antics of an idiot called Hitler who was stirring up the peasantry in Germany, and commenting on Russia's announcement of a new five-year plan, saying, "If they couldn't make the last two work, how do they expect this one to work?" There was little news of the thousands dispossessed by the Great Depression, the long lines of hopeless and rejected men and youths at soup kitchens in every major city of our great and prosperous land while the banks foreclosed ruthlessly on prairie farmers right, left and center. Nothing ever appeared in the papers because the press, in an unofficial silent conspiracy, hid the true facts from a nation and a world in economic despair and disarray. But any good news made headlines. If a company announced plans to build a seventy-five-thousand-dollar addition to its warehouse on Higgins Avenue, thus giving ten men work for two months, it was worthy of front-page play. A story as inconsequential as the sale of twenty-thousand bushels of Annapolis Valley apples to some obscure Caribbean British colony was hailed as a great boost to the Nova Scotian economy.

My father would read "Mrs. Thomson Advises"—she was the Ann Landers of the day—and say, "That crazy woman...." If we wanted to learn what that stern, socially correct, and liberated woman had to say about love, marriage, and The Great Beyond, we had to wait until he had finished. He never read the sports pages.

Sometimes, my sister and I, when we weren't at war, would play Snap and Old Maid and Rummy and Fish and Hearts and woebetide the person who failed to include a pack of cards in our luggage.

Monopoly was the rage those days, a worldwide mania, but we couldn't afford the game. The owners of Monopoly knew they had the world by the tail on a downhill pull and charged $4.50 for it and made millions. I read later that the man who invented the game sold it to a company for a pittance and died penniless.

But Raspberry Rendezvous had one feature which made it elect above the rest. A gramophone. The big brute of a thing stood on four shaky legs so that it wobbled when it was wound up. There was a stock of records, and night after night the reedy voice of Carson Robinson, the Willy Nelson of the thirties, would drift out into the night. I still remember the words to "I Learned About Women From 'Er" and "Abdul the Bulbul Ameer," two of our favorites.

There was also Cohan's "I'm a Yankee Doodle Dandy," the wailing "Brother Can You Spare a Dime," a dreadful tune with bad lyrics that became the marching song of the Depression, and many forgettable others. We sang the old favorites, "My Gal Sal," and "Swanee River," and the hit of that year, "Red Sails in the Sunset." If any record company wants to reissue "Red Sails" I can guarantee it will lose its corporate shirt, but we were young, innocent, and happy in those days and hadn't been introduced to the melodic tunes of the rock-and-roll age and the assault of a young man of nineteen with long hair earning hundreds of thousands of dollars pounding a guitar into matchwood while hollering 'I luvya, Iwannya' over and over until the record was used up.

About ten o'clock my mother would ask, "Who wants cinnamon toast?" Before we could answer she'd be reaching for the box of Eddy's matches, and one would flare. The kindling would catch and within two minutes there would be a brave fire throwing dancing shadows on the ceiling. The hand-held wire toaster would be loaded with two slices, and by the time eight were done and buttered, the pot was boiling with water for cocoa. It was always cocoa because a smart advertising man had come up with a campaign saying cocoa had no caffeine in it, thus preventing the long sleepless nights caused by the caffeine in coffee and tea. Years later I read that cocoa had as much caffeine in it as coffee and tea, and I only knew because a firm selling carob told me so in their ads. Carob, naturally, has no caffeine.

My mother always let us put on our own cinnamon because some like a little, some like a lot, some wouldn't care if they had it or not. I'll always remember those evenings, the shifting firelight on the ceiling, the warm pool of the lantern light on the oilcloth on the table, the four cups, all different shapes and colors, the big plate of toast, and the munch, munch, munch, and the slurp, slurp, slurp. 'Firelight' and 'cocoa' are still buzz words of happiness to me.

And as Samuel Pepys used to end his daily entry in his diary, "And so to bed...."

At 7:00 A.M. the call "Fresh fish, fresh fish" was heard in the land and my mother would take two quarters from the teacup on the shelf above the stove and I'd run out to join the small crowd around Manuel, the half-breed—now they try and add dignity to their wretched state by calling them Métis. Manuel was a huge man, always dressed in black pants and orange sweater, and his hands were forever bleeding slightly from nicks caused by his flashing fileting knife.

I loved that knife and I once asked him where he had got it and he said "I got me this here bastard file and then I got me another that was harder and I filed down that bastard file and that's the knife you see me with." Then he said, "See that there knot on that old poplar tree there?" Casually, he fired the knife from thirty feet away and it thunked into the center of the small knot. I was sure he was superb at everything he did.

Once I went out fishing before dawn, and as his old one-lunger was putt-putting us back to the beach where he did his fileting, he told me about his life. He did not mention the harshness, the poverty, and the discrimination his people accepted as their punishment for being born Indian. He talked and laughed his way through a half-hour's account of the good things in his life, the big pickerel catches, the tricks he played on other breeds, the weddings and dances, his three little daughters, and offhandedly of his prowess—"Sure, there's a lot of husbands for miles around here that hate Manuel's guts." That one statement, accompanied by his booming laugh, stays with me as the strongest memory of him.

The filets were the biggest, thickest, juiciest, and bone-free I have ever tasted and they were two for a quarter. When I bought four he'd always throw in a fifth and wink and say, "For your pussy. Gotta pussy, ain't you?" The men would chuckle and the women would look at the ground, and it was a couple of years before I learned what Manuel's joke meant.

Those pickerel fried in butter and served with heated stewed tomatoes and bread smeared thick with raspberry jam and a tall glass of milk were enough to send any ten-year-old, red-blooded Canadian boy rushing out onto the trail to do battle with the toughest kid on the block.

Later I would carry behind the cottage the half-dozen chunks of poplar and pine that had been dumped off outside and make little ones out of the big ones and then, if it was our day for ice, go down to the cavernous ice house and claim our bounty. About 10:00 A.M. there would be a devastating whistle, and it would be Dick, leader of our merry band of men. We would all be off to the beach, where the jolly sun would be playing spritely dancing tunes on the blue water. Offshore the string of rowboats from the rental at the lagoon would hold fishermen hopeful of a fish but not caring too much because the purpose of fishing is not really to catch fish. Some lazy afternoons I would take my bamboo rod down to the trestle where the spur line to Victoria Beach crossed the broad, turgid creek dumping into the southern part of the big lagoon. I always took my seat beside an old, old man of about fifty and we had many a long and interesting conversation over the years. He once said, "Barry, you'll find that fishermen are the nicest people in the world. Jesus must have thought so too because he chose five as his Apostles."

It was during one of those sessions that I cranked in my line to check the worm and I snagged into the belly of a huge perch. I stopped off at the store and weighed it and it was three pounds, some ounces. The old man said it was the biggest perch he had ever seen and one of the other fishermen said, "That makes you the fishing champ of Grand Beach."

Walking back to the campsite once with another fisherman he told me that my companion was the head of Western Grocers, a major firm in Winnipeg, and when I told my mother she said, "What in heaven is he doing here? A man like that, you'd think he'd have his own big place at Victoria Beach."

Behind that remark was the implied comment: He must be a Jew.

You see, Victoria Beach, smaller than Grand Beach but more rooty-tooty-snooty, did not allow Jews or even a gentile who had a Jewish wife. Grand Beach allowed Jews, but they mainly settled on Winnipeg Beach, sixteen miles across the lake. If you told a stranger you had a cottage at Winnipeg Beach, he assumed you were Jewish. In the old wild days of the frontier, being Jewish meant you were in a world apart, excluded by faith from all golf clubs and some hotels and resorts.

After frolicking on the beach, barging into a pick-up volleyball game, and having a hotdog—one third of the day's allowance—it was time to stand in the long line at the post-office wicket by the station and see if there was any mail. I cannot recall that there ever was, but it was a ritual. So was the scan of the bulletin board tacked to the station wall. If there was a message to phone someone, it could only mean bad news. However, the sun shone every day and there never was a message.

Then it was time to go to the store, untie the knot in the corner of my beach towel where two quarters were stashed, and buy a quart of milk, twelve cents; a loaf of bread, nine cents; maybe a few apples; and perhaps a pouch of Picobac, a tough, strong pipe tobacco that my father rolled into cigarettes and smoked. He never inhaled. A camel might have, but no human being.

Lunch, and then a short concert by Carson Robinson plaintively singing of the young British soldier returning from India on a troopship and meeting a sixteen-year-old girl whom he loved:

> But I didn't do such,
> 'Cuz I loved her too much,
> But I learned about women from 'er.

Afternoon, and the family headed for the beach. Though it had been all but deserted in the morning, it was now a tangled mass of bodies slowly frizzling in the sun. What a joyful madhouse. Into the water. Thrash around like a gaffed salmon. Out. Races along the beach. Perhaps a stroll to the lagoon, in our minds something out of a Louisiana swamp horror movie. We were positive that in those reeds offshore there lurked a huge and ferocious muskellunge ready to take off a foot as easily as a strongman would snap a two-by-four in half. Then back, searching to find the family camp of two blankets, a few magazines, and suntan oil. I always looked for my father's head because he wore a handkerchief knotted at each corner as a hat and an eyeshade of the kind newspaper editors always wore in the movies.

About 3:30, as if someone had shot off a signal rocket, every kid would head for the boardwalk and the concession stands to spend the second five cents of the day. My hotdog dripping with mustard would last three gulps. Then, because it was necessary that we beat somebody out of something, we'd sneak back and dip our fingers into the huge bowl of mustard and smear it on our faces like Indian warpaint. The hotdog man never protested; it would have been futile anyway and would have precipitated more intense retaliation on our part. Besides, he probably bought the stuff at two dollars a keg.

After a light supper at home, again we'd trek to the beach to watch the "Moonlight Special" chuff in. Every night it arrived loaded with couples, single men, and single girls, heading for an evening of fun and frolic at the huge dance hall equipped, the advertisements said, with the finest sprung floor in western Canada. Waltzes, tangos, the two-step, and every third round was for the jitter-buggers whose main aim was to out-frenetic every other couple. Hundreds of couples danced, and the single men prowled, seeking their prey, the giggly girls whose coyness made them obvious and actions made them an easy catch.

The boardwalk, or rather under it, provided another form of recreation. There was a legend around Winnipeg that every baby nicknamed Sandy had been conceived under the boardwalk in the soft, warm sand, while the tromp, tromp, tromp of a thousand feet resounded overhead.

One evening just before dusk I was walking outside that hangar-sized dance hall and suddenly, at my feet I spied a small change purse. It was the kind that old grandmothers peer into intently, eyes narrowed, lips drawn tight, while they fish in it for a quarter to pay the greengrocer for three pounds of Spanish onions. A hundred people may have walked over it and now it was mine. Mine! As I stood, looking into it, trying to count the fortune in one-dollar bills and change, a voice said, "Sonny that's mine." And a hand reached out and took it. I followed the arm up to the body and then to the face, and there stood a woman whose male counterpart I was to meet later on the parade ground of an infantry training camp. She handed over a dime, and said, "Your reward."

"Pretty white of her," was my father's comment later.

I raced for the hotdog man and gulped down one of his specialities of the day, with mustard. Then I walked down to the ginger beer man. I had always admired the tall glasses of brown brew he drew from a large urn, but a Coke was safer than an unknown quantity. Now, *now,* I would learn the secret of his success.

He passed it over, I took a long quaff and nearly exploded. The stuff was dreadful. Awful. Horrible. Beyond a ten-year-old boy's ability to describe.

"Don't like it, eh, kid?"

"No sir, I'm sorry. It's too bitter."

"That's what every kid says the first time. Here's your nickel back. Always chalk the first time off to advertising. You'll be back. Besides, that Coke has got a bad drug in it. Cocaine."

I hippety-hopped to the Coke concession and, with no thought for the morrow, tossed back a bottle of the stuff, letting it fizz and burn down and devil take the hindmost.

I was always drawn to the dance hall. Hundreds danced, getting in as many turns as possible before the Moonlight's engineer blasted out his half-hour signal and then the fifteen-minute warning and they had to run for the train and a seat to themselves where they could smooch. The young danced, while the old, the middle-aged, the not-so-old, and the kids stood like cattle in a corral and watched. Immobile, they watched. Every dance was the same length, the tune mattered little, and the couples danced as always, but still they watched.

It was rare for us to stay until the "Moonlight Special" backed out of the station at 10:30, but it was all too soon for the Moonlighters. They had had a Depression evening—a dollar a couple for train fare, streetcar fare to the station and back, forty cents; perhaps twenty dances, sixty tunes, for a dollar; a hotdog and Coke for two, twenty cents—a seven-hour date for $3.60. And perhaps he had persuaded her to go for twenty minutes under the boardwalk.

Others lingered, the young men and women who were staying at the hotel. If two girls each saved less than a dollar each week for a year—not all that easy on a shop girl's miserable wage—they could have a Depression vacation: a double room without bath, and three meals a day for $22.25 each a week. They could live like queens and spend each afternoon on the beach looking for boys and deliciously anticipating the evening dinner which, more often than not, was the same as the evening before. When the Moonlight chugged away and the old and young'uns left, they had the boardwalk to themselves. Well, not quite. There were also the boys who worked the concessions and in the ice room, the hotel, and the store, and they began stalking their evening's fun. Also moving in like sleek gray destroyers out of a fogbank were the young men, without city jobs, who camped in rude tents on the sand dunes all summer, cooking over fires of twisted sand roots and made a bare living "smashing baggage," a term that has lost its coinage these days. It meant that they would meet every train and, for a quarter, and sometimes fifty cents, they would haul the arrivals' baggage to R-9 or T-7. It kept them in groceries by day, and the girls from the hotel kept them in fun by night.

All too soon our summer was over. Last year's plans to explore caves and go on two-day camping trips in the big swamp had not been carried out this year because there had been so much to do, doing what we had always done. But we would definitely do them next year.

The last day was the worst. The cottage had to be cleaned because my mother was a scrubbed-white-and-clean person. My father had to go down to meet the 7:30 train to buy return tickets, each twenty-five cents, from those coming in. Everybody sold their tickets when they arrived because the return stubs were good only for a day. Four stubs, a dollar saved. That would mean twenty little boxes of chips. Well worth it, and so what if it was illegal? Everybody did it.

When the baggage smasher arrived with the luggage of the family moving into R-9, he was hired for another two bits to carry ours to the station. Then we had to wait, always one of us standing guard on our possessions until 10:00 P.M., when we would board the train.

I would take a long last walk on that mile of curved golden beach and say good-bye to the ginger beer man, although I had never bought another glass from him, and the hotdog man and the ice cream man. The ninety-minute ride home was a bore, and the race out of the Main Street station to the streetcars lined up for us was a bother. Then we were home.

I didn't know it at the time, but 1936 was to be the last summer we would spend in Grand Beach.

Forty years later I went back. The government had bashed in a two-lane highway, tight as a taut string, through farmland and swamp. In a car you do not get that breathless first look of the huge lake that we once did from the train. The town site was still there, but few spent the summers there, and fewer rented. Grand Beach was decidedly unfashionable. The gracious hotel was gone, and in its place stood a scruffy one-story structure, closed because nobody wanted to have an assignation or even knock back a beer or two on a sunny August afternoon. Besides, the five-cent beer of long ago was now six bits. The windows were broken and litter was everywhere. I remembered the tall, cool, white-painted building of other years and said to myself: 'Even if this thing was open it would be a pretty poor excuse for a hotel.'

I had been told the dance hall I had never danced in had vanished in a fire in 1950—and that probably killed the resort. I couldn't find the picnic grounds, the store, the ice house, the large gloomy dining room, the station, the rails. Every goddamed thing was gone. They had filled in part of the lagoon; it was a large parking lot, littered with about twenty cars on that bright day. And the final insult was that a bunch of bureaucrats had decided to buy it for a provincial park and had put up a booth at the entrance and were charging two bucks a car.

In the parking lot a couple from Ontario were parked beside me. They, too, had been making the pilgrimage. I took three beers out of the cooler and we talked for half an hour about other days. If he wouldn't raise his bottle in a salute, well then, by God I would. I said, "Here's to what we remember." He said, "Damned right."

> *I had a glass of beer about an hour ago*
> *And it's gone right to my he-e-e-ed....*

The Summer I Got the Farm Bug

The road runs straight as a gun barrel for miles, through a land benevolent and quiet and fruitful. In the measure of time as it is known in the West, settlements here are new because the first settlers began to file on homesteads only eighty years ago.

The towns and villages that dot the prairie grew up around the grain elevator buildings that the railroads built every nine miles along the main and branch lines. No farmer was more than a few miles with loaded wagon or sled from an elevator. Western Canada was opened up by the railroads for the benefit of their shareholders. The purpose was to carry the high-priced manufactured products of eastern Canada to the western farmer and to haul his hard-won grain and cattle back east at high freight rates, and west at exorbitant prices. Both ways, the farmer lost.

This is the country around Shoal Lake and Birtle, Solsgirth and Foxwarren, and many other widenings in the road. It is a small part of mid-central Manitoba's farmland, but the one I know best and the one I remember with affection because I spent one of my happiest summers visiting as a city boy from Winnipeg at my uncle's large farm six miles south of Birtle and twelve miles north of Shoal Lake.

The farm was half a mile off the highway, a road so potholed and gravelly that it was dangerous to drive at more than thirty miles an hour. Even so, that was a goodly speed for a car in the late thirties. The road from my uncle's corner to Birtle was maintained by a nearby farmer named Fred who supplied six horses and their feed and received slave wages in return. The government kindly supplied him with a rickety yellow grader. It was a neighborhood joke that he became the graderman because he couldn't make a living on his land, but then he spent too much time as a graderman to prove that he might have made a living farming.

These were Depression days and farmers a hundred miles to the west were trying to keep body and soul and family together on fried rabbit, boiled barley, Indian tea, government flour, and grease. The Birtle district never had a real crop failure, but times were always hard. Tales of barns full of fat cattle, huge bins full of wheat, and bank accounts full of money are largely a myth.

My uncle's farm was larger than a section, and though that it is very small potatoes these days, it was enough to make him perhaps the wealthiest farmer in the district back then. A family with only 320 acres could scrape by with judicial expenditure of imagination, hard work, binder twine, and baling wire, but those condemned to work a quarter-section had a very, very hard time of it indeed. As it is today, the successful strived to buy more land and the poor could only sell to them. Of course I didn't know any of this at the time. And if I had, I doubt it would have mattered.

As a kid I was nuts about the sea for several years. I had never seen it, of course. Despite the fact I wouldn't know the difference between an ebb and slack tide or a leg o' mutton rig from a spinnaker, the sea was for me. I'm reminded of the Royal Canadian Navy recruiting officer in the last war who said prairie lads made the best seamen: "...once we get them signed up and shipped to Esquimalt and they stick that finger in the ocean and taste that salt, we've got 'em forever."

I had cleaned out the neighborhood library of books on the seven seas and seafarers and moved on to the larger district library and finished up at the downtown Carnegie Library. It was all the romantic stuff of story and song—"Drake, Nelson, Beatty, Fisher, and still the grand tradition lives today." After devouring volumes on small-boat sailing, I spent hours at a time designing small and totally impractical and eminently sinkable yachts, sloops, ketches, yawls, and luggers in which I would sail to Tahiti or the isles of Greece. Each had a neat galley, a main cabin with a head, lockers full of food for ocean voyages, a light that would glow yellow and swing in its gimbals as we breasted heavy seas while I, pipe in mouth and ship's cat at my feet, would study charts and plot courses.

The futility of it all finally dawned on me and I set aside my dream. I knew that by the most diligent saving I could never put together enough money, especially since at the time I was delivering for Reid's Drug Store at ten cents an hour.

So I got the farm bug. The family owned several farms around Winnipeg, but they weren't quite what I wanted. For one thing, every yard seemed to be full of busted and rusted machinery and wandering scratching hens, and dogs that barked themselves into a frenzy whenever a car drove in. Another thing, each was only an hour's drive from the city, and I wanted something faraway, more exotic. When I heard that my Uncle John's farm was two hundred miles northeast and near the Birdtail River, that snared me. It wasn't that a river was nearby. It was the name "Birdtail." I saw it as quite wide, about thirty feet, and chattering away like a squirrel exploring new territory. It would be green and runny. I really wasn't disappointed too much.

So, all that winter I created a fantasy farm. It was really my uncle's unseen farm, or variations on the theme. In my mind's eye on my own farm the house would be here, small and trim, and the barn would be there, and between them a large garden. Fields stretched to the south, and there was a pasture for my horses and my thoroughbred runner and another pasture for my cattle. I drew diagrams. I measured buildings on my ruler to scale. I made sketches. I figured costs because in a feat of sheer legerdemain I had snaffled an Eaton's catalogue and through it I bought harness and pails, troughs, a blacksmith shop and a windmill, and I furnished the house in elegant but manly style, if there is such a creature. Through the prices quoted in the *Winnipeg Tribune* I bought cattle, pigs, ducks, geese, and chickens, and also pigeons—a mistake, I learned later—and I would shop around for a stallion and purchase some of the finest horseflesh this side of the bluegrass of Kentucky.

A librarian who could read kids like her books handed me a new book called *Five Acres and Independence* by a city writer who, with his wife, forsook the sad city life and moved into a played-out small farm in the hill-and-valley country of Indiana. It was a smash hit, the right book at the right time, because hundreds of thousands of Depression-weary Americans were looking at the hopelessness of life in the big cities and asking themselves, "Is this all there is?"

However, with my newfound farming experience, and possibly like many thousands of others, I concluded the book was a fraud. The couple were not farmers but just playing at it. They apparently had a bottomless well of money, and his reason for writing the book was to provide entertainment and make more money. They described their neighbors, every last one of them half-witted but wise, and their hilarious accounts of their mistakes and false assumptions and city-bred arrogance showed, if true, only their stupidity. I guess I learned one thing from that book. I would try not to be stupid when I got my farm.

So, it was arranged that I would spend the summer of my thirteenth year on the farm at Birtle and when my father put me on the bus and gave me four dollars for spending money, I was off on the great adventure.

It was a beast of a bus as it humped and grumped along, but I didn't care because it was my first time alone away from home and I gloried during that bright and clear morning in late June. Lunch was at Gladstone, a decidedly ugly town whose only distinction was that it had a Broadfoot Street and a Broadfoot Block, evidence that people of a finer culture had once passed that way. It also had the worst Chinese restaurant I had ever encountered in my life. I can say so today because I can never forget it. I remember that the windows were so dusty that one could not see inside. The floors slanted, the cakes and buns behind the counter were crawling with flies, and I heard the screeching of Oriental music played on a gramophone in the kitchen as we all trooped in. The driver said, "Liver and onions is the fastest, and we're running behind, so that's what I'm having." In other words, fifteen orders of liver and onions coming up. The soup was something soggy floating on something that was floating on grease. The squealing pigs in the yard behind were next in line for the stale bread and they got most of the liver and onions too. The chocolate pudding was edible but the tea was lukewarm and a man with a good eye could have speared fish in ten feet of it. I ate everything put in front of me and paid thirty-five cents, a high price in those days.

Farther on, the bus was waved down and we all sat, belching merrily, while a gang with shovels spread a large pile of rough gravel dumped in the middle of the highway. The driver—"Call me Ivan, let's be friendly"—called out, "Folks, you're looking at hard times. There's a DC-3 cat parked over there which could spread that gravel five times quicker than those fifteen guys with shovels can do it. It's called Make Work. These guys really aren't making ten cents an hour. The municipality pays them about seven dollars a month relief to feed their kids and they work it off at a dime an hour. That's what I call the Milk of Human Kindness and Good Old-Fashioned Human Spitefulness."

We rolled on into the afternoon sun and north of Shoal Lake, Ivan, who had more or less adopted me for the trip, pointed and said, "The Big Marsh on your right. If you're here in the fall it will have thousands of ducks on it. Four more miles and I'll let you off."

My uncle was waiting with the horse and buggy and he explained he'd come by horse because she wasn't getting much exercise. Everything was getting more and more mechanized. Besides, it was a nice day for a ride.

Who could agree more? Wild flowers grew by the road allowance, white daisies and black-eyed Susans and red clover. Meadowlarks triple-trilled as they spun off to circle over the green and rippling knee-high wheat. A gopher stood, soldier straight, as we passed by and my uncle said, "You can take the .22 and shoot those beggars. In town you'll get two cents for every tail." Wow! A redtailed hawk coursed the sky and someone at the farm off to the left was banging a pail with a stick to call someone home. I wish I could be a boy again to relive just that short drive through the clear afternoon with the black mare methodically switching big flies off her rump and the buggy wheels grating stones as we passed.

My uncle flicked his willow rod off to the left and said, "The farm." There it was—the huge hip-roofed barn loomed up like a Spanish galleon of my sailing days, and the long line of Manitoba elms planted long ago as a windbreak was a green curtain to all the treats that lay behind it. Coming into the yard, I remembered what Ivan, the bus driver, had said: "See a farm and if the barn is painted bright red and the house is looking mighty poorly, then the man is boss. House, she's nice and white with trim and the barn looking poorly, the lady is the boss. Both house and barn old and gray, they's poor folks." This house had a freshly painted coat of white with trim, and the barn was bright red, so I wondered who was the boss.

My Aunt Jessie met me at the door and said, "Well, well, so here we are."

I felt right at home and we went into the huge kitchen, half the downstairs of the house, and she opened the warmer of the big wood-stove and said, "Some cookies I just baked fresh and I'll get a glass of milk from the cooler. That's the separator over there," and it was the biggest I'd ever seen, bigger than the one I'd bought out of the Eaton's catalogue. "You'll get a chance to try it tonight."

The cookies were crunchy but the milk was sour, and when I made a face she laughed and said, "It's buttermilk."

A great farmer I was going to be. I didn't even know there was such a thing as buttermilk, the product of every farm that makes its own butter. My aunt said perhaps they could see their way to scooping out a quart of the real stuff from each morning's milking.

She showed me the parlor, a dark, cool room that took up most of the rest of the downstairs and was used only for visiting preachers, government people, and afternoon teas. Neighbors who dropped in as just-folks were entertained around the large, round kitchen table.

Upstairs were four small bedrooms, austere with narrow beds and dressers and a pole jammed crossways into a corner and nailed and used for hanging clothes. There was a large porcelain bowl decorated with pink and mauve flowers and in it a large jug for water and, on the floor, the thunder mug of great renown. It was rarely used because the two-holer with catalogue hanging from a nail was only one hundred feet behind the house on the way to the pig field. Today a prowler of antique stores would pay $300 for such a sample of prairie potty.

She said, "You should wander around and see the place. You'll find your uncle somewhere. The boys will be home in two hours and we can have a talk later."

I went to the barn, full of animal and hay smells and a huge horse in a reinforced box stall. He repeatedly kicked the wall. I found my uncle in the blacksmith shop, part of the long and low implement shed. He was stuffing wood chips under the charcoal in the forge, and he indicated the handle and made a turning gesture with his head and I began to crank up the blower. Slow, then faster, and even a city kid learned quickly that the force applied to the downstroke did the job. A rhythm was quickly set up, and the coal glowed and the metal bar grew white hot. Then I held the bar with heavy tongs and my uncle pounded sharp quick strokes with a hammer until the busy end of the bar became longer and thinner. Then he placed it around the snout of the anvil and hammered some more, and then thrust it into a pail of water—and he had a most serviceable hook for purposes I could not imagine.

I learned something that afternoon. The farm of a good man is his love, his joy, his obsession. He is never idle. Perhaps there was no need for that hook then but there would be later. It was not necessary to rearrange those half- and quarter-full cans of paint on the shelf. He could have waited for a rainy day with no fieldwork to be done to test that row of fenceposts to see if the barbed wire was tight. I wonder how necessary it was to yank the handle of the windmill so that it would pump another inch of water into the trough. He walked to the nearest field and, stepping gingerly between the rows, snipped off the stalks of a dozen mustard plants that bloomed obscenely among the wheat. We walked five hundred yards to a small field of barren soil, unfit even for cattle, and he was checking for fresh mounds of dirt that would indicate another gopher had set up camp and would have to be disposed of.

All that summer I watched him, and it was as if he had a long and varied checklist in his head. Nothing escaped him and if anything had to be soldered, wired, nailed, shored up, pulled down, replaced, moved, painted or washed, polished or sharpened, it was mentally noted and done soon. No superintendent in a factory could do a job so well. And yet it all seemed so casual. Moving slowly, deliberately, almost anticipating what he would find, he kept his eye on that farm—the cattle, the buildings, the machinery. The only thing he had no control over was the weather.

If I still had been in my sailing and seafaring period I would have said the farm was shipshape and Bristol fashion. A sailor can pay no higher compliment.

About five o'clock the boys came in, Walt with a six-horse team, walking behind them, since he had left the one-way in the field, and Doug, the older, riding high at the helm of the McCormick Deering tractor with the huge rubber wheels. The family pride and joy. No other farmer had one. It could pull like a sixteen-mule train and at a speed that was considered no less than astonishing. On a clear morning at seven one could hear the far-off bang-cough bang-cough of a neighbor's one-lung John Deere, while our tractor could be working in the field next to the house and you had to listen for its sound.

The cows drooped around the pasture gate after a long day of dissolution and trooped into the barn, each to its own stanchion, where they were snapped into place and began eating the fresh hay and the small bowl of barley that was their evening ration. Soon, the zing-zing of the flat trajectories of milk began hitting the pails, and the cats, led by Ginger, waited in the center aisle for a shot in the mouth. The milkers rarely hit the bull's-eye. Anyway the cats knew the milker, finished with his first cow, would pour out a bowl of warm and frothing milk for them and after they could go back to their job of hunting down the desperate field mice and barn rats. Farm cats never see the inside of the house. They are workers, like every other living thing. As each cow was stripped, it was released and left, filling up on water for the night while the windmill groaned.

I was told to carry the milk to the house, and I hefted one pail and a hard time I had of it, slopping it on my pants and on the ground. My aunt told me I should take two pails, and I did the next time, and she was right. Two pails gave me balance and were easier to carry than one.

My, but I was learning a lot that day to help me when I had my own farm.

Ever work a cream separator? There it stands, tall, all iron, and red, with a gleaming large bowl atop, awaiting the milk, and you grasp the handle and pull it toward you and nothing happens. The gears are locked, you think. Maybe you should push instead of pull, but even the dumbest engineer would not design it that way. You pull hard. Not so hard, my aunt calls. Pull it strongly but steadily. The handle moves. Slowly. Who invented this thing? You pull and then push on the downstroke, and soon it is setting up a momentum of its own. Then the brute begins its high-pitched hum and skim milk comes gushing out one sprocket and a thin stream of cream falls from the other. Around and around, faster and faster. Finally, the ordeal was over and, exhausted, I slumped in a chair.

I would not know until the morrow just how little I had been using those pulling and pushing muscles in my arms and shoulders. As time went by I got used to it, like one gets used to a steady diet of salt pork and spinach. In a week it was child's play and, taking that description at face value, they let me do it every evening.

At supper, the usual farm supper and then some, conversation was limited to talk of the noon prices on the Winnipeg Grain Exchange and questions asked and answered about the day's work. Walt said the one-way needed a new thingamajig bolt because a section was getting wobbly, and my uncle said he'd get one at the co-op in a couple of days. No, it should be picked up tomorrow. Can't, said my uncle. A neighbor was trucking in for service the next day and he couldn't be put off. I asked what service meant. My aunt looked at my uncle. He explained that the government selected a farmer for each district to keep a government bull and the farmer got paid for feeding him and got the service fee. There was no mention of a cow. It was a minute before I figured out what it was all about. I had seen the government bull and my uncle said it was an Aberdeen Angus; they called it The Old Man although it had a fancy name on its papers. A farmer driving to town had got out and talked to Walt at the fence about wheat prices that day; my uncle said that if McKee was selling a load today he was selling at the wrong time, but if he needed the money badly there was really no wrong time. There was talk of the chances of rain, the main concern of farmers. You get it when you don't need it and there's none around when you want it.

I was asked how things were in the city. There was really not much to tell. Everybody was fine. I had been given approval to miss my final exams of grade eight, so that was why I was early. My sister was taking tap-dancing and elocution. I had started piano but Miss Tease had suggested I forget about it because I didn't seem to have the hang of it although she would lose twenty-five cents a week from her meager wages. Too bad about her money, but the quitting part suited me fine. I said my dog, Bim, was OK and I wished I could have brought him along, and that got a chuckle. A city dog on a farm was no dog at all. His name, Bim, brought up talk of Bingo, a neighbor's hound that was corrupting every lady for miles around and was too smart to come within rifle range. Doug thought he had heard Bingo's siren call just two days ago.

As if on cue there was barking from the farm collies and the sound of hooves clopping up the lane and my aunt said, "Elmer."

A couple of minutes later the door opened and in walked a little man, not old in years but weary in his walk and eyes, wearing patched overalls and the biggest straw hat in Christendom.

"A big hat walking away with Elmer," chuckled my uncle.

A plate of baking-powder biscuits with butter and jam appeared and with his tea Elmer did himself proud, and four more biscuits and another cup went the same way.

He had been to town that afternoon and had brought the mail, a few bills, a government bulletin, and the cream check. The talk went around the table, little different from before. Elmer said nobody was raising hell in town, but if a certain girl didn't do something soon, there might be more to talk about. Everyone nodded. Elmer said goodbye. He hadn't taken off his hat. We heard his horse break into a gallop and Walt said, "A poor, old, broken-down plow horse with only a blanket for a saddle, but he's a fellow that wants to get home to his own barn and stock up on some hay."

My uncle explained that Elmer was a bachelor and farmed a run-down quarter-section two miles away. He dropped in quite often and during harvest he worked for my uncle in exchange for the threshing of his crop.

"He's lonely. He needs some company," said my aunt.

Later, I was sent on an errand with a message for him, and even my untrained eye could tell his land was just about useless, the buildings ramshackle, the machinery fourth hand. He seemed to be farming because his grandfather had been a farmer and so had his father, and he knew nothing else. When the war came along, Elmer was one of the first in line.

By ten, everyone was asleep and as I lay abed, the only sound was a faraway dog practicing his bark. I was glad I had not mentioned my dream of being a farmer. I had seen enough that day to know that the best farmer is a good businessman, among a host of other things. That night I vowed I would keep my folder of sketches, figurings, and pictures in my suitcase. In fact, I stuffed them in the stove a couple of days later. The farm of my dreams had no more reality than the false farm life of the city slicker who wrote that book.

Next morning I arose as the eastern sky was graying and a pot clashed on the stove and somebody turned on the windmill as if to say that its creakings started the day, as Chanticleer the rooster believed his first crow of the morning was the signal for life to begin again. Nobody got up at dawn in the city, except milkmen. Why, they didn't even hang murderers at that hour anymore.

Of course, I had it timed right on the nose when I came down an hour later, just in time to slosh my face with water and walk groggily to the red iron monster. I cursed that separator through every aching muscle, but I got her done.

Breakfast was as huge as the supper the night before had been, and my cousin Doug asked if I wanted to spend the day with him, summer-fallowing a quarter-section about two miles to the west. If I had only known, I would have taken a book or the .22 to shoot things. For two hours as the sun grew hotter I rode that big tractor, sitting on an uncomfortable mud guard, as we went round and round, doing contour work. Finally, my butt could take no more. I said I'd go exploring and be back at noon, and Doug pointed to a stand of scrub poplar and said he'd seen a lynx there last week. I went the other way. In a small, hidden field I came on a low picket fence enclosing two small crosses. It was a tiny cemetery out at the edge of nowhere. Who were the people buried there? Who had once lived on this marginal land? How had they died? When? Where were the people now who had once loved those in these forlorn graves, so pathetic and small beneath the lofty skies?

At lunch I asked and Doug said he knew very little. It happened long ago. A neighbor believed the graves contained two children who had died of pneumonia or diptheria in their parents' shack. Because the family had no money for a funeral or a plot, they had buried them on the brow of the hill, overlooking the coulee where the children perhaps had played. The name was lost, for no record existed of the family who had been visited by tragedy on a farm, alone and lonely. Doug said he painted the crosses and the fence every year. I later found that private cemeteries on the prairies were not uncommon.

My days were uneventful as I learned the pace of life, the swing and sway tuned to the season and the life on a farm. I found most jobs boring but absolutely necessary. I helped with the crushing, making bran for pig feed out of barley. Shovel and dump in the hopper and do it again and again. I slopped the pigs daily, bran mixed with milk, and the enormity of their greed and filthiness disgusted me. How was I to know that experts with degrees in agricultural science had proclaimed the common pig as having one of the highest levels of intelligence and cleanliness of any domestic animal? I know they never slopped those pigs.

I never learned to milk a cow. Either you can or you can't, and cows will bark like hyenas and sing Gilbert and Sullivan before I acquire the art. Oh, I tried, and had the bruised shins and face lashes to prove it. But I learned to herd, if that is anything to boast about. On the highway road allowance the grass grew lush where the dried-up coulee passed under the bridge. There was more than enough for the twenty cows I took out early from time to time. I'd pack a lunch, read, wave to passing cars, and take it easy because even a stupid cow will not forsake delicious forage for a smack in the rear from a freight truck. It was absolutely mindless work, but I know that the morning after a day of herding, perhaps one hundred pounds more milk passed through the separator.

Each day was long and I was on my own. I would go to town with my uncle or take an afternoon lunch and tea out to the field. I shot gophers and I wonder today if that so-called sport was the reason so many snipers in the army in the last war were from prairie farms. We sometimes visited neighbors and my uncle would be asked to put a figure on the bushels to the acre. I was amazed when he would quote a figure, provided the rain and the sun were on his side, and how the farmer would take his word as Holy Writ. I quizzed him once and he said, "Doesn't really matter how close I am. What we sell it for is important most of all."

One sunny morning when I must have shot every gopher on the place and the young crows had flown the nest to escape my wrath and I'd punctured the soccer ball I used to kick incessantly against the side of the barn, I offered to turn a twenty-acre hay field. My uncle and the boys exchanged glances. What does this city kid know about that, or work itself? Well, I knew a bit because I had played at it on another uncle's farm east of Winnipeg. So, choosing a light fork, I headed toward the field where the hay, in coiled mounds, had dried in the sun. It had to be turned in order for the hay on the bottom to dry. Things went well for an hour and then, as the sun climbed, the sweat began to roll and my eyes smarted; the hay dust got into my nostrils and mouth, and the tiny bristles worked their way without challenge into every part of my clothes and body. I had brought no water and I was perishing, and though I was making a dent in the situation I had created, I wondered if I could last till lunch. When I heard the truck horn blaring for me I hiked to the house, dutifully stacking a load of stove wood in my cradled arm as I reached the pile and dumped it in the bin. After sloshing my face and neck with water at the basin and washing my hands, I walked into the kitchen, ever so careful, like a drunk walking the white line.

My youngest cousin snorted, "Maybe we'll make a farmer out of him yet," but I knew it was a compliment spoken grudgingly.

I laid into those groceries as if they were the last I'd ever see, and after listening to the noon grain prices, which were meaningless to me, I filled up a jar with water and headed back to the scaffold of my own creation.

At three, my uncle drove up and handed over a package containing a sandwich, a piece of pie, cookies, an apple, and a jug of lemonade. He looked around, got back in the truck, and said, "You're doing fine."

Compliments, left and right.

That was all I needed. I was tired of being treated like a city cousin, and as he drove away I started to cry. A great big city boy of thirteen crying. I finished off the lunch and went back at it, twenty miles to the gallon. The dust devils kicked up earthy smoke all about me and the sun stepped up its assault and I was weary to the point of death. I kept saying to myself I was bloody well going to finish that field. When the horn blared for supper I walked in, picked up another cradle of wood, washed, and made myself turn that infernal machine again. I gained enough momentum so that I could lean into it and doze on the one-second downstroke. That night I was asleep before I walked into the bedroom. I finished that field at noon the next day.

Rewards came slowly. I'll always remember that summer picnic at the district school. Saturday at noon. A perfect sky. All the neighbors there, arriving by car, truck, buggy, wagon, horseback, or Shank's mare; everybody joking, laughing, exchanging gossip disguised as fact and vice versa. There were comments on the weather, the crops, the prices, and the railway—always the railway—the only real villain. And there I was, the city kid, ignorant and ignored. I entered the egg race and won easily. I cleaned up in the loose-shoe race because my city shoes stood out from the two dozen identical farm boots and I scooped mine up immediately. With a deadly eye I tossed three potatoes in a row into a basket thirty feet away. I may not have been able to milk a cow or ready a sow for the boar, but I had other talents and my three victories netted seventy-five cents. Nobody offered to fight me, and when we were gorging at the food tables a lady smiled and turned around a large plate of strawberry shortcake toward me, offering me the largest slice.

As the sun began to slide, everybody said their goodbyes, gave quick hugs, piled into cars, trucks, buggies, and set off for home—all except that rearguard of ladies who elected themselves the cleaning crew and took away enough uneaten food to keep them going for a week. As we drove into the yard the cows were at the gate, and I wondered if there is anything stupider than a cow chewing its cud unless it's a penguin staring into space. There would be no town this Saturday night because the groceries had been picked up Friday.

Town! Saturday night. Anything could happen, but never did. Work ended early, supper was served before the milking so as not to put the cows' machinery out of gear, and after the men shaved and everybody had spit baths and changed into their Sunday-go-to-church duds, we were off to Birtle. As we drove down the long south hill the main street seemed full, but a parking spot could always be found. The almost identical grocery order to last week's was left at Morris' store. The women strolled the three-block main street, covering a few feet at a time as pairs, knots, groups met and merged. Gossip the same as last week's was revived and continued. The men headed for the co-op or the hardware or the garage and then drifted down to the livery stable, which still advertised horses for rent but all you would get was a Ford coupe. Horses were on the way out, although many liverymen kept one or two and buggies for sentimental reasons. This big barn was the information center.

Many a young man risked his reputation by slipping across the main street, no man's land. The town's two beer parlors disgraced that part of the street, and if he had too many draughts at ten cents each he could be labeled a booze hound. Not that he'd really had one too many, but they'd call the bishop a booze hound just for drinking a few beers every Saturday night. Not fit to be in the company of decent girls.

I was a loner, slipping in to the Chinese restaurant for my milk whip—milk, sugar, chocolate flavoring, a foaming wonder for five cents. Feeling my oats, I might order a milk shake, with two scoops of ice cream, for ten cents. Then with my bag of Spanish peanuts, another five cents, I'd head for the show, and I am still amazed that in those days small village theaters got first-run films before Winnipeg's palaces did. The films were usually banal, very heavy on the new Technicolor process, and entirely forgettable.

After the show I'd squeeze in to the jammed café and gorge on another whip or shake with a glazed chocolate doughnut. I had a Winnipeg trick that hadn't reached the boondocks yet. You balanced the big doughnut on the tin shaker, put your straw through the hole in the doughnut, slurped and nibbled around the doughnut, and watched the reaction. The first time I did it, everybody stared. Two weeks later, all the kids were doing it. Great fun!

Then it was down the street to the dance hall where Mel and His Nighthawks were bashing it out on fiddle, accordion, saxophone, and a big bass drum. Waltzes, polkas, two-steps, but they danced to whatever rhythm was in their heads. A bunch of us kids would peer through the windows and make smart remarks. When it was gentlemen's choice, the young bucks would surge across the floor, aiming at the girls most likely to be lively later. It was great for the pretty ones, but rough on the girls who had been left standing behind the door when God passed out the looks. Ladies' choice separated the men from the boys, and the men they ran for were the best-looking ones, the ones who were considered fast, or those whose daddies had the most land and money. By midnight it was over. The last waltz had been played. Everyone drifted back to the main drag where the cars, trucks, and buggies stood waiting, loaded with boxes of groceries, sacks of meal, blocks of salt, and a bewildering array of other things. One by one, the cars with rear lights winking, the buggies with reflectors shining, wended up the north or the south hill toward home. The lights of the businesses blinked out and the village was quiet again for another week.

Sunday was a good day. I liked church service, held twice a month at the school by the coulee when an itinerant preacher visited. He could be United, Baptist, or Methodist, but never Catholic. Perhaps a dozen attended the service, the minister flailing away at the devil, greed, or licentiousness, in no particular order. While I passed the collection plate his wife sang as she pumped their portable organ. After a final hymn their car was loaded and they were away, over hill and dale, to deliver the word to more of the faithful.

Often there was a ballgame, and those farm boys with their sinewy arms could whip that softball past a batter with alarming speed. You swung at the best ones, and you were lucky if you connected; but when you did it usually went over the school-yard fence for a home run. Once a windmiller named Hooper disputed the referee's call, snapping, "Bullshit once, bullshit twice," and for a week he was considered to be a very rude fellow. Mothers warned, "Now, Sally, I don't want that fellow Hooper coming around here. D'you hear me?"

The grain turned golden and the binder moved into the field. A girl was hired to help the farm wives, and a hired man from the Ukrainian settlement to the northeast was hired at five dollars a week and he had to work like the very dickens to earn his pay. The loft of the barn was quite good enough a place for him to sleep. The utterly boring stooking went on and on, until the fields looked like the tent encampment of an army.

When the stooking was done the thresher was moved in and set up by the empty bins scattered about. It was my job, when they started to fill up, to climb in a little window at the top and, using a man-sized grain scoop, distribute the pouring grain until the bin held every bushel of grain it could. It was perpetual motion work at times, even for a skinny youngster who had built up his muscles and stamina over many weeks at jobs he had chosen for himself but didn't really want to do. In the afternoons I would often feel a warm trickle down my chin and, brushing it away, I would find it was blood from a nose bleed caused by exhaustion. A fifteen-minute rest would clear up the trouble, and then it was back to the bin. Bend, scoop, throw to the far corner, again and again. It was brutal work, but satisfying because I knew I had a rightful place in that circle of men and youths who gathered about three in the afternoon to gorge on meat and cheese sandwiches, apple pie, oatmeal cookies, and toss off cups of hot tea or cold lemonade.

Before I knew it, it was time to leave. Schoolbells would be ringing in a week. My uncle gave me five dollars for the summer's work, plus having given me two bits every Saturday night. So, one day at noon, I hiked to the corner and flagged down the bus. Dressed in my city clothes again, I lay back in my seat, closed my eyes, and then realized how tired I was. Not tired, but tired-tired. But I was rather smug because I had stuck out the summer and earned my way.

I fell asleep and, as the miles rolled away, I dreamed not of a farm of my own, for if I had I would have dreamed of Elmer and the hopelessness of a young man growing old farming alone. There would be no snug house fitted for every need, and a big red barn filled with fat cattle and fast horses, and good, deep, and black soil stretching to the faraway fence.

No, I dreamed of a small boat, a sloop, myself at the helm, the freshening wind on my face, the lift of the wave, the white sail slatting as I come about, and before me a shore and a tiny harbor in a land I had never seen before.

3

City Kid Days, Newspapering Daze

Today I can remember the Christmases of the Depression years in every detail: how bushy the tree was and how high it towered; how the large oak table filled the small dining room when all the relatives gathered for the plump stuffed turkey, the snowy mashed potatoes, the glazed yams, and the rich, dark plum pudding. Yet I have trouble remembering why I wrote that check for $135 just two weeks ago.

The street where I was born is vivid in my mind, and I can draw a map showing where small lakes formed each April on the wide and open prairie that stretched from our street—was it only half a mile?—to the broad, slow-moving Red River. I can describe every ragged member of the Baltimore Gang and rattle off the names of all our dogs—Bim, Sport, Rex. No high-falutin' pedigree names in that crowd, just one-syllable mutts. They played with us, ate with us, slept on our beds at night, and waited for us outside Riverview School, and when they died we mourned them and soon got another Bim or Sport or Rex.

Besides skating and building forts, and going to the movies, we had jobs. After delivering newspapers I became a delivery boy at the local drugstore. But work began in earnest when I got a job as a copy boy at the Winnipeg Tribune. *I was enthusiastic, eager to prove myself, and had some wonderful experiences with some wonderful people before it all ended when I went off to war.*

A few months ago, I got together with two of the old gang, Ray and Al, and for a couple of hours we regaled each other with "remember whens." And when we had finished with our memories, there was nothing left to say; so we said good bye, perhaps forever, and went our separate ways. The only thing we had in common, some forty-five years later, was our childhood, and we cherished each other for that, and really only that.

Who Remembers the Baltimore Gang?

Kids these days sure aren't like the kids we were back in the Dirty Thirties in Winnipeg. Today when a mother asks her sullen, slouching thirteen-year-old son what he is going to do on a sunny Saturday morning, he's likely to say, "Dunno. Guess I'll check the *TV Guide* and see what's on."

Mind you, I'm not talking about girls of today, for they might have something going for themselves, such as watching channel 5 while the boys are watching channel 8. When we were growing up in Winnipeg we had nothing, absolutely nothing to do with girls. Girls were either your kid sister, whom you tolerated, or the girls in Miss Alsaker's class, whom you hated. Girls got better marks and smelled different. They also giggled a lot.

When I was a kid, on a sunny Saturday morning in late spring, we would be with our gangs and all our dogs out on the prairie smashing the dying snowbanks with hockey sticks and whacking about at the field mice that ran from their holes into the jaws of the dogs.

Or we would be figuring out a way to pass the works yard of the River Park Amusement Park and see how much lumber could stick to our fingers so that we could build another swimming dock in June when the muddy old Red warmed up.

Or we might be hurrying toward our gang's assembly point, a telephone pole at the entrance to Fisher Park, to begin the four-mile trek to the Sherburne Baths where, for a nickel we could sport and fool around in the water heavily dosed with chlorine—a chemical that was supposed to cure all bodily ills but which only wrecked your eyesight for the rest of the day. We could have taken a five-cent streetcar ride each way, but then we couldn't have stopped on the way home and bought a steamy hotdog, globby with mustard, and a Coke, thereby spoiling our supper. I never knew what Mom meant when she said such goodies spoiled my supper because I always seemed to eat just as much.

In summer every July and August day was Saturday. We could oil and pump up our bikes, usually hand-me-downs from a brother or a cousin, and head for Lockport, twenty-four miles away, stringing out in a long line through downtown Winnipeg, whooping and cackling like a gaggle of demented geese. At the locks we would play for an hour on the banks, maybe fish and never catch even an immature bullhead, or play soldier firing the rusted First World War heavy machine gun monument. Then we would head for home, tired, pushing down hard on that old single-gear machine, and every downward thrust increased our weariness and our appetites.

We could hike along the trails of the Red about six miles to Wildwood Park, then a wilderness area, and at our destination pitch a pup tent and build a fire and toast wienies black. Nobody ever used that tent, but we put it up anyway. It was an unwritten law: on a hike you take a pup tent. In midafternoon, we'd take down the tent, roll it up, and off we'd trudge.

We might go down to Brandon Field, which was not an airfield but a float-plane base, and we'd perch on the brow of the bank and watch the bush planes make their run down the river, climbing sharply to miss the Elmwood cliffs, and head east or north to romantic places with names like God's Lake and Pelican Narrows and Norway House. We once saw a huge, bellowing ox being skidded into the *Flying Boxcar*, the biggest cargo plane in Canada, and it barely cleared the cliffs. We cheered like maniacs. Today I'll betcha not one in fifty residents of that neighborhood called Riverview knows there once was an airbase on his doorstep.

Almost every day in warm weather we went swimming in the Red, said to be the continent's third dirtiest river. Who cared! You became a regular at the dock when, with terror in your heart, you swam the two hundred yards across and then back, with arms dead and your gang cheering you on.

Three or four times a week there was a hardball game and since an uncle had given me a Louisville Slugger, I was always captain of one of the pick-up teams. The kid who had been told to go to Wright's

Hardware on Osborne Street to steal a ball automatically became the second captain, and when we had chosen our teams the role of captain disappeared because everyone proceeded to play his own game.

After the game, which ended whenever everybody suddenly became bored, we sat around by home plate on that prairie diamond and practiced our swearing. We had all the usual swear words, so innocuous that you hear them with boring repetition on television and in movies today, but we thought we were being wicked. We'd chant them faster and faster until the awful vocabulary became one long vocal blur. Then we'd bark them out and switch to yelling them, and there always were a couple of the kids who couldn't get the hang of using them naturally in a sentence. I guess I was one.

In August we'd have corn and potato roasts in a ravine over by the hospital grounds. Two or three of us would be assigned to swipe the groceries. We didn't need salt because we had a bag stashed at our meeting ground in the ravine, but one of us would have to snitch the butter from his mother's icebox. There were no huge and gleaming refrigerators then—just a boxy affair in which a man, twice a week, put in a block of frozen Red River water when a red card was placed in the front window. A blue card summoned the milkman, and another card brought a knock on the door from the old Italian who peddled fruit and vegetables from his horse-drawn wagon.

But I digress. Two of us would be assigned to steal the corn and spuds, and it was a tricky job because the best and closest garden was guarded by a mean man with a shotgun loaded with rock salt. The loss of a dozen big spuds and two dozen corn—corn selling for perhaps five cents a dozen—wouldn't have broken him. No, he just liked shooting running boys in the bum with his salt. When it hit, the stuff penetrated and my God, how it stung and burned! But that wound was considered a badge of honor. Welcome home, hero!

We shoved the potatoes into the ashes and put the ears of corn, still in their husks, on a wire grill we had found. When the cobs were done we ate them, grinning foolishly as the wonderful golden butter ran down our chins. When the spuds came out they had a thick crust of blackened skin and when it was chipped away, there was the steaming and delicious potato meat. No potato I have eaten since has ever tasted so good. The nefarious act of having pinched them added to the flavor.

As the late days of August began their slide toward autumn the time came for school again. Any kid who had failed one year at school was an older kid, as was one who had been strapped more than five times by Mr. Morgan, the principal. In those days families moved around a lot, usually by night when a truck would draw to the curb and friends and neighbors would load the household furnishings and goods—often very meager. The trick was to clear out before dawn when the landlord, knowing the ways of penniless tenants, might come around to collect his three months' back rent. So, new faces appeared in our class on the first day. The girls we ignored. The boys, well, that was something different. Yes sir, and the new boys knew it. Their moment of truth had come. In about two days everybody knew who was going to fight whom—an old boy taking on a new boy. The principal didn't mind. It was the way it was done. After four o'clock on the third day, the battle commenced. Not battles really. Not even honest-to-God fights. Just two guys stalking each other, each with the my-dad-can-lick-your-dad attitude. Then, without warning, they would be at it, hitting, clubbing, scratching, biting, kicking, kneeing, grabbing, and rolling in the dust— and then it was over. The ritual had been observed. No one won and the only casualties would be a bloody nose, a torn sweater, or a ripped pant leg. The spectators would drift away, old kids talking with new kids. No harm done. That's just the way it was.

It was this time of year that we would build forts. Dugouts, really. As I cast my mind back, I am amazed at how industrious we were. These were not foxholes but large openings perhaps ten feet square and eight feet deep; the amount of shovel work we put into them, after school and Saturdays, was truly astonishing. The floor was corduroyed with poplar sticks packed in with mud. More poplar was laid across the top and covered with strips of tarpaper expropriated from some housing site and then overlaid with the dirt. Small bush shrubs were planted for camouflage, thereby making them obvious to any searching parent from two hundred yards away. In the evenings we'd gather, claiming we had done our homework, and by the light of the fire—yes, we had crude but effective fireplaces—we'd talk while smoking cigarettes made out of the dried fluff of bullrushes.

We also again practiced the grand art of cursing in these dugouts. I remember I had been reading a *Reader's Digest* and came across the word "scrotum" in an article about some form of torture in a Central American banana republic. I looked up this very strange word and aha! I had a new swear word. I eagerly introduced it, explaining that it was the pouch containing the testicles, and we slipped "scrotum" and "testicles" into our ritualistic obscenity chant. Somehow these two words lacked the depth and vigor of the one-syllable standbys.

Hallowe'en! Hah! Little kids dressed as ghosts and wicked old witches would roam the streets, collecting apples and more apples. Why apples? As far as I was concerned in those days, if you ate two, you'd eaten 'em all. The rest went into applesauce and apple pie, so Hallowe'en was really a waste of time. Sure, there were a few suckers and blackballs and handfuls of peanuts and tiny boxes of Chiclets, two to the box, and Mrs. Pender always gave us popcorn balls. I still associate Hallowe'en with Mrs. Pender.

As we got into the thirteen-year-old bracket we switched to being buccaneers, pirates, vandals, Visigoths, robbers, and thieves, and every smaller kid was our natural prey. We'd stick one of our father's razor blades into a small pole and lie in wait, and when the little ghosts and wicked witches went past the bushes, out would snick our deadly weapon and apples and suckers would begin to trickle from the slit we'd made in the goody bag, and oh, it was such fun!

Farm boys are said to have put a buggy atop a neighbor's barn, or moved the two-hole biffy back three feet so, if someone answering the call of nature in the dark walked confidently to the two-holer, he or she could meet with a peculiar accident. I doubt it ever happened. I believe on that night everybody used the thunder mugs underneath each bed. A thunder mug? Well…it is not hard to describe but rather awkward to use.

The worst we ever did was to cut out a couple of streetlights and search for neighbors' garbage cans that we could kick over, but no sensible neighbor ever left his cans out on Hallowe'en.

I also turned my intelligence and ability to positive pursuits. Libby's, the Ontario company that sold most of the cans of spaghetti and beans eaten in western Canada, had a catalogue that showed how many labels from their cans were needed to get a nested set of cooking utensils for hiking and camping. There were many dozens of other goodies, from super knives to water bottles, to neat compasses, to hatchets and binoculars—we called them spy glasses—and boots just like the real mountaineers used, and pup tents—the kind you take on a hike, set up, and never use. My family would have had to eat Libby's spaghetti morning, noon, and night, 365 days a year, for five years, to get all the things I wanted. My business acumen, which never surfaced again in my long career, told me that other people also ate Libby's spaghetti. Didn't they? They sure did! So about twice a week, just before garbage collection days, there I was, with slitting knife, prowling the back lanes of Riverview, the great hunter closing in on that nested stack of utensils or the pup tent. I hunted through every can and the number of Libby's labels was incredible. If I had been able to turn all those labels in for money I could have purchased Libby's stock. In a couple of months I collected hundreds. I'm sorry they didn't send a vice-president out to see the Broadfoots, the Winnipeg family that ate so much Libby's spaghetti that they had to put on a second shift at the factory. As far as I know, no other kid ever did that.

Autumn was the time of revival of the Baltimore Road Stamp Club. Was that ever a con job! It went like this, see. Every kid collected stamps. Like taking a pup tent on a hike, collecting stamps was a thing to do. So we had to have stamp nights, didn't we? Stamp nights meant that everybody got together and traded stamps. So what were all those girls doing at our stamp night? If there were twelve kids from nine different homes in the club, then there were nine stamp nights and nine sumptuous repasts, as the travel ads say.

These Saturday night soirées started exactly four minutes after the end of the hockey game in Toronto when Foster Hewitt at the radio microphone once again had successfully performed the incredible task of telling the Maple Leafs how to score goals. No red-blooded kid missed Old Foster. The first two or three times, kids actually brought their stamp books. Just for show, of course. Then it just became fun and games and also the reason for the whole thing: food, food, food! Every mother, even with a cupboard that was bare, would go to extraordinary lengths to prepare a meal fit for us little wretches. We had psychology on our side. Every mother knew that each of us would go home and squeal on the amount and quality of the food as well as if Mrs. Gillespie had sold her mahogany tea caddy to make ends meet and if the Hill family still secretly kept those chickens in the basement, and many more awful secrets.

I clearly recall one member of the stamp club—a kid named Alistair. His nickname was Asser and he didn't go for this stamp-trading stuff. The moment he came in the door he would head for the dining room where the table was already laid out with goodies. Asser would stare and stare and then begin to drool. He never moved, never batted an eye. When a mother would suggest he join the other kids, he never even acknowledged the suggestion. When the signal was given, there he was, fighting for his gastronomic life. He always won. He was a two-fisted gulper and would be attacking one of the large cakes before the rest of us had dutifully finished our second sandwich. Once the battlefield had been wiped clean there was a rush for the door, Asser leading the charge. Nobody said thanks or goodbye. Nice, normal kids.

Thinking of Asser reminds me that we all had nicknames. None seemed to fit, but I guess that's why we have nicknames. Why is a very tall man often called Shorty, although a man named Miller is called Dusty and that makes sense? Asser went through the first fifteen years of his life with a scab on his nose. I mean when he was fifteen I joined the army, so all I can say is fifteen. Whenever the scab was just about healed he'd fall on his face again and it would start all over. Many years later I saw his picture in *The Financial Post*, and the article with it stated he had been made vice-president of a large engineering firm. I studied his face. Nope, no trace of a scab. I guess a man who becomes a vice-president learns not to fall on his face.

Robert Carter was nicknamed Foozy, perhaps because he was the first kid on our block to have a brush cut. Jim Best was named Ozzie. No meaning for that. Clifford Gill was called Beada. Somebody said it was because his little sister couldn't pronounce "brother." That sister, by the way, was known simply as Dirt. Leon Beaubien was known as Superman because he wore a red cape. Forbes Carter was called Forbosay, and one could figure that out. Dickie Geddes was called Prickly Lettuce, a variation of Cockney rhyming slang although we knew nothing about that. His mongrel dog, which had no tail what-soever, was called Oh Little Master of the Universe. James Rawleigh, whose short-cropped hair was like wire, was called J.J. Ron Galbraith, a huge and hulking hell of a nice guy, answered to Googli, even in school. Jack Purchase gracefully accepted his assigned name of Chips. My name was Mess. I never figured out how the original Broadie had been changed to Mess, no more than I could understand why Mess became Marblehead when I was in the army. Well, yes I can.

When the big guy in the sky was pulling the levers that turn the

Manitoba maple's leaves to red and orange it was time to think of cold. Bitter cold, an overnight snap that would freeze the water and crack every radiator in the country. We kids were not wishing ill will to the people with their 1929 Fords and their 1932 Durants and the two people in Winnipeg who could afford a Cord, but we wanted cold, a temperature low enough to slow, and then still, and then freeze the river before the first snows came filtering down from slate-gray skies. If the river froze hard enough we would have a skating rink two hundred yards wide and forty miles long, of slick ice, black ice, hard ice, and away we would go, down the royal road to Selkirk, a quiet fishing village a hundred twists downstream. "In and out the river is winding in the lengths of its long red chain," as Longfellow wrote of the Red River, although he hadn't been within a thousand miles of that turgid old fool of a river.

Every mother of a kid in the Baltimore Gang would pack a lunch, a bologna sandwich, a few cookies, and one of those apples left over from Hallowe'en. We'd trek down to the river, don skates, sling our boots around our necks, and then set off in long swoops, adventurers all. In a long line, taking turns at breaking the winds as geese do, avoiding the open water by the sewer outfalls, we would skate the forty miles to Selkirk. We knew how the soaring eagle felt. Total exhilaration! Effortless joy. Selkirk always came too soon, but when we gathered on the river bank and rustled up twigs and branches for our ritual fire and toasted our sandwiches on forked willow sticks, only then did we realize how tired we were. More talk. Perhaps a swearing contest. Then a short hike up to the streetcar line, fifteen cents and the long rattle back to town.

That night, after Foster Hewitt had again exhorted, pleaded, and screamed the Toronto Maple Leafs to victory over those bloody-minded Montreal Maroons, we did not exactly kneel beside our trundle beds, but we did offer up a silent prayer that no snows would come and we could skate again to Selkirk.

Then winter came, not with the rumble of thunder that presages a hard summer storm, but first with a few flakes, then a flurry, then six or twelve or eighteen inches silently covering up all men's sins of summer and autumn.

The rink then became our lives. Every kid made his way to Nick's Shoe Shop on Osborne Street, and that kindly old Italian would grind our skates and pound in a few tacks to repair the ravages of the year before. On Monday, Wednesday, Friday, and Saturday we played pick-up hockey, as many as twenty kids of every age chasing one puck and it didn't matter which net we fired at. Just grab the puck, stick-handle, and fire a low, hard smoker. Did I say "net"? Try two broom handles or sticks frozen into the ice. No kid wanted to play goalie. Everyone wanted to be where the action was. A goalie was the kid who skated on his ankles because the only blades he had were his brother's, three sizes too large.

In our neighborhood we were lucky. My father and three others got the idea of a community club. The city gave them a chunk of land taken back for taxes. The Canadian National Railways donated a boxcar for a clubhouse. Planks for the boards were scrounged, as were the two forty-five-gallon oil drums that were welded together and fitted with a door and a chimney. It kept the shack warm. Poplar wood was bought for about three bucks a cord and a caretaker was hired. He was "Whitey," a fellow from Arnold Avenue who hadn't worked for years, but he sure worked now for his ten dollars a month.

He had to open up the shack at three in the afternoon. If there had been an overnight snow he had to clear the rink, often a task so enormous the poor fellow barely summoned the strength to sip away at his daily bottle of moonshine. He was a kindly man, Whitey, and his job allowed him to operate a small concession stand—hotdogs, soft drinks, skate laces, and such, and if he did bootleg a package of Turret Cigarettes, five smokes for five cents in the stores, his profit on his ten-cent under-the-counter price was nobody's business.

I had my first smoke in that shack, one of Whitey's Turrets, and I took a deep drag just like I'd seen Hoot Gibson do in the movies. It rolled down my throat in a fiery ball and I thought I would die. I was twelve and I swore off cigarettes for life—a vow I kept for two years.

It was in that shack that I learned a fundamental lesson of life. I had roughed up a kid named Albert Swangard against the boards and he challenged me to a fight. Usually these fights were held behind the shack. This one was inside. We were evenly matched and, though I didn't have the desire to fight, good old Arnie, my friend, wasn't going to let me get away. There was a code of honor in those days. So, I was hammering him right well until I backed him into a corner and then he became a tiger. Lesson: never back a desperate kid, man, or animal into a corner. Always leave him an escape route. I still won, but...

Tuesday, Thursday, Saturday nights, and Sunday were family skating times, and if there is anything to unite families into a community, it is family skating. It is also hell on wheels for romance, kid style. I remember a girl named Marni. Gee, I didn't know what to do and a big guy named Tom Rockwell moved in with all the *savoir faire* of an avalanche coming down a mountain. Ah, blue-eyed, golden-haired, and sweet-smiling Marni.

There were races for old and young. Ever seen a three-legged race on skates? More fun than laughing at fat ladies. There was pom-pom-pullaway and snap-the-whip and British Bulldog and afterwards hot-dogs and cocoa for a thin dime, one-tenth of a dollar. What kid today knows British Bulldog?

We didn't spend all of our time out of doors. The Park Theatre was an important part of our lives. God bless you, Rudy Besler. He was a short, stocky Jew who had run a movie house in Melville, Saskatchewan, before coming to Winnipeg and opening the Park. His wife was the cashier and his two nieces were the usherettes, and there had to be someone else up there in the dark running the projector. He loved kids. I mean he *really* loved kids. We always called him Mr. Besler with a degree of reverence we held for no one else. The Saturday afternoon matinee was his special gift to kids. Five cents, which will only get you a curse from a dead drunk wino beggar today, got you into the show. You saw a full-length movie, a Silly Symphony cartoon, usually a Fitzpatrick travelogue, and the Pathé News. The price of admission also included a large caramel sucker. We'd suck that caramel down to the nitty-gritty and then, as we all trooped up the aisle after the show ended, it was the thing to do to gently place the gooey stick against the hair of a girl you hated. What reason for hating her? She was a girl, wasn't she?

If I could talk to Mr. Besler today, I would ask him if he hated cowboys and Indians movies. I bet he would say yes.

When one came, and they came frequently, our gang and other street gangs would arrive armed with trusty cap pistols and a one-hundred-cap roll, ready to do justice. Let the Indians circle the wagon train. We, the Baltimore Gang, were there. When the fighting got intense and the war whoops splintered the air, every kid was standing on his seat and firing at the screen, picking off Geronimo or Crazy Horse or Sitting Bull with an ease that astonished us. The sound of a hundred cap guns blasting away almost drowned out the screams of the girls. The acrid, blue, sulfurous smoke almost obscured the screen.

Mr. Besler would signal for the movie to be stopped, a spotlight would throw his shadow on the screen, and he would say, "Children, if you do not stop this I will close down the show."

We didn't think he meant it until a tough guy from the Arnold Gang dropped Mr. Besler in his tracks with nine fast shots from his six-shooter. End of show. No more killing movie-house owners.

Mr. Besler's normal evening prices were two bits for an adult and ten cents for mean kids, a rate structure he maintained until 1957. Show me another businessman who maintained Depression prices through to 1957 and I'll show you... well, I'll just show you. No one can tell me that at five cents a shot for kids during the Depression he made any money. I know why he did it. He loved kids. A very nice and kindly man. I salute him.

All was not fun, whacking field mice, stealing lumber, skating, putting caramel suckers in the hair of little girls. Every kid wanted a job, and when Keith Howard, who had a forty-eight-paper route on Baltimore Road, looked for an assistant, I got the job. On sheer merit. Twenty-five cents a week, rain or shine, snow or leaden skies. When I quit the job five kids fought for it as if there was no tomorrow.

My next job was as a delivery boy for Alan Reid, our local druggist. I was thirteen. Ten cents an hour, winter and summer, but I remember the winters most. I worked Christmas Eve, Christmas Day, New Year's Eve, and New Year's Day. Mr. Reid was one of those Depression businessmen who remained open until 11:00 P.M. to catch that last wandering quarter. His method was to put each of his delivery boys into business. Smart business. We had to have a float, about five bucks in quarters, nickels, and dimes. When we took out an order we paid him the amount, and it was up to us to collect the money. Needless to say, none of my customers—for that is what they were—was allowed credit. When Mr. Reid locked the door for the night, he would pay Johnny Roy and me sixty cents for a tough night's work and make us five-cent milk whip—the equivalent today of a buck-fifty milk shake. We repaid his outstanding gratitude by swiping everything we could when his back was turned.

I'll never forget *that* New Year's Eve. A call came in from the municipal hospital at the foot of Morley Avenue: a few cases of Coke and cigarettes. I was told to go around the back to the nurses' recreation room. When I knocked, a woman opened the door. She wore only a bra and a pair of panties. I remember them still today. They were pale blue. There were sounds of partying in the dim room. She paid and then looked at me and said, "Kid, do you want to come in and warm yourself? Looks like your balls are ready to drop off."

My God! Did nice girls really talk that way???

I think it was then I realized Marni might have something more to offer than blue eyes and a sweet smile.

Next summer I worked in the harvest fields owned by a farmer named Johnson at Deloraine, and for slaving from dawn to dusk I got $1.50. I was fourteen.

I have mentioned gangs. They were not the kind of gangs that people think of today. They were just kids from the same neighborhoods who went to the same school. Ours was the Baltimore Gang, but we had members from Balfour, Oakwood, and Maplewood. Ah, but there was the Morley Gang. What a vicious, rotten, stinkin', lousy, riotous, and dastardly bunch of hoods. They also went to school with us. Played on the same teams. Great guys in school. Crazy apes outside the schoolyard.

They had to be challenged after six of them walked down our street one Wednesday night looking mean.

I was chosen to issue the challenge. I did so to a lout named Dennis Royston who sat beside me in Miss Elliot's class. I said we would meet them Saturday on the field of combat: the vacant lot on Oakwood. There was no way they could back down from such a forthright challenge, although we hoped they would.

Ten A.M. that fateful day. Eight of us—the other four had found very important things to do. Nine of them, big and mean brutes, exactly my size, which was perhaps five-foot-two. Heavy, maybe ninety-eight pounds, as I was. We were armed with the tops of garbage cans as shields and sharpened lathe sticks. They were armed the same. No guns, no knives, no hand grenades, no bazookas, no atomic bombs.

"Okay, Broadfoot, you invited us here."

"Yeah, Royston, so you're here."

"Yeah."

"Sure, yeah."

And then I saw Billy Gill, no relation to the Clifford Gill who was nicknamed Beada and who had a sister called Dirt. He was coming out of his garage and he didn't have a garbage-can lid and a sharpened lathe stick. He had a great big stick. He was one of the guys I thought had something more important to do, but I guess he had just been looking for a stick of the proper size.

Let me tell you about Billy Gill. He was English. He was Jewish. His father was quite wealthy. Billy played the piano very well, and the rest of us thought him a bit of a sissy because we had all quit our lessons after three visits to Miss Tease, the neighborhood teacher. Billy collected butterflies. He caught tadpoles and raised them to frogs and then dissected them. He would run away at least six times a year and the police would catch him on the way to Morden where the Dominion Experimental Farm was situated. I understand he could talk learnedly with the agricultural scientists there, the few times he broke through the dragnet. He was thirteen that year. Six years later he died when his bomber crashed on a raid into Germany.

Billy walked resolutely up behind this hulking ninety-eight-pound killer lout and swung his club and when Royston was falling, he slammed him once more. Then he walked back to the garage. Holy cow! This was supposed to be a fight where nobody got hurt. Now there was Royston lying on the ground, dead as Joe Schnaf's dog.

The battle line of the vicious Morley Gang fell back in horror. So did we. Nobody was supposed to get hurt. Then Royston got up and staggered off to the north, leading his sordid band of thugs and the field was ours. A great victory!

When my mother heard of it she told me she would slap me silly if it happened again. So much for the heroes of a latter-day Agincourt.

So much for the battles of our childhood, on the fields of our innocence, surrounded by the people who loved us so much. A few years down the road there were real and terrible battles to be fought.

"You're Going to Be a Writer"

I always wanted to write. Oh, there was nothing mystical about it. No star appeared in the East beckoning me on and I heard no voice calling me when I slept, and this is the first time I have disclosed that perhaps my maternal grandfather was the one who got me into the racket.

His name was Walter Scoular. His family had owned mills around Kilmarnock in Scotland and were quite wealthy. After he had sired six children he packed up everything and came to Manitoba where six more children were born. He tried ranching and failed. A try at farming failed too. Being essentially anti-social, he took his family into the bush twenty miles east of Winnipeg and carved another farm out of the wilderness. He could have purchased cultivated land a few miles to the west but, no, that was not his way. When he retired, if indeed he did, he had built for himself a small house on an acre two hundred yards from the farmhouse where his youngest son Ben lived with his family.

He was a tall man, heavily built, with a stern face and piercing blue eyes, and for years he lived alone, and apart from sleeping on a bed with boards as a mattress, he spent his time in the long, narrow kitchen. He conducted a one-man morning service every day, hammering out hymns on an old piano and reading from the large family Bible. He made his breakfast of thick porridge, cream, toast, jam, and tea. My aunt brought over his evening meal. He ventured outside rarely, usually only to fire both barrels of an old twin-hammer twelve-gauge shotgun at birds that sang in the tall poplars around his house at 5:00 A.M.. He hated robins with a pure fire.

The rest of the day he sat in a huge leather armchair, cushioned by deerskins, and read the Bible and the pulp ten-cent editions of Zane Grey and other Western writers. But he would occasionally delve into the Doc Savage genre of early science fiction. Nothing in between. He was an incessant pipe smoker and was the one man I know who could keep one going for long periods. The house reeked of smoke, but it was good tobacco.

On an autumn day when I was about thirteen I cycled over those god-awful mud roads to bring him some medicine, and we sat and talked while drinking tea. On the wall was a large framed print of Rosa Bonheur's "The Horse Fair" and next to it a print of a large and noble red stallion, probably torn from the *London Illustrated News*. He used to stare at these pictures for long periods and then thump his heavy oak cane on the floor and say, "Great horses!" He loved horses, but from tales I have heard, he was very hard on those he owned.

This afternoon he looked at me, thumped the floor twice, and said, "You're going to be a writer. Write about horses."

His remark shook me and on the long ride home I thought about it and I said, "Maybe I could be a writer. I don't see why not."

That same autumn I pedalled to the neighborhood library for my weekly fix of three books and I took out T. E. Lawrence's magnificent account of the guerrilla war he conducted in the desert against the Turks in the First World War. My friend the librarian said, "Surely you're not going to tackle *Seven Pillars of Wisdom*? I said yes and when she asked why I could only mutter that it was the biggest book on the shelves. When I returned in a week and she asked me what it was about I gave her a fairly accurate appraisal of content, narrative power, and style of writing. She appeared impressed and said, "I do believe Winnipeg might have another writer one of these years."

The third hint of things to come was the next year, in grade eight, when my English teacher, Mary Nethercutt, threw away the rules and had the class do short essays on topics like "two pages on a bush pilot on a mercy flight approaching a storm," or, "two pages on a forest fire nearing a small settlement." Instead of two pages I would do four or five, scribbling as if my very life depended upon writing six pages. They were drivel, of course, but at the end of that year she took me aside and said, "You're going to be a writer and don't forget it."

So, at age fourteen, I began my first novel. From my savings I bought ten notebooks and some pencils and, remembering my grandfather's advice, I set out to write about horses. Although I had read many Western novels, they were about people and not horses. Horses were just to get people around the country or fall from if they were shot by the bad guys. But I was going to exclude people and deal only with horses—an undertaking that even the finest writers might hesitate to try. I had never been on a ranch and I knew little about range horses, but I had this idyllic ranch in a valley in the west and a fine, free-running herd of mares and colts. Up on the ridge was a wild stallion. I did not know the ratio of stallions to mares, but I felt just one would be enough. I'm not sure I really understood exactly what stallions did to mares, but I had a rough idea. The trick was to either get the stallion down to the mares without the rancher capturing him, or get the mares up to the stallion. I learned two things. Never try and put yourself in the mind of a horse, as years of betting the ponies later taught me. Secondly, if you don't know what you're writing about, then, for God's sake stop writing.

After reading over seven notebooks of the nonsense I had written I realized that nothing was happening. The stallion was still up there and an adversary hadn't even come out of the hills to challenge his domain. The mares were still down in the valley and probably getting horny. The colts were growing up and wondering what the hell was going on. So, after two hours of reading, it was only six paces to the fireplace, and I made the long journey and that was that.

In the few years left before high-school graduation I fooled around with writing, getting a few short pieces printed. After graduation it was logical to pay a visit to the *Winnipeg Tribune* because, after all, they had printed a few of my things on a children's page. I didn't tell this to Fred O'Malley, the managing editor, when he interviewed me for a copy boy's job. Fred was short and wiry, had red hair and was crosseyed. He had an Irish temper and many's the time I saw him lurching out of his office when the city edition was delivered to him, and as he descended on the news desk, he was circling headlines with a red pencil. He would be beet-faced and shouting at the news editor, and he would throw the paper in his face and run with a funny hippity-hop back to his office. The news editor would pick up the front page, chuckle, and pass it off to a deskman for corrections. As long as one headline was rewritten, Fred was pleased. He didn't seem to care what went inside. All that mattered was how Page One looked when the householder picked it off the porch, although any newspaperman knows that the subscriber knows or cares less about Page One than he does about Dear Abby.

The first time I saw this performance, I thought, "Boy, oh boy! The big time!"

Yes, said Fred, I could have a job. A senior copy boy was going into the navy in three weeks. "Give my secretary your phone number, and, by the way, don't you want to know what the pay is?" I said well, yes, and he grinned and said, "Eight whole dollars a week."

Through a neighbor's influence I could have worked on a telephone gang for eighteen dollars a week plus free room and board. Instead, for three weeks, I toiled in the men's clothing section of the Eaton's mail-order house, monotonously piling, robot-like, pants and work shirts and underwear and socks for twelve dollars a week. I vowed then and there that I would never do anything that did not involve a minimal amount of intelligence.

On the appointed day I reported to the copy editor, who introduced me to a fat lump of a thing nicknamed Jackie who immediately tried to hang the nickname "Blue" on me because she said everybody had a nickname. I was to report at 7:30 A.M., run copy to the upstairs composing room until 8:00, then to to the *Winnipeg Free Press* six blocks away and pick up ten copies of their morning edition and drop off ten of ours. Then it was run, run, run...run copy, clear the teletypes, listen for bulletins and flashes—wartime, you know, and nothing was happening—and then fill out the stock tables from another kid phoning in from the Stock Exchange, and clean and refill paste pots; run more copy upstairs and go for coffee and bacon and tomato sandwiches for the reporters and answer their phones when they were in the can or out of the office; put two bundles of papers on the Morse Place streetcar and be sure to be at the stockyards in faraway St. Boniface by 4:30 to pick up the day's cattle sales and mark them and then take them up to the composing room for overnight setting.

There were four other copy kids and, apart from the one who phoned in the stocks for half an hour, to this day I am damned if I know what the others did. New boy, so sock it to him!

We also worked Saturdays, 7:30 to 1:00 P.M., and the city editor was a cagey one. Saturday was the day he gave out any free tickets, or other little goodies that came his way, which he didn't want, and if a kid didn't show, then no streetcar tickets, no theater passes, no circus passes, no hockey passes, no nothing. Besides, what was there to do on Saturdays anyway, and especially when you could tell your friends, casually, "Oh, I'm working at the *Trib*." Sure as hell beat digging telephone pole holes with a bar and spoon or stacking men's overalls in Eaton's.

Because the *Trib* was short-staffed, I was a asked if I wanted to do some night assignments. Of course I said yes. My first was to review a traveling show, sponsored by the government and on a Canadian tour to show civilians what kind of entertainment the boys and girls in uniform were seeing. It was a good all-round performance, snappy and fast and funny. I went backstage to get more information from the manager, a Colonel Blimp type I grew to hate when I joined the army. He thrust a clipping from the *Toronto Star* at me and said, "Here, kid, just copy this one out. They did our show last week and it is a good story."

I read it, and every sentence was pure puff. I thought, "Why, you jerk," and I went back to the office and typed out my review, and every act that deserved any criticism I gave it to them right where Lucy wore the beads.

When it appeared, all magnificent eleven inches of it—worth $2.75 at space rates—the news editor, Carlyle Allison, handed me the clipping and asked if I had written it. I said yes and he asked—heresy in any newspaper executive—if that was the way the show was. I said yes, it was. I also asked what was the matter with the piece.

"Nothing; damn good," he replied and I felt I had scaled the heights.

My next night assignment was to cover Burns Night. A strange assignment because our publisher was a big noise in the society and a lover of the Scottish Bard. Sending a sixteen-year-old kid to cover it was madness. I went and was assigned to a table for eight, the other seven being high-powered business executives and politicians of the type who composed most of the city's upper echelon. I recall now that, as I filled up my plate with many dollops of gray and greasy haggis, they looked on horrified. I thought the meal consisted of haggis and only when one old Scot rumbled, "Easy, laddie, easy," did I stop. Each put one dollop on his plate but I was damned if I'd back down and I ate the whole plate, perhaps a pound of the stuff, while their embarrassment for me changed to admiration. I went very easy on the roast beef, let me tell you, and skipped the dessert.

Then came that time-honored ceremony, with The Toast to The Haggis and then The Eulogy to the Bard. The guest speaker was, to put it mildly, stinking drunk. Everybody ignored this as if it was the custom. It fascinated me. Beside him was a little court jester of a man whispering him lines of Robbie Burns to repeat. The man wavered about, spluttered, took sips of his grog, went into short periods of muttering, and then it was over. Great applause and no one seemed to notice that the man was incapable of even stirring his coffee.

I went back to the office and wrote the story, leaving out nothing.

Next morning under my watchful eye the city editor read it, looked at me, handed it to the news editor, who took it to the managing editor, who hippety-hopped into the editor's office. It came back down the same route and the city editor called over an ace reporter, James C. Anderson, and handed him my story with a few quiet words. Jimmie came back ten minutes later with the rewrite that showed up on page two of that day's paper.

When I was delivering coffee to him later he said, "Meet me in the men's room."

When I got there in ten minutes Jimmie was doubled up laughing and Ted Schrader, our columnist, was reading my story and Johnny Buss, the day sports editor, was saying, "C'mon Jimmie, take it easy. Watch that heart of yours."

Jimmie shook my hand and said, "Kid, that's the best story that has been written for this paper in a long time." Schrader was giggling so hard he couldn't speak.

I asked him how he could write another, leaving out everything I had written but the names, in such a short time, and he said, "I covered the one last year so I just used that, the quotes and things. Nobody will care." And care they didn't.

But Jimmie had the girl in the library mimeograph about ten copies of that story and passed them out to others and they, in turn, made mimeos of it. Years later I would run into some guy in the Toronto Men's Press Club or the National in Ottawa who would say, "Great story you wrote on Burns Night."

The next day Carlyle Allison said, "I think we'll put you on the night desk. You show a lot of potential." He had a twinkle in his eyes then, but during two memorable battles I had with him much later that twinkle disappeared.

So, I began my career in newspapers.

My job was to clean the teletypes and arrange the copy by national, provincial, international, and various war zones. It was an important job. Copy kids who do it now on big dailies get more than two hundred dollars a week. My salary had been increased to twelve dollars a week. I also monitored the police radio, and many a good story was put together by the overnight police reporter from my clean notes. I had the knack, which I have never lost, of knowing by the tone of the dispatcher's voice or the replies given to him that something very big was up. A murder, a shooting.

Another job was pasting up and editing the minor items that came in on the telegraph from our far-flung rural correspondents, and during that time I kept a horrible-horrible file of the most bizarre. Alas,

I lost it. One was from Fisher Branch, way back in Hunkie hillbilly country whose representative in the Manitoba Legislature made one speech a year, deploring the increase of wolves in the district and urged the legislators to "thank about the poor passants." The town was dirt-poor and had only two cars. They collided one afternoon, demolishing each other, and each driver claimed he was innocent because each was avoiding a wagonload of pigs which at that moment had overturned on the one and only short street.

During this time I met a most remarkable man. Most dispatches from Ottawa, Washington, and London from the correspondents came in at night, so a CN telegrapher did four hours' duty until midnight. I remember him only as Bill, a small, friendly man who had lost one hand. I'd be talking to him and his wireless receiver in a tin tobacco box would begin to rattle and he would keep talking, often for two minutes. Remember, this was his transmission. Then he would excuse himself, swing around, and begin tapping with one finger at furious speed. Remember, too, perhaps two full sentences had been sent before he began typing, so that he had to remember them, word perfect. Also remember that he was always two sentences behind and when the clicking stopped, he was still typing for about two more minutes. It was the most amazing performance I have ever seen. It was uncanny, and when I would ask him how he could do it he would say, modestly, "I don't know. Just something I can do."

Then, by God, my big chance! One night about 7:30 I got a telephone tip telling about a C.P.R. engineer who, while hauling a string of empty grain cars to Brandon had looked out and seen, in a small river alongside the tracks, a kid struggling in a hole in the ice while his two companions stood around, helpless. The engineer slammed the train to a stop and jumped out of the cab, yelling to his fireman to unhook the engine. He raced out on the ice, slid himself across to the drowning kid, and hauled him free. He carried the boy to the cab, hoisted him inside, and, pouring on the coal, raced the engine to the nearest town while the fireman tried to revive the unconscious lad. A mile from the station be began blowing his whistle, a sure sign to the townspeople that something was very wrong. They got the kid into a car and rushed him to hospital and his life was saved. Helluva story, even on a good news day.

I contacted the engineer at his Winnipeg home but, believe it or not, his phone was out of order. I jumped into a taxi and hustled my butt out there, and by sheer good luck caught him just as he was leaving for the Legion. I drove him to the Legion, interviewing him and getting his C.P.R. pass because it had the only available picture of him. I returned to the office with his story and, again with sheer good luck, reached the parents of the half-drowned kid. I had it! My first scoop, although today it is called an exclusive.

Elated, I wrote the story as best I could, threw it in the overnight editor's basket, finished off my chores, and caught the last streetcar at 2:00 A.M. Famous at last! I hardly slept that night.

Next morning my mother said that Mr. O'Malley's secretary had phoned and I was to see him at 1:30—inconvenient as hell for me because I didn't start work until 6:00—but after all, I was to get a mighty round of applause from my co-workers.

I walked in to his office and he said, "Where the Christ were you around eight o'clock last night?"

I said I was out in East Kildonan getting a story about a kid who had been saved from drowning. He shrugged that off and said, "I phoned at eight and there was nobody in the office. Why did you leave it unmanned? You know goddamed well something might have happened here. Mr. McCurdy might have called."

I exploded and yelled, "Screw the publisher. I got a damn good story for you and besides, I was only away from the office for one lousy hour. Read the story."

He picked up the city edition and there bang and big on Page One was my story and O'Malley said, "I should fire you but I won't. Just don't do it again. Yeah, pretty good story. Might have given you a byline, but we don't hand them out to kids."

That was newspapering forty years ago, or one man's idea of newspapering.

Then came the word I was dreading. I was being put on the casualty list, a thing that even today I cannot believe existed. Casualties from the war were beginning to come in and filled up a part of every paper. Brutal losses in Italy. Heavy casualties in Bomber Command. Warships sunk in the North Atlantic. Men killed. Boys wounded. The kid next door missing in action.

The editor, whichever one it was and may God have mercy on his soul, decreed that the *Trib* had to carry pictures of the dead, the wounded, and the missing. The paper really didn't give a damn about the casualties, but several head shots would "brighten up the page." In other words, these pictures would have a nice cosmetic effect on an otherwise dull page and so boost the ego of the editor who lived and died by how his pages looked.

I was sent out cold, with a list of the casualties to be run next day, and told to stay out until I had at least four or five mug shots. Few people in the poorer parts of Winnipeg—and it was still a city hung up by the worst Depression in history—had telephones and it seemed that most of the casualties came from these areas. The men joined young and early to escape the terrible poverty of their lives. So with my list and a taxi, I would cruise the city knocking on doors trying to find pictures. It was a pin-in-the-list sort of thing.

The family had been notified three weeks before, but still their grief was palpable.

How many times did I walk up to an open door that summer and hear the sounds and conversation of dinner and when I knocked, silence?

"Mrs. Berkovitch, I'm Barry Broadfoot of the *Winnipeg Tribune* and I've come about a photograph of your son."

"Oh, my God! My God! Boris, Trudy, come here, come here. There's a fellow here who wants a picture of Nick. Oh, God, my baby, my baby, he's alive. He's coming back to us."

There didn't seem to be any other way of going about it, but as a youth I should not have been sent, if anyone should have been sent at all.

As gently as I could, I would have to explain to this crying family that I did not know anything about their son; that all I wanted was a picture of him "so his relatives and friends can see him in the paper."

As the sobbing mother was led away, how could a seventeen-year-old kid explain to the ashen-faced father that I wanted the picture in order to dress up a crummy newspaper page? To make the page look busy, in newspaper jargon.

Often I met hostility because some understood the real purpose of my visit. But more often I was invited into the parlor and made to sit beside the mother, with the others watching while I was taken through the family scrapbook. Nick as a baby, in his first pair of long pants, after his high-school graduation looking happy but serious, camping on the Red River, and then the inevitable picture of him in uniform, much larger than the rest and tinted by the photographers who used to travel the camps and bases doing these photos.

I did this job—call it a gruesome one if you will and I won't argue—and then, like a pilot after a thirty-op tour of duty in a squadron, I was relieved and another cub reporter given the task.

Life returned to normal—chasing fire wheels, interviewing high-ranked and officious officers of the Empire passing through and giving pep talks to Rotary, Kiwanis, the Men's Canadian Club. A duller gang of goofs I never want to meet again.

A famous English singer came through alone, singing to Rotary, Kiwanis, the Men's Canadian Club, et cetera, promoting something like Bundles for Britain, and her marvelous voice soared on many records during those years.

I interviewed her in her room at the Fort Garry Hotel and the time passed, so interested was I in her story of wartime Britain, and she appreciated someone who was genuinely interested. When she went to the washroom, the Canadian Army public relations captain who was escorting her during her Winnipeg stopover said, "Kid, will you kindly shove off? I've got to get her to a concert tonight and after, if she hasn't got three good romps in her, I'll be a very disappointed man."

The entertainer walked out as he was speaking and then ducked back. When we shook hands, I'm sure the captain could feel the chill. She said to me, "Why don't you meet me in the lobby of the theater at 10:45 and we'll have dinner?" Then she turned and smiled at the captain, whose face had become a map of fading pleasure trails. We went to Child's and had breaded veal cutlets with tomato sauce, mashed potatoes and turnips, cheesecake and coffee, and I insisted on paying the $1.90 bill. We talked until 2:00 A.M. and I walked her back to her hotel, wished her a happy journey, and went home, the happiest guy in the world. I knew she didn't want me to go up to her room, but she had desperately wanted to talk with someone who understood who she was and what she was trying to do for her country, and mine.

She was a very nice person, a fine lady. And when I think of that damn-fool captain and his boast of sexual prowess, I wonder why so many officers I met in those days were like that? She probably had him pegged from the start.

I will always remember one girl about my age named Selma. Her volunteer job was to bring in stories and articles about the activities of the city's large Jewish community. She would write up meetings of

Jewish lecturers on tour and the activities of the Jewish movement on the University of Manitoba campus and a myriad of other activities, and I noticed a pattern woven through everything she wrote—the persecution of the Jews in Germany and then in countries overrun by the Nazis. Her stuff was treated with no more import than the activities of any other ethnic group or the weekly column of Boy Scout news. To be fair, she didn't do a good job of telling the story. Even so, in retrospect, I find this surprising because although the Jews kept a deliberately low profile, there were many in Winnipeg with a great deal of financial clout.

I was intrigued, and since her twice-weekly visits seemed to coincide with my 9:00 P.M. lunch hour, I asked her out for coffee. I explained that I did not feel she was getting her message across. I also said I did not know what that message was. She burst into tears and then became hysterical.

When she calmed down, Selma said, "The Germans are killing our people. By the tens of thousands, Jews all over Europe are going into concentration camps and are dying. The young and the old and the sick, they go first into these flame ovens, and then when the strong ones get worn out they are burned too. Everybody knows it and nobody wants to talk about it. This is what the whole war is about. Not land, but killing off our people."

I said I had heard little or nothing about this and she screamed, "You won't. The Americans won't let it get into the papers and on the radio because they will make billions of dollars making guns for England and Russia and for their own soldiers. If people knew this truth they would hate Americans, and they love to be loved."

Of course, her reasoning escaped me because even if the world knew what was happening to the Jews, how could that possibly speed up the war and a victory for us?

Anyway, I interviewed her and she brought two other men who had got out of Germany in 1938 and still had pipelines into Germany and Occupied Europe. I thought, they must be desperate, to talk to a seventeen-year-old kid when some of the world's most high-powered columnists and commentators should have been at their service. I found out.

I wrote a long story piecing together what I had been told and the little I could glean out of the publications they showed me. The *Trib* would not print it. I never received an explanation. In those days a cub reporter, or even the star reporter, did not ask. But when my story was refused, I began to wonder if it was all worth it—this romantic exciting, crusading newspaper game.

Only after the war had been won did the stories of Dachau and gas ovens and S.S. atrocities come out, as they had to; then the world's greatest journalists tumbled over themselves to tell the story of how six million innocents were exterminated.

Working on the *Trib* was probably the best time in my long newspaper career. I remember going into that long and noisy, cream-painted city room each day with eager anticipation. If you had to work seventeen hours one day, that was fine. You felt you were accomplishing something, and that something was important. The newspaper was the center of all that was vital and interesting and exciting because it was here where it all started. If the heartbeat of a good newspaper slowed, and it became older and sloppier and stodgier and afraid to take that next big step toward the excellence that eludes every paper, then you could almost feel the heartbeat of the city slow too.

There were characters, like Cliff Hayes, a bush pilot in the north who decided he wanted to be a reporter. The first time he sat at a Remington we knew he was a star. A natural. He dressed like a Hollywood reporter, talked out of the corner of his mouth, made references to several wives he had had when two was the absolute limit even the most rotten of cads would have in those days. Bush pilots were exempt from military service but reporters weren't, so to evade carrying a rifle he joined an American company with a contract to fly bombers to Britain via Florida, Brazil, the Azores, and up into Blighty. He wrote me but one letter which said, "These crates we're flying are powered by Singer Sewing Machine motors and I doubt if I'll collect by first pay." He didn't. The bomber he was piloting disappeared somewhere in the mid-Atlantic.

Then there was Tony Allen, the city editor with a Harvard degree. One day the agricultural editor gave him a very weirdly shaped egg— his correspondents were forever sending in funny-looking eggs and carrots—and Tony remarked that the hen must have had a rough time of it. Then he casually tossed it over his shoulder to the big wastepaper basket. He never missed the toss—but this time he did. Four stories down. Minutes later a well-dressed businessman appeared at the

counter and told the receptionist: "I…Want…To…See…Somebody!"
Tony was already walking toward the man and he took out his
checkbook, wrote a check for $125, and handed it to the man, saying:
"I hope this is satisfactory, sir?" The businessman looked at it and said,
"Yes, this is fine, and good day, sir."

Tony walked back to the city desk remarking, "Hell, who needs
three weeks' pay?"

By the way, the agriculture editor was also editor of the religious
page on Saturday because he was a defrocked minister. It figures. He
was a truly decent man, and when I started as copy boy he took me
aside and said, "Barry, it is not true that newspapermen drink a lot,
and I hope you won't," thus predicting my career in journalism. I said I
wouldn't, although I had a smoke in my hand and had been drinking
beer and rye for a year.

When I joined the army a few of the guys gave me a small farewell, a
couple of cases of beer they had managed to scrounge up in those days
of rationing and some sandwiches made by the wife of Jack Robertson,
the night editor. We guzzled, talked, joked, told stories, and broke up
at the awful hour of midnight. As I walked part of the way home with
Ben Lepkin, still the best theater and movie critic I have known, I
thought, "What a hell of a send-off for a twelve-dollar-a-week cub
reporter," but I was so pleased.

At parting, Ben shook hands and said, "You didn't have to volunteer.
Wait till you're called up."

I said no, I'd get it over with now, and he laughed and said, "Okay,
but you'll be back."

I did come back from war service and I wondered why, at the time.

My twelve-dollar salary was increased to fifteen dollars a week. I
also found out as the years passed that newspapering really didn't have
much to do with writing, but it was a hell of a good way to waste time
until the real writing had to begin.

4

A Hunt Ends, a Quest Begins

It's funny how things happen. I was back in Winnipeg after the war, studying at the university, when I ran into old Mr. Grant. I had not seen him in many years, but I remembered him well. He had taught me how to play chess. When he asked me to take him duck hunting, I said yes. Neither of us knew at the time that he was about to teach me something else.

I was very disenchanted with my life at that point and the future seemed to stretch emptily ahead of me, but in the few hours I spent with that fine old man I learned that I must start looking again through the proper end of the telescope. I can't really say that he inspired me—and were he alive, he would be horrified that I might think so—but that morning he showed me that one who lunges for life savagely will not always find the inner peace that makes life worthwhile.

So I returned to university with a new perspective, determined to find ways to express myself, ways that were fulfilling. There was a lot of laughter and some heartbreak, and yes, a definite sense of achievement. I did not strive for academic honors; the rewards were intangible but no less real.

The laughter stayed, the heartbreak went quickly away because we were young and there was a new world out there. When I graduated, I put my degree away, said good-bye to loved ones, and headed west, to Vancouver and every challenge that lay on my road.

Last Flight off Netley Marsh

In Manitoba there is a time of year, autumn, when hunters go north to Netley Marsh to see the late flight of northern ducks before they wing down the Great Central Flyway to their winter havens on the Gulf of Mexico.

It is a time of clear and crisp nights, warm and tangy days, when businessmen in Winnipeg, meeting on Portage Avenue at noon, ask not, "Improve your handicap this summer?" but, "Have you filled the locker yet?"

Duck-hunting time; shooting behind blinds on the barley stubble of a farm field or, at dawn, crouching in the weeds or balancing in a punt, waiting for the birds to come streaking down from those miles of silent and mysterious marsh.

Marsh shooting is the best, spotting them moving in off the water where they rafted for the night, picking one bird and telling yourself you will stay with it, snuggling the twelve-gauge into the shoulder, leading, swinging smoothly as they come within range, twenty more yards closer, then the crump of the gun, the thud of the recoil, and the forlorn tumble of death.

I knew a man, a doctor, who said he hated shooting, hated eating ducks, hated killing; but he did it so effortlessly and so surely and so amazed his friends that every time he went to the marsh with them it was an ego trip.

However, killing ducks on a cold, wet morning with the birds coming in on a tailwind is a challenge few men handle well.

And this takes me back to another time, in the late thirties, when I was a boy. There was a man who lived down the street from us in a small and ugly brown house with a wide verandah across the front and a *Caragana* hedge giving him some privacy. He was retired, and I knew his wife had died because my parents went to her funeral with a few neighbors. His son had moved to Vancouver and his daughter had married and gone to Toronto and he was quite alone.

He used to talk to us, the Baltimore Gang, when we were hanging around the mailbox, our rendezvous, and he was posting a letter. He would tell us about the natives of New Guinea and how the Laplanders raised reindeer as Canadian farmers did cattle. He knew a lot about

Japan and China and he could go on at great length about tiny, naked natives in a desert in Africa living on roots, bugs, and a large type of lizard. They could throw a poisoned spear a long way with great accuracy.

He was a small man and he told us once he had arthritis and he'd have it until he died, but worse. He was a veteran of the First World War and whatever he wore—a suit, a jacket, a sweater—he always had a large and garish veteran's button on his lapel. My father told me our neighbor had worked at a number of jobs, but he thought he was basically a clerk. He had a small log cabin down in the Whiteshell Forest Preserve where he went for two weeks every summer.

His name was Mr. Grant.

One evening our phone rang and Mr. Grant asked for me. I did not know he knew my name from our conversations around the mailbox, but he was asking if I could come around the next day, Saturday, and throw a cord of split poplar into his basement. The boy who did it was sick. I said I would.

Now, a cord is a lot of wood when cut and split into sixteen-inch lengths. After throwing it through a two-foot-square hole into the cellar and then stacking it, I felt I should have earned fifty cents for a morning's hard work. He gave me twenty-five cents and I thanked him. He invited me in and we walked up a short flight of stairs into a big, warm kitchen and he gestured toward the table. "Both children had their tonsils and adenoids taken out on that. I call it the operating table. None of this Children's Hospital business in this house," he said. The dining room was small and opened into a large living room, full of old and stuffy furniture, brown or dark rose in color. There were a couple of bookcases against the walls, and on the floor by his easy chair were stacks and stacks of *National Geographic* magazines. He nodded toward them, saying, "My jungle library, thanks to the Grosvenor family." I didn't know until years later that the Grosvenor family were the be-all and end-all of the *National Geographic.* Those magazines were his window looking out on the world.

There was a stand with a row of pipes, and this seemed appropriate because to this day I can never associate Mr. Grant with a cigarette or a stinking cigar. A smoking jacket was draped over the big chair—a Christmas gift from his daughter in Toronto? In a corner stood a cage and a canary—a silent canary as I recall. It was a room with little going for it, and the gloom caused by the closed blinds added to its lack of character.

I sat down and he went back to the kitchen and returned with a large piece of apple pie and milk, and a glass of some kind of whiskey for himself. He asked me what I thought of the coming war in Europe and about Mackenzie King, the prime minister, and my answers, I'm sure, were pretty childish. In school it was readin', 'ritin' and 'rithmetic, with some geography and history thrown in to sweeten the pot. All in all, however, the conversation was heady stuff for a kid of eleven.

Beside him was a leather hassock, which was a fixture in every lower-class living room in the land in those days. This one was green and white, and on it was a chessboard with ivory pieces. When I glanced at it, Mr. Grant asked, "Do you play chess?" I said no and he asked if I wanted to learn, and more out of politeness than desire I said I did. He replied, "A wise choice. You'll never regret learning the game."

So every Tuesday I would walk down to Mr. Grant's house at 7:00 P.M. and the board would be set up and we would play several games and I always lost because he was good and I was learning. He was patient in the instruction. After our games, there was pie and milk or tea for me and a whiskey for him. This went on for many weeks, and soon we were playing only four or three games a night because it took him longer to win. One night I beat him. The next Tuesday I did it again. The following week I beat him twice out in four games. In no more than a month after that double win I was his master. To me, it was embarrassing. I had not even got through the four books on chess he had loaned me and now I was the winner. I wasn't making any brilliant plays, but I was anticipating his moves, knowing how he would attack, on what side, with what pieces. I also understood what pieces he was prepared to sacrifice. I can't say I was better, but he was the attacker because of his confidence and knowledge, and also of my ignorance. Chess is war. The attacker always has the advantage, and I was the defender, and mistakes made were made by Mr. Grant.

It all ended when I won three games of four and he stood up and said, "I seem to have lost my zest for the game. I can't see any point of you coming back to play again." That was it. Dismissed. There was no pie and milk that night. I felt sad. He was my friend.

Time trudged, staggered, and fell down and then it was 1947, ten years later. I had graduated from high school, joined the *Winnipeg Tribune* as a cub reporter, volunteered in the Canadian infantry and my non-war. Now I was back in my home town, enrolled at the University of Manitoba and not liking it at all, on the basis of about five weeks of it. The first-year classes were filled with veterans with their brown-dyed uniforms not quite concealing the stitches of patches, stripes, marks, and other stuff we used to clutter up our uniforms to prove we were somebody. I knew very, very few of them and my mates from high school were now all in third or fourth year. They had taken the way of sons of wealthy men and gone to university instead of fighting for God, King, and Country, or in whatever order you wish to put that trinity.

To me, the kids coming in from high school were just youngsters, and after several lectures in each subject I felt the instructors were almost up to the level of the high-school kids. I was like a new boy on the block. I attended only the classes I had to and spent afternoons going for long walks and drinking beer in the Pembina Hotel.

One gray afternoon I was walking toward the river where a path went for miles up to the hotel and I heard someone calling my name. It was Mr. Grant and he was waving from his verandah.

"C'mon in, c'mon in, boy," he called. So I was still a boy, eh? Same house, same living room, same big chair, the same unidentifiable smell, and the midafternoon gloom was still there. Bigger stacks of the *National Geographic.* The green and white hassock beside his chair, but no suggestion of a game. Same pie, but this time I had a whiskey with him.

We talked, he anxious to hear of my experiences in the army, and while he fingered that big First World War button on the lapel of his cardigan he never mentioned his war. I felt the time was not right, but I could have told him of a camp where a chess master had taken on forty chess players from our battalion and beaten thirty-nine of them with lightning moves as he went up the line of boards. He had a draw with a guy from Saskatoon, a Jewish kid.

Another year went by and I was getting settled in, had bought a 1933 Plymouth sedan from a widow, had a girl friend, and things were fine. One night the phone rang and it was Mr. Grant and without any palaver he said, "Seen you going by in that car of yours. Used to sell cars before and partly through the Depression. Know my cars. That

'33, she's light but a good one. Plymouth makes good cars. C'mon down here if you can make it. Got a proposition."

Hah, I thought, he's found a new book on chess and mastered the problems and he's going to give me a licking.

But no. When I got there he didn't beat around the bush. Just handed me a whiskey and asked, "Ever hunt ducks?"

I said yes, ducks, geese, partridges, prairie chickens, Hungarians. I said I used a twelve-gauge with barrels of Damascus steel and he told me to throw the thing away before it blew up in my face.

"No, give the damn thing to a museum. Tell them it was used in the Crimean War."

Then he said he wanted me to take him duck-hunting and not next week but the next day. All I had to do was bring my car, my gun, my shells, and dress warmly. Now I knew why he had called me. I agreed, and we went.

As we drove out of Winnipeg the next afternoon I thought, Christ, he must be seventy-four, seventy-five, by now and, apart from piss and vinegar, he's pretty shaky and he's got enough gear piled in back to outfit a platoon.

Yesterday he had said, "I want you with me. Carry things. Help, anything goes wrong. This is something I can't do alone."

He kept up a running commentary and I wondered if he hadn't been dropping the level in his bottle of whiskey. When I asked where we were going, he said, "Boy, up on the edge of the big marsh. Late flight. All the fools will have blasted the sky apart long ago. We'll be alone for the flight. Late autumn."

We turned off and headed north on a muddy road and he told me to get into the ruts and keep my hands off the wheel and we'd get there. He waved at stooped workers, men, women, and children, cleaning up their potato crops, and he said, "Galicians. Don't know them but I would have known their poppas and mammas. Used to travel, selling. Took a politician with me once and we stopped at every shack and he poured every man a big, big glass of white lightning, home brew, fire water, from a keg he'd worked into the back seat. Don't know if that did it, but the bugger got elected again."

An hour later as dusk began to set in he said, "That mailbox there. That's my hunting lodge. Turn in," and we wheeled into a Galician farmyard, whitewashed house, late-blooming geraniums by the homemade plank door, a log barn, a couple of straw stacks, a hay pile, a large mound of manure, a pigpen with the pigs out of it, in it, a rusted tractor, one-way, hay rake and rick, iron-wheeled wagon, and that was about it.

A man, and a woman standing behind him, were at the door, and when Mr. Grant clambered out he called, "Evening, Stan, and a good evening to you, Mrs. Peters."

The man came forward quickly and shook Mr. Grant's hand hard and said, "Not think you come, Mr. Grant. Three year now. No phone call for me to neighbor. No letter that kid help me learn. Maybe you dead, wife say. No good. Come, bring him."

Mr. Grant turned to me and said, "Guns, shells, gear, everything, yes, and that brown paper bag. Bring everything into the house. His English neighbors are thieves, and his dog doesn't bark."

I thought, My God, now he's a sergeant major.

As I lugged everything in and dumped it, he was saying, "...and we'll leave early to catch the morning flight, over by the two bridges. They should be fat as butterballs. That barley stubble south of the tracks. Many guns about?"

Stan said, "Many, then some, now maybe just few. Not much boom-boom," and he clapped his huge hands twice.

Mr. Grant turned and said, "This is Stan Peters. Used to be Stanislawzcicki or something, all *c*'s and *z*'s and when I first came here I told him just to change his name to Stan Peters. Nice name. Easy to hear, remember. Not legally done, of course, but legal enough. Where's that brown paper bag?"

I handed it over and he dug in and pulled out a handful of chocolate bars—Cadburys, Baby Ruths, Krisp-Kwicks, Almond Squares—and threw them on the linoleum-covered table and said, "Call kids."

Stan gestured toward some sacking covering an opening and hollered something in Galician and two towslers, a boy and a girl, came out. He spoke to them and the boy, about nine, marched over and gravely shook our hands. The girl, six, curtsied.

They each took a bar and put it in the side pocket of their overalls. Stan handed the bag of goodies to his wife and spoke to her rapidly. She nodded and began putting out plates and cups and a loaf of bread and pickles. If they didn't know we were coming, then why this huge meal with bowls and pots of steaming food being brought to the table?

As she hustled, Stan hauled a gallon jug from beneath a stand-up washbasin and filled three hefty tumblers. It was clear in the jug, but when poured it became milky and after one pull, I thought, can I survive this? I did, just managing to finish it when the last dish reached the table. The stuff would have knocked a plow horse to its knees.

Mr. Grant was telling Stan he should buy more beef cattle and sell butter and cheese in town and feed the extra milk from his small herd of milkers to the pigs. Buy more pigs. Forget the milk truck, which was irregular and sometimes just didn't come. I thought he was mighty uppity telling another man how to farm and then he said, "I've been with Stan a long time. Give him money to start this farm, money from my father's estate, or else he'd still be a hired man for some Englishman back near town. I said Libeau country was best because the land is very cheap and it will grow. Paid off every cent. This is Stan's second wife, second litter."

The food was hot, nutritious. Turnip and beet soup, I think, thick stew. Black bread and jam. I turned down an offer of another glass of Murder First Degree and so did Mr. Grant and Stan put the jug away, so we still had our wits about us.

An hour later we went to bed, a big handmade bed with a huge European-style comforter and pillows like rocks. On the wall there was a picture of a man and woman at their wedding festival and beside it a cheap white cross and a picture of Jesus.

I said, "Hell, this is their bedroom! Where are they sleeping?"

Mr. Grant said, "She's probably with the kids and he's curled up on the floor or in the hay loft," and he blew out the lamp and said, "Go to sleep. Morning comes early in this country."

Mrs. Peters woke us up at five, banging the lids on the iron stove. I hopped out of bed, dressed, sluiced my face down in the pail by the stove, and dried it with a bit of gunny sack hanging there. I went out, into night sharp and crisp, and I wanted to reach out and grab a fistful of the air and squeeze it for its goodness. As I looked at the sky I saw the first blush of northern lights of the year and heard a dog howl nearby, not a howl to greet the morn, but an "I've-been-kicked" howl as he received his punishment for letting a bleary-eyed farmer trip over him.

Breakfast was sowbelly and eggs, bread and tea, and I hated to leave that warmth of lamplight. I wasn't really The Great White Hunter at

6:00 A.M., but there I was, loaded down with a small packsack of food, a shell bag, shotgun, and a gallon of water slung over my shoulder with a piece of binder twine. I questioned Mr. Grant about so much water but he was insistent, saying it was necessary and ending up with: "Water is the staff of life and cannot be done without." I did not correct him by saying the word was "bread," not "water." But I did know I was going to have a sore shoulder after two miles of walking. I'd have a groove that would never go away.

He knew where he was going, even in the dark. To the ragged road, and on it for five minutes, then over a stone fence, across a spongy field, down a path through a large stand of poplars where the going was rough, and then up on the railway grade. The stars were still hanging up there in the tent of night. He must have had cat's eyes to get us to the tracks. We walked for twenty minutes on the ties, he telling me not to worry about a train because only three freights came by a week and it just showed how stupid railroaders were, spending tax-payers' money on useless lines like this one. Then he said that there were two creeks ahead, side by side, and he would shoot at the first trestle where the creek drains off into the marsh and I would take the second. He told me to leave the food sack and the jug by the water barrel on the first trestle, although why they would want to prevent fire from destroying this useless line he didn't know. I wondered if Stan hadn't slipped him another tumbler of Murder First Degree.

Far away another dog started an insane, insistent barking. A gang of crows in trees south of the track were waking up, the convention chairman calling them to order, and a debate began whether they should take off for the sunny southland today or tomorrow. Stay or go? Like hicks outside a carnival girlie show. To go, or not to go?

Mr. Grant began giving me instructions on how to shoot ducks, where to locate, where to look, how to stand, how to shoot, how to recover, how to keep still, when to shoot, and "For God's sake, boy, if you've got a wounded one on the ground don't bash its head in with your gun butt. Wring its neck." I was laughing to myself.

And then, "Shoot like you play chess. Not flashy, just steady," and that was the first reference since that day so long ago as we measure the time spans in our own short lives.

He said, "I'm going," and he slid down the grade. I dumped the gear and water by the barrel on his trestle and walked across my trestle, testing every footing because the last thing I needed was a broken leg. I slid down the grade, worked my way forward, and found a perfect spot, close to the edge of the water of the marsh, a place where willows grew waist high. I set up camp.

I slipped in two red, shiny shells and stared out at the marsh and I tested my swing with the gun, pushing the butt hard into the cup of my shoulder, squeezing on the dead triggers, and I waited. More sounds of coming day. Another dog, farther to the west. A light breeze knocking the last dry leaves of the poplars to the ground and tinkling the lacy ice along the marsh.

False dawn began as the giant machinery of the universe slipped into a higher gear and the night began to turn into day. You could see now, but it really was only the sensation of sight. I heard a whiss-whiss over my head, high, and then twos and threes went over. No use trying. Waste of shells. Ducks that God didn't want to be killed.

Fifteen minutes later, as the machinery began to move faster, I heard two booms from the other side of the first creek and I thought, "Jesus, has he got two already?" Then I was kept busy, firing, loading, searching out the incoming, firing, opening holes in the heavens— elation, frustration, joy, desperation, hey hey! I heard Mr. Grant's gun booming away, and other reports from other parts of the marsh, but far away.

The ducks were hurtling in like Typhoons going after German tanks isolated on a dike in Holland. The light was perfect now. I was lucky and got three in five minutes, dropping them only a few yards behind me. Mallards. I hit another and it fell into the marsh and was lost. A fourth. I picked it up, held it to my cheek, and I could feel the last of its heartbeats as it died.

Just when I thought the morning flight was finished, I spotted two more goofing over the marsh, and then they made a charge for the shore, the drake in front and his lady friend a few yards behind. I thought, *You're for me.* As the big mallard came in range I waited a second, rose, my gun now an old friend, and when the boss saw me he flared upward and honked a warning to his mate. I squeezed and his wings snapped into his sides and like a well-thrown dart he planed into the ground a few feet behind me. I shot for the hen but missed and she went over, came around, wandered out of range for a minute or so, and then back in down the fire path. I knocked her over but only wounded her, and she flew, slipping and veering, out to the marsh to die.

The sky was clear. The flight was over. I cleaned up camp and crossed over to the grub bag and the water and found Mr. Grant sitting with his legs dangling over the creek, smoking his pipe.

"Well, how many?"

"Five. You?"

He tapped his pipe bowl, slowly hoisted himself to his feet, and replied, "Not one, son. None. I told you the birds were here and they were. I just couldn't reach them somehow, or, well, maybe it's these old eyes or this old trigger hand or this old man himself. Years ago I could have filled a sack. I got one, a stray, and it fell out in the water. Couldn't have hurt him much 'cause he swam away. Maybe I just surprised him. Fell down out of shock."

I thought of his fine gun booming away so confidently, like Wellington's artillery at Waterloo. All I could say was, "I'm sorry, sir. We'll have a good feed on mine. They'll cook up fine."

"No, son, those are a treat for your folks for having to put up with you," and he slapped my arm and chuckled.

I laughed and held out the jug and said, "Have a drink of Adam's Ale?"

"Thanks, son, but we don't need it. Fact is, why did we bring it all this way anyway? A thermos of coffee would have done better. Just that in the old days we always brought along a jug of water. I don't know why now. Just did. Sling it into the creek. No sense carrying it back. Then you and me better be getting on. Flight's over."

He started down the track, his beautiful gun held at the infantryman's trail and when the last gun of the morning roared somewhere, he turned toward the sound and snarled, "Damn fool. Probably shooting at a mud hen. Flight's over." He was tired.

At the farmhouse the woman came to the door and gave us a note that read: Gone Selkirk with neighbor. Buy oats. Come again. Mr. Grant read it and handed his gun to Mrs. Peters and with gestures indicated that she was to give it to Stan, but he failed in trying to get across that it was a gift. She called inside and the little boy poked his head out and Mr. Grant patiently explained and the lad nodded, took the gun, gravely shook hands with both of us, and we loaded the car and left.

"That was nice of you to give your gun to Stan," I said.

"Yes. A fine man, Stan. We've shot over that marsh many a time, me with a gun it took me three years of saving to buy and he with a thing you'd be afraid to shoot a mad dog with. Maybe it would backfire. Stan will know why I gave him the gun. Glad he wasn't home. Best after all."

I knew it was his last hunt.

"Son, you can take me home now."

We Vets Came, Saw, Conquered Academe

It was the best time of the year and the best year of our lives.

We, so many tens of thousands, had our discharges from the Canadian Armed Forces and something was happening that we would never have thought possible: we were going to be university and college graduates!

The vote-chasing Liberals, through the new Department of Veterans' Affairs, had swung wide the doors of the country's universities and colleges, and we could get a degree, just like the rich kids. D.V.A. would pay us sixty-five dollars a month living expenses—those with wives got eighty dollars—so long as we made good marks and were good little boys and girls. The schools could not object. What were a few thousand new students in the year 1945? Besides, those lean and hungry institutions would prosper mightily from our fees paid by the federal government. But something went wrong, because the politicians had grossly underestimated the number of us veterans who rejected previous ways of life and saw a bright and gleaming future ahead, all wrapped up in a neat diploma and tightly knitted with our hopes, dreams, and ambitions.

Yes, it was the best time of our lives and if we had joined up to make the world safe for democracy, democracy was now making the world safe for us.

In the twenties few Canadians had a higher education because, as they say, it was just not done. We were a nation of the lower middle class, the poor and the rural, and few were the numbers of youths who could find jobs good enough to save money to put themselves through four years of grind. Of course, if Daddy were middle class, all was possible, and those who then graduated ran Canada as surely as the sun falls behind the mountains of Vancouver Island. The great majority of these young men came from southern Ontario, an area pinned to the unknown mosaic of Canada by the City of Toronto's hatpin.

These early graduates knew it was their right to run Canada, a nation so young and naïve and gentle that it really required little administration. What had to be done was done in a Big Brother fashion. Things were done to make the country work, and no more. That way southern Ontario could dominate forever.

During the Great Depression those of the middle class—especially those who worked for the government—could put their sons and daughters through university or college because, with severe deflation, even a little money was a lot. A dollar had great buying power.

That era, like the twenties, mitigated against those who wanted higher education. Most universities had an unwritten law that prevented Jews from entering the chosen professions *en masse*; only a few were allowed in as doctors, dentists, lawyers. Jews were thought to be too smart and would therefore shake the foundations of southern Ontario's fiefdom—Canada. Girls who wished to be teachers could go to Normal School—but was that really higher education? Farm boys could go to agricultural colleges, which really were not colleges at all. Other boys stayed on the home farm; city youths found jobs wherever and if there were any.

Rarely was an ethnic seen in the colleges and universities: It was considered presumptuous of a lad from a Ukrainian farm in Saskatchewan to want a better way of life, and the son of a Polander in Manitoba was thought to be doing well if he could buy a quarter-section after ten years of working for his father or neighbors. As for negroes, Canada had a few railway porters and shoeshine boys. The existence of Indians was not acknowledged except as a tourist attraction when the proud Blackfeet staged whooping and yipping rain dances at the Calgary Stampede.

Chinese high-school grads were expected to follow their fathers into the family laundry or restaurant; Japanese students, perhaps the most eager for advancement, were expected to work in market gardens, stores, and on fishboats as their life's career.

Scandinavians were certainly tolerated and often could be considered as okay and the First World War suspicions of all things Germanic seemed to be fading and, of course, there were the French, who had their own colleges to turn out a priest for every family.

But in the main Canada was truly WASP Country.

And then came the surly rumble of Panzer divisions and our nation was at war, and there was so little time to look backward again.

Then it was all over, first in Europe and then in the Pacific, and there we were, milling about, passing in and out of the tiny, cramped registrar's office at the Osborne Street campus of the University of Manitoba, dozens of us that day early in October, just as there had been dozens on each of the previous thirty days.

In a way I, like the rest, moved about hesitantly, all of us perhaps fearful of what we would find. I had not expected to go to university but to return to newspaper reporting. Were four years of university to be an interlude, or was I about to chart a new course in my life?

There were so many of us. The man who fought the wobbly controls of a crippled Lancaster bomber returning from a night raid to Essen and who would marry an English girl and bring her to Canada as a war bride. The man who had been in that terrible house-to-house fighting in the destroyed Italian town of Ortona, the Stalingrad of the Western Allies, and he wanted to engineer highways. The lad who had never seen the ocean, so he joined the navy and manned a Bofors gun in the awful days of the Nazi submarine wolf packs in the North Atlantic. The nurse who had watched helplessly at a field hospital at Caen in France and who wanted to take Interior Design and make life a nicer place for people. Those were people who could have been there that October morning, and probably were. There were also the ordinary Joes, be they slobs or sluts, optimists or brooders, thinkers or doers, the good men and the bad men, the jokers and the scroungers, the happy-go-luckies and the Plain Janes, the kid from next door and the kid from Melfort, Saskatchewan. Truly a melting pot.

So, on this happy morning as we milled about, looking for faces we had seen or known in some camp in Canada or some far-off place, we were essentially children again, as bewildered as we had been when we enlisted. In the services we knew only too well what it was like to be screwed, blued, and tattooed, blancoed and snafued, rushed somewhere in half a day to wait nine days for something to happen; the unnecessary but required paperwork for which the forms were missing or which would be thrown away anyway, and the unending blather and gossip and I'm-in-the-lifeboat-Jack mentality. Each of us, in our own way, had learned to cope with the stupidities of service life. Now, seeing the disarray and confusion, we wondered if we were running into it again.

Suddenly I saw a familiar face in the crowd, a guy named Heffer, a tall, scrawny type who hated me and I hated him when we were stationed in a camp far away. He let out a shout and I let out a yell and we shook hands and fired off questions, neither of us answering the other's. He'd been through this pig scramble two weeks ago and he took me, yanked me, pushed me, and in ten minutes he had got things done, a process I had thought might take the whole day and far into the night.

I had filled out forms, signed them, and been given three cards; I had been handed a large sheet that showed what subjects I was required to take and where and when they were, and another sheet with a list of books I would need, and a booklet stating the rules and regs of the university, all emphasizing what a lucky guy I was. I threw the booklet away and whenever I needed to know something I asked someone who knew. Army style.

I had to assume that the university had been told and warned and also cautioned that this tight little island was about to be invaded and would never be the same again. I imagine the deans and professors and lecturers and administrators had all nodded, smiled, and said yes, we understand. We were to be treated no differently from the boys and girls coming in from the high schools. But again, yes, we were to be treated differently. They were told to treat us gently, carefully. Some of us, they were told, had been away from the real life for two, four, six years. Our learning habits would probably be somewhat different. We might want to know something that came up at a lecture and we'd want to know it now! That must have terrified them! Our social graces might not be all they might have desired because after all, so many of us had been deprived of the cultural advantages of the high-school monthly dances. We might try to take control. After all, hadn't many of these chaps, good fellows all, but hadn't many taken part in controlling the world? They might have been told that many of us had learned that the way to make something work was by bloody well making it work. That is different from controlling. You can make something work and then turn the machinery back to the one who had controlled it but couldn't make it work.

To my knowledge, the "civilian" student body had not been briefed, and why should they have been? After all, weren't they only kids, the reason for the university?

They could have been told that the bronzed and handsome s.o.b. who wanted to steal a senior's girl had been a wing commander in Burma and he had the R.A.F. moustache to prove it. Don't mess with the little fellow in the dyed battle-dress jacket: he had been a commando and you could lose your front teeth by getting into an argument over who was next in line in the cafeteria. The chap who waited until the end of a question period and then fired in a zinger that stopped the professor cold might have commanded a destroyer off the Normandy Beach on D-Day.

Funny, everybody expected a lot of things to happen. They didn't. Not right away. What we were doing in that first year came to us naturally. In those heady days we were in the Fields of Academe and reconnoitering the terrain.

What we really wanted was so simple—an education and some happy times and, most important of all, some quiet times to think things over.

So, after all the confusion of moving up to the start line, we did get sorted out and those who wanted an Arts degree to put away somewhere as a souvenir were shoved one way. So were the future chemical whizzes who took Science. The lads who wanted a bank for their very own headed off to Commerce. We all went where the instructions told us to go. Just like in the service.

I remember well my first English 101 lecture. I had missed several by being late in registering, and there must have been four hundred in that amphitheater, rows upon rows, stretching high to the gods. A year before, the professor might have had a hundred goggly-eyed freshmen.

The professor was late and from my seat way up there I surveyed the multitudes and thought, my God, is this a class or are they going to hold a basketball game down there? Nope, just a lecture. The poor, dumpy man with the scraggly red hair and wearing his professor's uniform did his best in a squeaky voice to explain Robert Frost, an American poet whom he obviously revered. I later wondered what this man felt when Frost was revealed to be an arrogant bastard and was rather discredited in the world-arranging department.

We listened to him ramble on about a doctor driving a horse and cutter through woods on a snowy evening, and I vowed then and there I would never take any notes because I might miss something important.

Before my first week was over I knew, as I'm sure everyone else did, that Arts was little more than an extension of high school. The diploma we wanted would not prove that we had received an education but only that we had paid our dues to a society that demands we appear to have received an education. In four years, nothing I recall at university disproved that theory.

During the year in English 101 we turned in a couple of essays, one on Chaucer, who I thought was a gutty guy, and received them back with neat *B*'s and *C*'s on them, but no indication that they had been read. In the spring we wrote a three-hour exam and I suppose all four hundred of us passed.

Before the start of the second year I went to the Dean of Arts and Sciences and I said, "Dean Argue, is there any reason why I should take mathematics and chemistry? I'll never use them. They are as useless as tits on a bull to me and the time I am wasting on them I could put to better use. After all, I'm not planning to blow up a bridge in Quebec...."

He was a sweet little man with a kind word for everyone and totally ineffectual—which made him important in the academic scheme—and he replied, "Dear boy, you wouldn't do that, would you?"

"Do what, dean?"

"Why, blow up a bridge in Quebec. You said..."

He had taken my joke literally, proving again that he was absolutely suited for the job.

Dean Argue explained that the university curriculum had evolved over many decades, based on the English system, or was it the American system? The Albanian? He said chemistry and maths would sharpen my perceptions and he said French would broaden my base of understanding. Facetiously I said I knew the molecular properties of water and that two plus two equaled four. Since *Les Miserables* had already been written, I felt no need to continue in French. Or maybe the good dean said that these three subjects would make me more aware of life. I had seen enough already to make me quite aware of life.

The upshot was, I took three subjects I didn't want or need because the system said I must. I passed second-year chemistry by cheating on lab work and on the exam, and failed math and also the supplementary exam in the autumn. I was given a third exam so that I could move into third year. I know I failed the third, that special test, but as I was by then apparently the only guy who could run the semiweekly *Manitoban* newspaper I got a phoney mark and moved upward and onward to the pleasant Fort Garry campus, away from the low ramshackle set of buildings that was the downtown campus.

That downtown campus was truly an arsonist's delight. He wouldn't have needed a can of gas. An ordinary kitchen match would have done the job. It didn't even have a men's common room, thus defying Stephen Leacock's dictum that a university, before it had lecture rooms and professors, must have a common room. But it did have a canteen, a hike along a long, dark corridor lined with lockers, down a flight of steps and into a dungeon filled with rickety tables and chairs and a counter serving sandwiches, hotdogs, pie, coffee, tea, and soft drinks at prices that should have paid off any operating deficit the university might incur.

It was in this bastille basement that we'd gather—the vets at their tables and the civilian students at theirs—and we would hold forth, talking not about our war experiences but about the things any groups of young men would talk about—mainly the girls of our classes who wore sweaters and skirts—remember the New Look?—and appeared to be skipping as many classes as we were.

We were blending into the scenery by now, discarding our dyed battle jackets and pre-enlistment duds and blossoming out in tweed jackets and brown pants and shoes. I must say we looked kinda nifty. We were discovering the girls, a process we'd gone through years before and which we were experiencing again.

When you are billeted in a garrison town or in camp near any town or city, you quickly learn that the King's uniform makes you a pariah to many townsfolk. Hence, you don't see much of nice girls. You remember what they were like from the poster of Betty Grable and her round, little bum, and sultry Rita Hayworth in a low-cut nightie slithering across her hot silk bedsheet toward you. Those two looked pretty good, but they were just paper and colored ink and these girls were flesh and blood and they were right there.

However, there was one trouble. They were afraid of us. They must have read too many magazines or their mothers told them too many stories. But slowly the ice began to crumble around the edges and by second year every fellow had a girl. Or thought he had. The girls, with that kind of competition, decided they could have two or three fellows. One to talk to after he bought them lunch. Another to go for long walks and discuss her philosophy of life with, and the third to use as a Saturday-night date. To them, we were just fellows. What they were really looking for was the pre-med student because, after all, every mamma wants a doctor for a son-in-law.

And, damn it all, the vast majority of these girls were nice girls!

If you and she were kinda serious in her unserious way, she'd want to go dancing at the October Freshie Frolic and watch the Glee Club have another whack at a Gilbert and Sullivan operetta and have a big night at the annual presentation of the choral club. Or go in costume to the Beaux Arts Ball in February or watch the Manitoba Bisons fumble another against the Bemidji basketball team.

One girl I knew felt that a satisfying evening was to study at the downtown library and then go across the street to the Salsbury House for a nip and hot chocolate. No, a nip was not that. It was the Winnipeg version of the 1947 ten-cent hamburger. A red-hot Saturday night was playing in a foursome at bridge at her sorority house. A big date was going to the Uptown Theatre to watch the sneak preview of a first-run movie that had already played in Lac du Bonnet.

What we wanted was to buy a case of beer or a jug of rye and borrow a car and drive out to a secluded park on the Assiniboine River and get laid.

The best way, if you wanted it was to pick along the grapevine until some stud came up with the name of some girl, preferably from out of town but good-looking, who had been kicked out of the women's dormitory and was now living in a basement suite, alone. She might not come across but at least you know her mind was moving in the right direction.

I eventually succumbed to what Satchel Paige would call "The

Social Ramble" and I saw the insides of some fine liquor cabinets in some fine homes, but I only did the trip as an act of self-preservation. You see, in third year I was informally engaged to one girl and on very good speaking terms with two others, but this fact should in no way make anyone disputatious of my good intentions. At that period I led one hell of a busy life, attending a few classes, editing the student newspaper, and doing my social rambling. The ramble only lasted about three months. The three ladies knew each other, and I imagine got to comparing notes in one of their rec rooms while "In the Mood" was softly playing.

So, labeled a pariah, I stepped up my visits to the scruffy Aberdeen Hotel, where a waiter named Bob would sell twelve glasses of froth for a dollar. I asked him why, as each glass cost him a dime, and he said, "I sell a hell of a lot more beer than the other guys, so I get a bigger bonus."

You just can't beat the logic of a beer-parlor waiter!

The beer joint was called "The Abbey" and if you frequented it enough the ruling body of student drinkers canonized you. It was a heady feeling because someone poured a glass of beer over you. These were rowdy, self-proclaimed intellectuals who had a deep disdain for all the ideals that ex-servicemen are supposed to have. Therefore, they considered the U. of M. a place for clods and sods and were only attending it so that they could get jobs teaching English Lit at the rotten place.

I got into student politics in a strange way, considering that I had no desire to be a politician and had even less ability. Under a crazy system first- and second-year Arts students had one vote toward the election of an Arts representative to the University of Manitoba Students' Council. Third- and fourth-year students had two votes. Through *The Manitoban* I had good friends who ran the student end of the Arts Faculty and they lobbied mightily on my behalf among the senior students. Lo, I won.

As junior and then automatically senior rep I was responsible in a way for the health, wealth, and happiness of about two thousand students. It was bizarre. Half the students must have had more interest in student politics than I did, but I went dutifully to every council meeting, was put on committees, worked on reports, and attended the odd conference—and they were odd, consisting mainly of consumption of Demon Rum. I managed to survive, as did the priests in the French Revolution.

I remember my first meeting. I must say, the veterans were beginning to emerge in strength in student politics. They had waited almost two years, and now they were ready to go for it all. They were moving in on the councils, the newspaper, the public relations committee, Mock Parliament, the debating union, the radio society, the glee club, the yearbook, and virtually everything else except the curling club, which the agriculture students from rural Manitoba controlled.

My first meeting showed their Lib-Tory-CCF minds at work: diffuse, defuse, dissimulate, debunk, delay, deride, declare, deter, dominate, destroy.

A major item on the agenda was the scheduling for the year's final exams and these novitiates were popping up saying that the schedule was unfair, too many exams were bunched too close together, too many were too far apart, and besides it was all a commie plot. The battle raged.

Finally clear-eyed and innocent me got up and I asked how long this scheduling had been going on. The advisor from the administration said this was the way exam scheduling had been for many years.

Had anyone, any council, complained before? He said no, not to his knowledge.

"Has this system worked in the past?" I asked brightly.

"Yes."

I asked one of the loudest bitchers if he or anyone else had a better schedule for exams, especially since they were only two weeks away. He glared, his look telling me in no uncertain terms that I was a jerk for being so impertinent.

I then asked, "If nobody can suggest anything better and this system has worked well for many years, why won't it work well this year?"

Uproar. Table pounding. Shouts of commie. Et cetera.

The council president banged his gavel and said, "Well, that seems to settle that matter. The next item on the agenda, and let's move right along on this one, concerns the quality of coffee in the cafeteria on the Fort Garry campus."

My God, but those were exciting days!

I was glad to get out of student politics, but in a way I did enjoy it. Despite some absolute donkeys, there were just enough good and sincere men and women involved who tried to make the university a better place. On every campus there are such people. Reading the newspapers, I see that some of those donkeys are still acting like damn fools and are still getting elected. The good and sincere ones got into useful lines of work. Anyway, I was glad to be part of it all.

Of course, there was backroom politics too. Five men of high repute on campus sitting at a table in the Clarendon Hotel beer parlor would come up with decisions that would affect the student body for years to come. In the Arts Common Room, four men, members of the Booze, Broads and Bridge Club, would come to intelligent conclusions that would be in effect for years. I suppose that when all the captains and the kings depart and the politicians have shouted themselves into imbecility, the backroom groups prevail and this is the way our so-called democracy must function.

My greatest satisfaction was the three years I spent on *The Manitoban*, two years as news editor and the third as managing editor. There, too, I found politics at work and I ignored those involved. I found them more repugnant because they were playing at intellectual politics. I tried to put out the best newspaper I could, and I did. I was secure in the knowledge that intellectuals, however sincere, have never run a good newspaper and never will. When it comes down to the dollar and expediency crunch, they are the same as everyone.

If I had played my cards right I suppose I could have been editor of the paper, but when I began to argue before the selection board—composed of the editorial-page intellectuals—I knew I was doomed and I ám glad. The winning contestant—a drinking buddy of the selection board—suggested that *The Manitoban* be increased from eight to nine pages. I knew when they said his suggestion was a good one that none of them knew the difference between a page-one ear and a back-shop hell box. It would have been a unique experiment: no newspaper in the world has nine pages, although thousands have eight or ten pages.

I believe I was the only managing editor to put out an extra. The president of the university, Dr. Albert Trueman, had resigned suddenly after a final argument with the incredibly stuffy university Senate over how the institution should be run. He was a small "l" liberal. That says it all. He was truly loved by the students and probably disliked by the faculty. I decided to send him off in fine style and I hustled up to the paper's office with two of my best reporters, put together a front page, four good stories, and a picture, tabloid size, and shot it off to the printer and by Saturday at 8:00 A.M. my edition was being read on campus.

I guess my major mistake was in not asking permission from the editorial board, but then, I had never asked permission before. I was reprimanded, not for putting out an extra but for my rather severe editorial comment in the main story on the page. One did not spit in the eyes of the august senators. The edition blew back on the editor and for that I am sorry. But I was young and full of piss and vinegar in those days.

Now, most university and college papers should be sent to the town dump as they come off the presses.

I had a good, eager staff—there was even some talent—and while a few have gone on to greater things in journalism and publishing, the brightest and the best of them went into law or banking or business and did very well. Who said printer's ink gets into your blood?

Perhaps the fault lay with me because at our many beer-and-bull sessions I hammered into them that newspapering was the greatest game in the world. It was also self-fulfilling and rewarding, but when they got out into the nasty world they found that it was just another grubby and grimy business. Remember, idealism is for the young. The rest of us have a living to make.

I also had a weekly column dwelling mostly on campus, civic, provincial, national, and world affairs. The remaining 20 percent of the column was sophomoric drivel, more or less. I had it for a year and signed it 'C.A. Daver' and in all that time nobody caught on. That pleased me.

I gained impressions of the faculties during those years and they have never left me, although they were completely false. For instance, engineering students worked very hard but they had to because they were stupid. I've gotten to know a few engineers since then and realize they are not stupid, but take themselves very, very seriously. Commerce students were interested in snaring campus jobs that paid honorariums and in coaching the girls' teams, drinking coffee in the cafeteria, and telling each other where John Maynard Keynes went wrong. Agriculture students, when not curling, always seemed to be driving home in their pickup trucks to hunt deer. Lawyers began practicing how to look wise while lighting a pipe for the twentieth time in twenty minutes with big wooden matches and saying, "Of course, when I article with my uncle's firm I'll start learning the law. I'm just wasting my time here." I never did find out what Science students did, but I suppose they efficiently learned to light a Bunsen burner and bend glass tubing and how to daub a white lab smock with various chemicals to make it look authentic. Weren't these types the guys who put together the atomic bomb?

I don't want to malign the middle-aged ladies of today who took Home Economics, but all they seemed to learn was the makeup of a calorie and how many there are in a slice of bread, and to exhort their girlfriends in other faculties to vote for the girl from Home Ec who was running for women's president. Girls in Interior Decorating were nice but had a disturbing tendency to become pledged to those earnest young men in the Faculty of Architecture, possibly as insurance that they would get jobs doing the interiors of the buildings their husbands would design.

But it was Arts, my faculty, that was goofiest. Arts students seemed to have no specific goals. Arts students in their graduation write-ups said vaguely that they were headed for a career in teaching or journalism, law or social work, external affairs or politics, housewifing or secretarial work, modelling or just being a "free thinker." One said he'd like to become an industrial czar and another, who was not involved with the theater, thought it would be nice to be a film director. See, some direction but no firm commitment toward a career. I understand most did well, especially the many who became housewives and mothers. Arts faculty was a hunting ground for girls looking for eligible husbands and I even remember one tall basketball player who stalked an heiress for two years—and got her!

Arts, in short, was fun. Sure, there were drudge courses like Economics and now I only remember the Law of Diminishing Returns, which I never did understand. Psychology was a joke taken by students who wanted a fast and easy two units toward the degree. And Sociology, well! Another two units. I signed in at the start of the year, attended no lectures, read the textbook front to back the night before the exam, and got one of the highest marks in the class. I just used my common sense. History to me was fun because of a professor who had fled a prestigious eastern U.S. university for the sticks because of politics on campus. He was a delight. However, though I remember him with fondness, all I can recall was that Philadelphia and Smyrna were two of the eight religious cities of Asia Minor and most Roman emperors came to a rather sticky end. English Lit, my favorite, was a bore because of the way it was taught—twenty-five- and thirty-year-old veterans being lectured to as if they were high-schoolers. "And, Mr. Broadfoot, when Antonius was making fun of Lepidus, what effect did he hope his remarks would have on Caesar?" "You tell me, Professor Jones. I don't have Coles' Notes with me, but I'm sure you have." That ended that.

I went back three decades later for a debate and a small dinner and there they were, many of the instructors and lecturers I had known and now all in positions of high authority. How can this be so? I asked myself. Then I thought, if a high-school student gets a job with General Motors tightening four bolts on the assembly line and waits it out, why, he, too, can wind up as manager of one of the automaker's divisions. Why not at university? After all, it, too, is a factory.

But despite it all, I spent four of the most happy years of my life there. Nothing to worry about. No boss, no pushing for promotion, no wife, no kids, no wee house and big mortgage. Just sunlit days of autumn and early spring, lying on the brown grass talking to a girl and planning some devilment and hoping she was doing the same—with me. In the library the joy of having a lass you've been eyeing sit across from you and say casually, "Care for a coffee?" The satisfaction of having the managing editor of the *Winnipeg Free Press* write a note saying that you were putting out a good paper and please drop around and see him soon. You didn't, but the offer was there. Recognition. Finding that Professor Paul Hiebert in the Chemistry Department had written Sarah Binks, the awful, gawd-awful poetry of the "Sweet Songstress of Saskatchewan." Having the one good English professor open your eyes to the joy of Shakespeare by acting out the plays. Getting in sharp shots at the pompous asses on the student council. Baked beans, heavily laced with molasses, and buttered toast at a beanery on Broadway. Slow, slow dancing on Saturday night at the Winnipeg Auditorium. The smell of burning maple leaves. Winter afternoons in Moore's Restaurant and ordering borscht and laughing when my friend said, "But I thought it was served hot."

And then it was spring of 1949 and all over the nation the veterans of

1945 were graduating. It was the beginning of about twenty-five good years for Canada—heavy crops, plenty of jobs, new factories, booming cities, new towns, prosperity on every hand. Anybody could get a job and everyone was confident that he or she was in line for a better job. The vets became eminent lawyers, rich businessmen, top journalists, well-known writers, brilliant doctors, important industrialists, leaders in architecture, prominent in education, the arts, dominant in the sciences. They also became the politicians.

It was Canada's time, those years after 1949, when those thousands of veterans rushed eagerly and joyfully at life.

5

Hello North, You Still There?

I still chuckle when I think of that crazy summer.

I spent it in the North, on a surveying crew with a wacky French cook and a gang boss who drank too much and told a million stories. Among the cast of characters was a Métis roustabout who could move silently through the parkland and pine, sniff and whisper, "There's one over there," and drop a buck with one shot from his .22.

It wasn't the "True North Strong and Free." As the crow flies, it was perhaps two hundred miles northeast of Winnipeg, but if one defines the North as isolation and the back of beyond, our camp was right in the middle of it. No road but the one we were making. A mine village nineteen miles to the west. Abandoned mines and falling-down trappers' cabins with calendars advertising long-forgotten medical miracles of fifty years before. Every valley had one or more lakes. There were twenty billion pine trees and forty trillion tons of rock and, though no one back in the city would believe me, there was permafrost everywhere.

The country was also full of characters—if you could find them. Usually they found you, and usually a half an hour before supper.

I was twenty-two, and I didn't mind working for sixty-five cents an hour. The work was hard and monotonous and the muck was like setting concrete and the mosquitoes—oh, Christ! The mosquitoes! The food was plentiful and good and the crew's talk was pure gold. At night, while everyone was asleep, I'd walk to the lake for a short swim, and before I returned I'd count a million stars.

Molly and Me, and Jerry Makes Three   🐾

I had come off a rough time. Too many parties and not enough studying. Two days before, I had written my last exam, a three-hour Economics II affair at the University of Manitoba and I was betting 5 to 1 against myself. Also, I had had a strange romance for the last three months with a tall, thin blonde named Jennifer.

There was no way I wanted to go back to the newspaper for another four months of chasing firewheels and covering municipal councils, and I didn't really care if Fair Jennifer dumped me for some smoothie whose father owned half the grain elevators in western Manitoba. When Colonel Dickens, Ret., offered me a job as chainman on a government surveying crew north of Manigatogan, I graciously accepted. He had known me since I was in short pants and he said I would get $6.50 a day, a big white tent I could call my own along with nineteen other guys, and all the fresh air I could inhale.

So, on a fine day in early May I was having a final drink with my sister. She was drinking tea. She said, "No more for you. Time to go," and I shoved the bottle into my army duffel bag and we headed for the steamer dock on the Red River. She drove my car. Didn't ask for the keys. They were always on the dashboard.

I asked her about Jennifer because they were friends and she said, "Let's say you're doing okay and leave it at that. You're probably doing the right thing, getting away like this. She'll be around when you get back."

"Ambiguous remarks like that warm the cockles of my heart," I replied.

We reached the old wharf at five o'clock and there was the *Clara III*, a wispy trail of smoke drifting from her rusted funnel. My chauffeur said, "Well, it isn't exactly the *Queen Mary*."

I said, "A ship is not an it, she is a she, but I wonder what the *Clara I* and *Clara II* ever did to deserve such an offspring?"

She laughed and I felt good. We were still pals-together. I got out and hauled out the duffel and she kissed and hugged me as we stood on the dock. She said, "Take care of yourself," and got back in that old '33 Plymouth and I warned, "Use the heap all you want, but make sure she's always got lots of oil. She drinks it like a lush. Insurance papers are in the glove compartment." She wheeled around and as she went up the gravel road I got a shave-and-a-haircut-two-bits salute.

I walked up the gangplank, maybe looking for someone in absolute authority in a snappy uniform and gold embroidery on his cap and dripping in braid and important medals. I found him. He was short and grimy with a roughly shorn wheatfield on his face and wearing GWG blue overalls. He was yelling and waving his arms at somebody out of my sight. The man at the winch, I figured. They were loading freight.

He broke off his ballet and rasped, "Grab a bunk in the cabin. You're our passenger list." I answered, "Thanks, captain," and he grinned and replied, "Yeah, and you're cute too."

The old freight boat only had one cabin, amidships, dark and low and smelling of sweat, urine, whiskey, and that sharply definable nose tickler of puke. That cabin with its twelve bunks must have been a regular Skid Road barroom when she was full and one could never guess how many years she had been pushing a bow wave up and down Lake Winnipeg, putting into little villages, an Indian camp, or standing by impatiently while a lonely settler or trapper rowed out to get his groceries and mail.

The other interesting fact about Stateroom A, Upper Deck, was the overlay of diesel fumes and smoke so thick you could carve out chunks of air and handle them like cardboard boxes. I decided I wasn't going to spend a night in there. It would be on deck for me, come hurricane, scurvy, or high water.

Overalls-And-Stubble was wrong about the passenger list. There was another body stretched out on a bunk by the door, crooning aimlessly and balancing a bottle of booze on his chest. It was Jerry Lister, a fellow I knew in a stand-off fashion at university, a playboy fooling around until his daddy decided to take him into the family business as a vice-president. The Listers were in the cartage business, and big! They were great at taking things from Point A to Point B and not smashing your Ming vases. Jerry grinned and handed me the bottle and said, "Welcome aboard, Captain Hornblower." I turned and held the jug up to the light. There was about two inches left. I said what the hell and drained it and dropped it on his chest. He picked it up, shook it, and delivered this pronouncement: "Well, you sure took care of that little problem."

Then he recognized me and yelled, "Old BB! The bloody colonel said he was doing me a favor for the summer. Said there was another smart-ass type aboard. Didn't say who. Going surveying?" I said yes and he said good, he had brought his chessboard with him.

As I turned to leave, Jerry asked, "Say, is that guy a real colonel? Didn't seem too bright to me."

"Sure, he's a real colonel but he also answers to major and if you call him Sport he'll come to you and wag his tail if you pat him."

I went out on deck and lugged my duffel into the cabin for safekeeping, and in the ten seconds I was gone Jerry must have sighed deeply, rolled over, and gone to sleep. He was out.

I regretted now not taking up the colonel's offer to fly up on the Norseman with the supplies because I could see unpleasantness ahead with Jerry. We really didn't care much for each other, little as we knew one another. You could say that he and I operated on opposite sides of life's ledger. Like missionaries and traders, our accounts didn't balance.

I leaned on the rail and looked over that old and bedraggled excuse for a ship and wondered if she didn't sink at this wharf would she make it to St. Andrew's Lock. However, I decided that one should never underrate an old hag. They have learned the business of survival. She must have had countless thousands of miles under her keel despite being manned by incompetent crews and hammered by those vicious Lake Winnipeg storms. She reminded me of a line in a poem: "...she was stubby and square and she didn't much care." Her hull and houseworks could have stood a thousand hours of hard work with a steel brush and a carload of marine paint, and God knows what she looked like below the waterline.

One day she would broach in a huge sea when her steering snapped and she would roll and go down and few would mourn her passing, although many would remember her with affection.

A Moore's taxi came fast down the road, shooting out a rooster tail of dust. Maybe the driver was eager to deliver the freight safely. A tall man in uniform got out and fished out a valise from the back and a big paper bag that tinkled. He walked, yawing five points to port and then correcting his course by steering ten points to starboard. As he worked his way across the gangplank he looked at the funnel as if for a heavenly sign. He went by me forward, not even glancing my way.

"The captain," said a voice behind me. "Hasn't been sober since 1941 when he came off this boat as mate and the navy gave him a commission and he spent his war skippering a big, shiny garbage scow around Halifax Harbour. Kinda soured him on a home on the ocean deep and a life on the briny wave."

I looked behind and up to a small deck on the top of the cabin where a woman was standing. She was the kind of lady you felt should always have her arms akimbo. She was wearing a man's bush shirt, an ugly combination of green and purple squares, and she wore a long white cook's apron. She came down the stairs and I saw she was barefooted and about six feet tall. She leaned on the rail beside me and put her hands on the rail, as if displaying them; big hands, strong and rough and red. If she had made a fist with one and walloped you, you would stay walloped.

But strangely, her voice was almost childlike. Unusual in an Amazon. It was smoky with the smell of peat fires and there was the feel of greening flax between stone fences and of a mist that is almost a rain. I knew if she became angry there would also be the sound of seas battering a rocky western shore. With booze bubbling inside me I almost made a smart remark about the Irish and then thought of those hands and the pounding waves.

"Drunk. 'Tis a wonder of the ages how he manages. Oh, he'll get us there, never fear. The *Clara* is the first boat out from Selkirk after the ice goes out of the river and the last one in, her sometimes looking like an old hen caught out in the wet all night. People out on the lake love him. A fair man, a good man, and only mean when he's on a real bender, so he's got a built-in mean streak, but a good man."

I told her my name was Barry and she said she was called Molly. I caught that. She was called Molly but that may not have been her name. As happens often with people, a short history was in order. She had been a cook all her working life, working on the boats in summer and in private homes or in a restaurant in winter. She wasn't married and didn't intend to be. She liked a drink more often than not, and when she died there might be some profound discussion in high places as to whether she would go to heaven or hell.

Molly's life history was just about the shortest I had ever heard.

"They'll be finished loading in a few minutes and we'll be pulling the hook. Grub's on soon as we're moving and if you don't like the thoughts of my cooking, after all these bloody years of trying to please roughnecks and not doing so well, then you can eat in Selkirk. There's two Greeks and a Chinaman in Selkirk, but don't blame me if you don't come back. They'll find you in the gutter, and poisoned you will be."

"Molly, I shall be delighted to partake of your bountiful repast, made, I'm sure, with all the love and skill you have within you."

"Save that guff for the girls," she barked and walked aft to her galley, next to the dining room. I waited until a deckhand flipped the lines aboard and the man at the wheel gave three hoots and the *Clara III* edged out into the muddy, swirling river and was caught by the spring flood and moved gently and pleasantly downstream.

For ten minutes more I watched the blindsided, ugly brick river-front warehouses and factories fall astern. A plane drifted downward in the soft air toward Stevenson's Airport, and on the grassy banks, as residential streets appeared, old men and young boys dangled worms in the current. Not hoping to catch a fish, just fishing.

I was singing a few bars of "Sweet Molly Malone" when I entered the small dining salon and I got a glare that would have chipped concrete. The table was laid for eight and in contrast to the rest of the ship, Molly's stomping ground was clean as a penguin's vest.

"You'd better knock off that blather right now, mister," she rasped and I replied, "Okay, Molly, but that's the only part of the song I know anyway." She said, "Fine Irishman you'd make when the pubs close down on a Saturday night in Dublin." We both laughed.

It was beef stew, chunky, heavy, spicy, and bubbling. Hunks of bread torn from a fresh loaf were on a plate and a pound of butter on another. There was a side plate of fresh onions and a huge bowl of peaches and cream. There was a convoy of smaller bowls accompanying the big one, so I figured the idea was to dip straight from the stew bowl. I dug in, daring my eyes not to water, and the stew was the best I have ever tasted. I told her she deserved an award and she stood there, arms akimbo, and said, "When we dock at Selkirk I'll give you some money and you can bring me back a case of beer. Ask if they have stout, but they won't. It's a bloody plot against the Irish."

One of the deckies clumped in, a man without the grace or wisdom to admit he was not a Scotsman. He sat down across from me, grunted a jovial hello, reached for a heel of the loaf, crumpled it in his huge hand until it was the size of a large marble, and threw it into his mouth and snarled, "Stew again, Molly. Always stew. Molly, we deckload a couple hunnerd cases of fish south every trip and there's big oceans either side of this godforsaken country, and you can't even come up with fish. Not even once a week?"

"One more word, Swede, just one more word..." and she let the threat hang there.

He clawed the main bowl of stew toward him and gulped half of it down faster than I could have eaten a lemon tart. Two more chunks of bread followed and half the onions; then he dumped peaches into his stew bowl and slurped them down. He rose, the job done in five minutes, and said, "I'll be back for my quart of milk later."

"A Scandihoovian. He'd be better if he got drunk twice a week like the rest. No manners. Reads and reads again those pamphlets the Lutherans give him, but still no manners."

No one else came in and she got talking and her life story continued. She was born Irish, but in Boston. The Irish City, as she called it. Her father had worked in a tannery and their house smelled like one, and when he decided he wanted land of his own they had moved to Manitoba. She said he had heard that the Irish and the English weren't always fighting over religion and politics there.

"He got land all right. The railway agent skinned him of his savings and gave him one hundred and sixty acres of rocks and gulleys and wolf willow, and he had so much land he didn't know what to do with it. Being Irish, if they'd given the poor soul five acres he'd have done fine, but he used to get up in the morning and look at those one hundred and sixty acres and then go back into our bit of a shack and start another day's drinking—the bootleg he bought down the road. He moved us all into Winnipeg and got a job in a tannery again and so the small shack we lived in there also smelled like the Boston house. It was grand, I'll tell you.

"I got to the fifth grade, so I could do writing and reading and numbers, but I couldn't tell you what the prime minister does or why they have a thing called the North Pole. I've been my own woman for thirty years now and I've done a lot and I'm not old, but I gotta act old and mean on this tub. Keep my wits, or I wouldn't be around too long. Cooking is what I like best. Now go out on deck and I'll bring you a cup of my coffee."

I leaned on the rail and wondered why good cooks always referred to "my pie" and "my coffee" as though they had invented it. The narrow but long farms first worked by the French Canadians were now slipping past, although most had been taken over by Galicians, and their whitewashed houses and onion-domed churches came into view and fell back. I wondered how so few people could have so many churches. Disputes, feuds, I guessed. In that department they were no different from any other bunch on earth. The devil must be laughing.

The second deckhand came along from the front hatch where cargo was still being arranged, paused at the galley door, and said, "Cap'n." He stood two feet from me, not looking at me, looking at nothing, and humming a tune. Over and over. I finally recognized it as the first line of "Pretty Red Wing." Oh, the moon shines tonight on Pretty Red Wing. Molly came out in five minutes and handed him a casserole with a spoon wrapped in a napkin. The deckie wandered away.

"The captain's meal. Cream, three eggs, lots of breadcrumbs, butter, and paprika on top. He calls it his omelet. Never eats anything else. I call it mush. That kid. One of the dumber ones I've seen. Wants to be a sailor but doesn't know if the Pacific Ocean is east or west. Had a job as deckhand on the Hudson Bay trading boat *Fort Severn*, going to all those Eskimo places last summer. Thinks he knows it all. Knows nothing. Before he came to us this spring I think he spent the winter in his home town being the village idiot, but he got fired because he couldn't get the hang of the job. He read somewhere that a captain is called 'Cap'n,' but on the *Clara III* we call him 'Captain' or 'Mr. Carruthers' or 'Why-the-hell-can't-you-keep-your-eye-on-the-channel-markers-Carruthers.'"

She went back to her galley and returned with two big crockery cups two thirds full of steaming coffee and carrying a half-bottle of Three Star Hennessy. I took one cup and she put the bottle to her mouth, yanked out the cork, and spat it overboard.

She filled our cups to the brim and said, "Compliments of the captain. Never knows how much he drinks before he passes out, and before I pound on his door to wake him at five o'clock I sneak a look and if there's a bottle I take it. Then it's mine. Keeps the ice worms away."

We drank and when our cups were half empty she poured out the rest of the brandy, dropped the bottle over the side, drank deeply, blinked, and said, "Whooosh!" I did the same, although slowly, and we watched the real estate pass by.

"Ever read about this river?" she asked. "A lot of history and nobody cares too much. Been in the museum in town; nothing in it, but I read about what we're seeing. The French. The *voyageurs*, you know. All the way from Montreal looking for furs, paddling with those savages in tippy canoes. Hudson's Bay people. Nor'Westers. God, but they were a scandalous lot. Soldiers of the king. Indians. Those hopeless settlers that Lord Selkirk brought in. About 140 years ago, and nothing awaiting them but meanness and ill-spirit. Traders, cheating, robbing, stealing. Murder. Native girls being ravaged. Missionaries. Those Presbyterians, Scots all, and every last one of them buggers. Anglicans. The R.C. priests, the black crows, I call 'em. Furs, everybody wanted furs to make top hats for London gentlemen. York boats. Buffalo by the millions, and now all gone. Every last one that was wild. Lake boats. Icelanders. Fine people. Tried to set up their own republic up on the lake. Swedes could take a lesson from them fellows. Nearly married one, but I guess my hair wasn't blonde enough and I didn't have curves in the right places. They say once a long time ago Vikings from Norway came down this river and down into the United States. They think they found some of their stuff down in North Dakota. Seen a lot, this old Red River. Now, just a dirty stream, unfit to drink, too dirty to fish in."

Another crew member, probably engine room because of five pounds of grease on his hands, came along and I dropped my cup in the river and went back to the cabin and rousted Jerry up and pointed him toward the grub.

We went through the lock, along with two Ghoulie fish boats and a millionaire's yacht probably heading for his private island up the lake. The huge, gray-stoned fort a few miles downstream came into view: Lower Fort Garry dominating its cliff, one of the few major forts in North America that was not besieged. Then into Selkirk, a quiet, river-front town with elm-shaded streets where the big news of the week would be the departure of a waitress in one of the cafés because some local fisherman had knocked her up.

Jerry, full of stew, was rarin' to go and I got a tenspot off Molly and we headed to the River Hotel. The waiter didn't want to serve Jerry, convinced he was under twenty-one. I spent five minutes, while the customers howled, convincing him that Jerry was my brother and was twenty-one. Jerry would be about nineteen, small for his age and still drunk.

The beer parlor was dingy, dirty, full, and noisy, but we found a table and I dropped a buck and told the waiter to leave four.

A couple at the next table, smoothly, from long practice, slid into our two other chairs and the woman said, "Make that eight." Jerry, full of the Old Nick, told the waiter to make that ten beers and added, maliciously, "There goes your tip."

"I get a tip in this dump, I call a town holiday. My old man's the mayor," replied the waiter sourly.

I looked at the couple. Lower class. Typical. Freeloaders. Half a buck to their name and four kids somewhere crying for milk. I was about to tell them to shove off when the woman, sensing so, bored through my attack and asked, "Sir, do you know anything about the law?"

If this was a trick they regularly used it was a good one. She threw me off guard. I really knew nothing about the law except that there are laws and if somebody kills somebody, a jury finds that somebody guilty and he gets hanged.

The woman, straggly hair, nicotine-stained hands, and a blubbery smile, said, "Fred here," and she waved a hand, "Fred is my husband." Fred looked like he was missing about fifteen bricks from his wheelbarrow and he said, "Fred, that's me, and this here is Ella and she and me live over toward East Selkirk. I drive truck and she does washing."

Ella said, "Neighbor's trying to kill Fred. Got us worried."

The waiter came and Jerry ordered another ten and the woman leaned across and sniped two of my British Consuls, handed one to Fred and lit them up.

Fred put the conversation on an intellectual plane by studying his smoke and drawling, "Knew fellow in the army could make smoke come outa them ears of his."

"Fred, will you please keep that big trap of yours shut. I'm talking real earnest to this fellow. Knows about the law. Now, Fred sold a truck to Jack Eaton for one-sixty and Jack never got it more than a mile down the road when the engine fell out and..."

Fred cut in: "Drive shaft broke. Not any engine falling out."

"Will you kindly shut that big trap of yours, honey. Next morning Jack comes around and he's mad. Wants his money back. Well, we didn't have it. Bought stuff with it soon as Fred got the money. My sister who needs this funny operation got sixty of it. Charitable thing to do. Kinfolk. Jack is so mad he says he is going to kill Fred because that damn engine fell out…"

"Drive shaft broke."

"Fred, that's the last time," and she neatly lifted two beers off the next tray before the waiter could put them down. "So, I been collecting this here evidence, you see. I got it here," and she pulled a child's school scribbler from her purse.

"What kind of evidence?" I asked.

"All kinds, case that Jack Eaton comes at Fred with a gun. What he said to people about me and Fred and things like that."

"When did this truck break down?" I asked.

"About seven months ago and Jack still is talking mean even now, all because of a silly engine falling out…"

I cut in this time and said, "Look, this distinguished friend of mine is an expert in criminal law and you explain everything to him and he'll tell you what to do," and I leaned over to the glassy-eyed Jerry and told him I was going to make a phone call and buy some beer and we'd better get down to the boat within fifteen minutes.

I carried two beers into the lobby, ignoring the waiter's shout, and drank them chug-a-lug while I dialed back to Winnipeg. Jennifer's mother came on the line and asked who I was and then I goofed and gave my right name. She said, "Jennifer's not here." So much for future mothers-in-law.

I went back into the beer parlor and the redoubtable Ella was turning over page after page of her evidence and talking to Jerry. He was staring dumbly ahead.

I bought three cases of beer with Molly's money and whistled at Jerry and walked out. If he was going to miss a summer in the pines over a lousy murder case, then let him go to it. He caught up to me on the hill down to the wharf, taking long and half-running strides. As he went past he said, "Jesus, that woman's plain crazy."

"Her husband's no blue-ribbon grand champion either," I called.

We boarded and the unseen face in the wheelhouse got three more toots off his conscience and we swung into the stream and moved along, sedately, as an old lady should. As we passed an Indian village with half-naked kids tumbling in and out of rowboats and canoes and scrimmaging on the beach, our helmsman gave them a double dose of compliments of the season. They waved madly and I felt like a locomotive engineer on the prairies passing on the word that civilization was just fine at either end of the C.P.R. track.

Molly and Jerry and I were up on the small upper deck and our great criminal lawyer was demonstrating how he could give himself a cut lip by snapping off the cap of a beer bottle with his teeth. Molly laughed and took the bottle and did the job neatly, and on two others too.

We talked about how great it was to be on the river at dusk.

The mate came topside and gratefully accepted a brew, drained it in one long slow pull, and Molly laughed and said, "Well, as the old lady said as she threw the dishwater into the garden, every little bit helps."

The mate was off duty and had been nipping at something and was feeling no pain. Jerry probably hadn't been sober since noon. I was feeling high, but content. Molly was in good shape.

Two herons flew across the bow and the mate pointed. His name was Summerville and his dourness when we were loading meant nothing now. "Flying west. Two cranes in Russian mythology means good luck. Cranes are about the same as herons, so this is going to be a good trip."

Molly asked him how he knew anything about Russia with a handle like Summerville, and he said he had been on the Murmansk run during the war and had got to know a bit about Mother Russia. He told us about the convoy where thirty-seven of fifty-six allied ships were sunk, and his voice got slower and lower when he got to the point where his own ship had been torpedoed. Then he brightened up and started to tell dirty jokes, each one filthier than the one before, and he prefaced each one by saying, "And with due deference to the lady amidst us..." and then he'd be charging forward again.

We talked back and forth about nothing as the night deepened, and occasionally the searchlight from the bridge would skitter across the water to pick out a white buoy. Jerry had passed out. Summerville was singing "The North Atlantic Squadron" to himself. There were only a few bottles left and they kept sailing out into the water. The river widened. The stars shone brighter than they did in the city. The forests had dropped behind and the big marsh enveloped us with its smells and presence. Molly had gone to the galley and brought back a sackful of spuds and was peeling them for tomorrow. The man at the wheel had turned on a radio to catch the 11:00 P.M. news. I was thinking that at this very time the night editor Alex Roberts would be slipping into the slot on the desk at the *Winnipeg Tribune* and reading the memo off the live spike that said I would not be in this summer, having decided to go surveying. He would say to his assistant, Dalgleish, "So Broad-foot's gone north. Wonder what's got into him?" Dalgleish, who would always play three ways against the jack, would probably say, "Well, I wonder if this work really suited him. Besides, the guy's a nut."

The mate had crawled away to his bunk. Jerry was sawing up cords of wood. Molly had finished peeling the spuds and gone to her cabin. The beer was gone, the bottles floating far behind us. I went to the cabin and hauled up two narrow mattresses for my bed. I smoked and watched the stars and Molly came up and in the dim light I could see she was holding another bottle of brandy aloft.

"Spoils of battle," she cried and added, "Forgot the cups. Mind if we drink from the neck?"

No problem. There was more than half a bottle and we counted it out in small sips. I heard much more about Molly's life, a rambling account that only elaborated on what she had told me. Always working for other people. No family left of her own. Too many drinks and too many hangovers.

Jerry awoke, groaned, and stumbled off to his bunk. The brandy level vanished and we left the marsh channel and hit big water. I felt the fresh breeze on my face and the *Clara III* heeled to a new course. The wheelsman rang for more speed and the old engine muttered and the old tub settled in for a long run.

Molly stood up, wavering a little, and hurled Three Star Hennessy off into the dark and I yelled, "Dizzy Dean. Strike three."

She muttered something that sounded like "Goodnight" and I lay down on one mattress and pulled the other on top. I watched the stars tilting.

I was happy and fell asleep after doing some befuddled thinking about Jennifer. I decided it was something I would have to figure out later. Far too complicated now. Maybe I'd send her a love letter.

A Crazy, Hazy Ride to Camp

Molly dropped the steaming towel on my face at 6:00 A.M. and yelled, "Rise and shine. Grab your socks, let go your cocks, the sun's come up over the docks."

I rolled out from under the mattress and laughed and said, "Ham and eggs, Molly. All that booze wants some company."

"Wish I could but Mersey Landing's just ahead, and after we unload you two and cargo we're pulling out for Norway House. You eat at the landing. Thanks for the beer."

"You bought it and thank the captain for the brandy. He's got a heart of gold."

I went down to the cabin after scrubbing with the towel and roused Jerry and toted my duffel toward the gangway as the *Clara III* blew three times and ghosted through the mist of the narrow channel to the dock.

I shook hands with Molly and told her if she were rich she'd be a grand rich lady and she said, "Off with ye," and we stepped onto the rotting planks. An old man said, "Passengers, eat up there, if you please," and pointed to an old gray house. The kind you see on dead farms abandoned in Saskatchewan in the Dirty Thirties.

As Jerry and I waited outside the house the *Clara III* gave three more unnecessary toots that bounced off the granite facings of the channel and she swung out, hesitated, pushed her butt backward a few yards, and then steamed for the lake. The next time I'd hear of her would be in an advertisement offering her for sale "As Is, Where Is," and the where of it was a reef off Black Island, put on the rocks by a helmsman of dubious distinction.

Ever the gracious maître d', the old man said, "My daughter will have it on the table by now, so will you step this way, gentlemen?" I looked at her. Hell, she could have been his wife. Old before her time. And years of cooking had taught her nothing—or maybe she had learned once and decided it wasn't worth the effort. The platter of eggs must have been fried the night before. Bacon from a mean old hog and toast that had been burned three days ago. The coffee was hot and wet and that's the most charitable thing one could say. I ate four eggs, half the bacon, four pieces of toast with jam, and three cups of java and paid fifty cents. At least the price was right.

We went out into the sunlight. The mist had cleared. Jerry heaved up his breakfast against the silvered boards of the house. In his Harris Tweed jacket, tailored pants, and loafers he looked exactly like what he was: Joe College.

"We're supposed to go to the mine, up there somewhere," I said to the old man. "Which way is up?"

"Partway I drive you—I got bus. Then a boat on the river. Then a bus. Then the mine."

Sure enough, he drove an old bus around from the back of the house. It was yellow, rusted, minus the door, more like a Mexican mountain jitney, but it had a motor and four wheels.

Jerry said, "If he drives that thing, I walk."

"Shut up, stop shivering, and straighten up."

We loaded our gear and a bunch of boxes, sacks, and cartons off the dock, and banged and clattered into the bush, missing stumps and holes, with branches slashing the sides, and negotiated one back-and-fill turn. We did everything but fly low and ground-loop. One bulldozer in a day could have made an honest woman of those seven miles.

We came to a clearing and there was a small boat pulled over to the bank. On the stern, waiting, was a woman and two kids. She turned out to be the wife of the manager of the mine, staying a week at the company's summer cabin half a mile below the landing. She said her name was Mrs. Marwell and the two kids were Monica and Andrew, both bright and shiny as polished McIntosh apples. There was also an Indian, lying in the grass, drunk, with a bloody handkerchief stuffed in his mouth. She said he had come out of the bush ten minutes ago with a bottle of beer, broken it off at the neck on a rock, and then gashed his mouth when he tried to drink. She asked the old man if he'd take him back to Mersey Landing and he said, "Naw. That's Rufus. He'll be okay. Let him go. He told me last night he's got a job at the mine, so let him go."

We loaded, went aboard, and the Indian staggered forward and lay down and went to sleep.

The captain stepped out of the wheelhouse and asked if it was okay to cast off. He actually used the words "cast off." Ocean liners cast off, not thirty-foot riverboats, sad, in need of paint, and with a cranky old mill grinding away below. Anyway, she nodded, and he went back to the wheel, looking ridiculous in his gold-braided cap and his greasy overalls.

The river was twisted, dark brown, cold as the heart of a glacier, and in spring flood, but the tub moved along surely enough and I talked to the kids and their mother, told them a few dumb stories, and Mrs. Marwell told me about the town.

"Call it a village. Call it nothing. That would be better. The mine, the miners, half of them D.P.s. Displaced persons from Europe. A hotel— the rooms are always vacant and the beer parlor is always full. What else is there to do? A fairly big store. Whatever you want, they haven't got; it is their policy. A restaurant—kind of a nice place, a log cabin, friendly, good food, run by a widow and her two daughters, who do a few things on the side—so the story goes—but nice girls. Oh, there's Frenchie's place. And there is a barber who is also a taxidermist and I've never been able to get the connection. A doctor and a nurse hired by the mine and a policeman who is big as a prairie silo. People say he is hired by the mine, too. Oh well, the mine is the town. No two ways about it. That's it. There's nothing else except a vast number of yapping dogs and the roar, roar, roar, all day and night, from the mine."

I said, "You mentioned a place called Frenchie's?"

"Oh yes, you might call it a roadhouse if there was a road going by it but there isn't. Everybody goes there Saturday night to drink and dance, and about midnight everybody chooses somebody else's wife or girlfriend and they fight for an hour as to who gets what. A fun place. When we've got executives from headquarters in Toronto out visiting, we take them there. I guess they talk about it for a month after they get home. That's it."

We were coming into another landing, a dock, fitted with several new planks and the piles shuddering as the current came sweeping around a bend giving the structure a hard belt with its shoulder.

Another yellow bus was waiting and the driver was whapping away at its innards with a blunt instrument. "She's feeling mean this morning, Mrs. Marwell. Give me a few minutes and I'll have her going again."

We unloaded gear and groceries again and sat on a grassy spot and Monica, as pretty as a wood violet, all six years of her, and Andrew, a manly little fellow of eight, begged for more stories. I said I'd emptied the package of those on the boat, but showed them the great and mystical Disappearing Coin Trick. Behind me, the bus stuttered, grumbled, coughed, whined, and then caught with a bang.

Mrs. Marwell sat next to me on one of the worn, lumpy seats, and in fifteen minutes she said, "Next stop, nowhere. A mine and a lot of frustrated people. A lake so cold you can't swim in it and so dirty from tailings the fish can't live in it. Planes come and go, people come and go, and that's it."

It sounded bleak, and I was having second and third thoughts about my decision to go north.

The bus swung off the sandy road and up a small rise to a large house, and mother and kids got off. My guess was that the mine manager's house was the only decent one in the surrounding thousand square miles.

The driver let Jerry and me off at the store. Inside, dark and gloomy and not a customer. There were three clerks, but getting served was an interesting proposition. They were all too busy, each supervising his own little colony in this retail empire. One was meditating over his Campbell Soup cans. A second was polishing a string of Horsepower beaver traps. The third picked up an orange from a display, smelled it, looked at it, and put it back.

I tapped the cash register with a quarter. No action. Then harder. Then damned hard.

"Kick the counter," said Jerry.

"Kick it yourself," I replied, but I did. Then I kicked it harder.

That brought Mr. Keeper Of The Soup Cans over.

"Yes, what do you want?"

"I want a diamond drill outfit and an airplane on floats, a Norseman, and half a ton of jerky and I want it quick. There's gold in them thar hills."

"And two whores," chimed in Jerry. "The best you've got in stock. Clean ones. Fresh as daisies and with flashing eyes and big tits. And four burros and six cases of Hudson's Bay rum."

I added, "A jeep and a sack of pineapples and throw in a bulldozer and a government assayer. That enough, Jerry?"

"Naw. Ask him if he's got 128 round-nosed shovels, eight axes, a ton of dynamite, and a ball of twine."

Behind the counter the poor guy's eyes were bugging out and I felt like leaning over and pressing them back into his skull. The joke, if it was one, had gone on long enough and, besides, I had seen Mr. Big In Charge Of Oranges sidle over to the phone.

"Okay, skip all that. Give us two cans of peaches and a box of crackers and I'll be obliged if you would open the peaches. I left my can opener down in the valley," I told him.

Big-city smart-alickiness obviously didn't go over well in this neck of the woods.

We sat on the porch eating dry crackers and spearing peach halves with our fingers. While we were having a smoke a jeep came gunning down the road.

At the wheel was Man Mountain Dean, except he was The Law. He was big. Lord, but he was big. Five feet, twenty inches of big man. This guy could clean out a barroom just by looking in on it. He sauntered over with that easy grace of big men with authority, especially big policemen with all the authority in many hundred square miles. Here was Clancy of the Mounted.

"Gentlemen?" A question rather than a greeting.

"Did the storekeeper phone you?" I asked brightly.

He ignored my sally and asked what brought us to town. God, just like in a corny Western. Two strangers arrive and nobody can spot a telltale bulge under their buckskin jackets, but everybody suspects the worst. The marshall seeks them out as they lounge nonchalantly on the verandah of the store. What brings you to town? Who are you? Where do you come from? Ever been in trouble with the law over in Tombstone? We don't like troublemakers in these parts, stranger.

I laughed and said, "Morning, officer. We come in peace. We just came in on that yellow bus from the landing. We've just finished our lunch. Now, we've got to find a Mr. Carter who has the government road camp around here. Can you help us? We're told in Winnipeg he'd be here, or somebody."

Now the Mountie was one big smile and he called into the store, "Harry, phone the hotel and see if Carter of the road gang is there. Say there's two of his guys here, wondering what to do."

While we waited we chatted and smoked and he said, "If he's not in the beer parlor— which he probably is—but if he's not, you've got a long way to hoof it. It's not much of a road out there, more of a trail, and no vehicles have reason to go there." He pronounced it "vee-hickle." "Maybe I can bend a regulation or two and take you out there. Pretty country and I might find my fly rod hidden in the jeep."

I asked what the camp was like and he said, "Canvas. Naturally. Worked-over gold country. Lakes, lots of 'em. Camp, she's nineteen miles out. About thirty men—some roughnecks, a few I wouldn't play a single game of crib with. Half a dozen Indians, most of them axemen, and one shoots deer for the pot. Seems the government plane is always losing the lake they're near. Two weeks ago it brought in three tubs of halibut in salt brine. Just that and not a damned thing more. If they'd been on a ship they'd have had one of those mutinies. But the cook somehow got them through. He's a Frenchman—not a French Canadian. No, a Frenchman from France. I've seen a lot of them cooks around and about up here, and if you see a cook whose whites are spotless, then I figure by my reckoning he's a good cook. This fellow's whites are whiter than white. He can't speak English, but he's got two sentences. One is 'You be dead duck,' and you will be if you make any mean noises about his food. It is damn bloody good. The other is 'Okay, Charlie, I got ya,' which means nothing to anybody else, but it seems to work. You know, somehow I think he does understand some English. Else, how in the hell could he find his way out here, all that way from France?"

I said, "I'll find out. I speak French."

He looked at me thoughtfully, rubbed his chin with a big paw, and said, "Ho." Then, "So." Then after what is called a pregnant pause, during which you could see his brain going "hmmmmmmmmmmm," he said, "Tell you what. If you hear anything out at that camp that seems funny, would you let me know?"

I grinned. Sure, horseman. If anything is wrong or funny, the cook would be the first one to know. He's the guy who is always looking and listening, and especially if all he knew in English was "You be dead duck" and "Okay, Charlie, I got ya," and if someone spoke French they might find out that he spoke a lot more English and knew a lot more than he let on.

The Mountie smiled and looked at his watch and said, "Sure, maybe I can invent an errand and get you out there," but as he spoke I saw another jeep racing down the road, boiling out a contrail of dust. It had to be Carter. It was.

As the jeep braked, the Mountie said, "And when you come to town I don't want no trouble. There's enough out there on the road as it stands now, with a bunch of Scandinavians, Indians, and the rest. Just last week had a Finn in here all cut up with a knife. A mess. He wouldn't say who done it, but I know he had a fight with another Finn. His goddamed cousin. Went at each other with knives. Know why, for what? They got to arguing who was closest to the peg in a stupid horseshoe game and so, they're at it. Some of those guys have been out in the bush there since Christmas."

He looked at Carter as he stepped from the jeep and shook his head. The man was obviously drunk. Good and drunk. He was a big man, with a face that, in profile, could have been on a coin celebrating a great victory of a Roman general. Front view, it had obviously taken some batterings in its time. It was a secondhand prize of a face. He was big-shouldered and wore those devil-may-care duds, khaki shirt, pants, and high-laced boots of a soldier of fortune in a minor war in Central America.

"You off the boat? You for my crew? University, I guess. What you taking?"

"Arts," Jerry said.

"Arts. Jesus, another one. Well, if you can't use an axe or stretch a chain or hold a rod straight, we'll use you to organize singsongs in the evening and read cómic books to the crew by candlelight."

He may have been drunk, I thought, but he sure had a touch of the Old Merry in him.

The Mountie told him to protect us from the likes of Carl and Cree Henry and Big Swede and a few other names I missed, and Carter, slipping in behind the wheel, said, "Hell, they got to learn sometime."

We drove around to the float-plane ramp and loaded up with a sack of flour, potatoes, onions, cans of this, tins of that, and a side of beef—stuff that had been dumped off by the pilot on the morning run. Then he raced furiously toward the hotel, braked, killed the motor, and yelled, "C'mon, one-eyed jacks and deuces wild! We got business in here." So we trooped into a room half full of drinkers.

Carter gestured toward them and said, "Graveyard shift. Nobodies. Forget 'em. Over here. Executives' table. Now, this is the way we do things. Each throw in a dollar. We draw on that."

He fished in a beaten-up wallet and pulled out a single, and Jerry and I threw in. A skinny little guy came over shortly with twenty beers bulging over his tray and then he came back with ten more, which sort of filled in the holes.

"Welcome to the land of lost hopes and busted dreams and disillusioned heroes—and count me in on all three," Carter said, and picked up a glass and hurled the beer down his throat. I mean hurled. I did the same, opening my gullet and letting her fly. How long does it take three guys to drink thirty beers? Fifteen minutes, with this maniac. That's the way it was.

My head was beginning to buzz when Carter picked up the glasses one by one and fired them, using a wrist flick, across the room straight as a bowstring into the hands of the little bartender. The guy was standing there grinning. Twenty-eight, twenty-nine, and thirty, the room of guzzlers was chanting, observing the most fun they would have all day.

Carter pulled another dollar out and I thought, no, I can't last another round, but he threw it on the table and said, "Thanks, Emil," and got up. "That puts things into their proper perspective," he said to us. "Time to high-ball."

The three of us stumbled out into the sunshine. The Mountie's jeep was parked next to ours and he started talking low and fast to Carter. I couldn't hear but an idiot could understand what he was saying. A man who was drunk as a fiddler's bitch by noon, a long and dangerous road. Something needed saying.

"Relax. Take it easy. I understand. Just relax. I'll tell him so. He's got to be in better shape than I am," and Carter turned on me. "Hey, kid. You drive this here fool thing? Just down the road until I get out of the clutches of this Christian gentleman."

I got in, snuggling the vehicle between my knees as I had done so often in other times. I flicked through the gear positions, tested the wheel play. A lot of it. It would be a dangerous thing to handle, even on a gravel road, let alone a road made up of too many potholes and too little gravel.

I said to the Mountie: "Okay, point me," which was like saying, "What time does the midnight ferry leave?" There was only one road and we were on it, pointing east.

"How are you?"

"Fine, officer. Just a little drunk."

He leaned over and his eyes sought out the engineer scrambling to get in and he said, very low, "When you're near the camp you'll see a spring on your left. It's boxed in a white butter box. Stop and let him freshen up and then he can drive into camp. About a mile. Better that way. Eh?"

I nodded and half a mile down the road there was the boss, head bobbing between his knees, occasionally hitting the dash with the top of his skull. Out cold? Sleeping? Playing possum? Jerry had made a nest in the confusion of boxes and bags and was laid out on his back, watching the clouds drifting along in a handsome fashion.

I passed the last cabin of the oldtimers, prospectors, and trappers too old to go foot-slogging and just waiting for the small pension check. Counting the days until they could hike into town and buy grub and have a few beers. How many times had they tramped over new ground and then deeper into the bush and found nothing and come back over their trail and found the ground staked by others and already sold to the big companies for a good price? They called it "Running Fever," that urge to get out because they had a hunch, but found that Lady Luck had dealt them the three of hearts to their four-card spade flush draw. The old story.

It sure was nice country. I passed a neat little lake about eight miles out, sitting as pretty as a princess's tiny sky-blue bonnet, flanked by a littoral of tall gray-green timber and a granite ridge rising higher behind. I wanted to stop but I had to get my load of dangerous cargo home.

Rounding a corner, I nearly rammed an old porcupine steaming along like H.M.S. *Renown* plowing up the Straits of Malacca, headed for an insurgent native village where her big guns would teach those filthy heathens the lesson of their lives. Porky wasn't going to move, or even stop. I could see that determined look in the critter's eye, natural to others of his species. I jammed the brake and spun to the side and Jerry muttered, "For Christ sakes, drive this thing, will ya."

Thank God they were too lazy and dumb to put decent roads into this north country. If there had been a ditch we'd have been in big trouble. The skid to the left rolled Carter over against me, and getting back on course rolled him back, head still down, bobbing and weaving like the punch-drunk fighter he was.

I was sweating like a navvy and at the next bumbling stream I eased the jeep to a stop, got out, and washed my face in the deathly chill water until I heard the engineer mutter, "C'mon, kid. That can wait. Sure, wait. Won't do any good noways. You know, I always say one good sweat will wash away the old sweat." When I got in and turned the key he was bobbing and weaving again, fighting his world.

I hit a pothole to avoid another and heard a clink and on the floor was a flask that had worked its way out of his pocket. I slowed and held it up. Half full? Half empty? I worked the cap off and smelled. Nothing I recognized. Jerry reached over and took it and said, "Smells bad and shakes funny. Comes out all milky."

"White lightning," I replied. "Gimme," and I put it down where I'd found it. If I had taken a crack at it he would probably have known to the half an ounce how much I'd stolen. No sense in that.

Jerry said, quietly in my ear, "Think we got a hard case here?"

I thought, sure. Government ain't like industry. In industry he'd have been out on his ear in jigtime, walking toward the elevator on the executive floor carrying a Birks' box with a gold watch in it. In government they get a spooky one and ship him out to places like this, as far as they can, and hope they can get half a decent summer's work out of him.

I thought of his face again. He may have been fifty-five. His hair was jet black. He had a wide forehead with a deep and flaming scar over his right eyebrow, to which a dozen things had contributed. His eyes were blue, his cheekbones were high, Indian fashion, and broken blood vessels snaked through his nose. His mouth was wide and his teeth were white and perfect. False, obviously. It was a face that demanded attention. It said, "Look at me." Somewhere, many years ago, some woman had loved him desperately and he had given her babies and each time he went out into the bush she would say, "Oh, come back soon. I love you so." Then she began to say it less, and now, perhaps never. It was a good face and I liked it and him, but right now that face was down between his knees.

I was hunting for the spring and soon I saw it, where the Mountie had said. Someone who knew about camp water had boxed it properly. I stopped and the engineer's head snapped up and he got out of the jeep, as sober as a Hutterite preacher.

He said, "I'm going to do about fifty yards' walking up in the pines, and then I'm coming back and if one of you takes a belt of that popskull, you're welcome to it. It'll kill you."

As he had said at the hotel, that sure put things in their proper perspective.

He came back and spent five minutes sloshing his hair and head and face and hands in the little pool formed below the spring. He blew, he bubbled, he gargled, and he said, "Well, that puts the ginger under the horse's tail."

A bulldozer had tipped up and toppled a large flat rock and he sat on it. "Gather around. Court's in session. Well, fellows, I'm not a booze fighter any more. I lost that battle many years ago," and he pulled out the bottle and slugged two inches off and slapped the cap on and went, "Aaaahhhhgh! Nothing like Rice Krispies with thick cream for breakfast to make life worth living.

"Now, camp's ahead. We got a cook, a dilly. I heard from the office in Winnipeg he was decorated by King George the Sixth after he served in the French Underground. Maybe so, maybe not. Just don't cross him. There's a bull cook. He's fourteen and the cook brought him along. He's a good kid, when he's working, and trying to become a big movie cowboy star by practicing on that cheap guitar. There's four truckers, Gem Trucking, who brought their outfits in on the ice last winter, so they're stuck here until winter again. They're not happy. There's Carl. Scandinavian first name, French last name, Indian and all mean, but he's a good camp man and can smell a deer a quarter of a mile away. You'll be eating a lot of venison. He can tell a lot of good stories. Stay away from him unless he talks to you.

"There's Cree Henry. Used to be a pilot on the lakes. Said once when he was on the big lake, as first mate on a freighter, the captain asked him their position. Were they lost, he asks. One hell of a son of a bitch storm going on all around him. Cree Henry said they weren't lost—he just didn't know where they were. His wife or girlfriend chopped off his hand with a hatchet. Cree Henry said whichever done it, she was jealous. He uses it for a club, so don't ever tackle him and don't try to bust up any fight he's in. That arm will split you like you wouldn't believe."

"There's Alex Marsden. My transit man. Just graduated from engineering. Good man, but screwed up with some girl. I had him last year. Okay. Deverell on level. He loves that instrument so much he takes it to bed with him. There's Don Rhys. Says he's a Communist but wouldn't know the Hammer and Sickle from a knife and fork. He has a woman with him and they have a tent out behind the cook tent. Her name is Gerda. Yeah, against regulations, but what the hell. And listen, you punks, she don't share it with anyone."

One by one he continued the list, taking small sips, and when he finished the crew the bottle was finished and he hurled it hard and far, the way a good cricket pitcher would, and I wondered if he'd played the game. I suspected he had gone to a university where they would play effete games because, while he tried, he could not disguise his breeding and education.

The bottle splintered on a rock somewhere out of sight and he said, "Bring the flag down to half-mast for a dead soldier."

He pointed at me. "They always send me too many of you. Too many fathers with kids like you who must play Tuesday-night poker with the district superintendent. Anyway, you look intelligent and can drive the jeep, so I'm going to make you my chauffeur. That way you'll be able to keep tabs on the breed girls in town. You can also be my executive assistant. Always wanted one, and shit, the boss of a big outfit like this should have one. If you've got any first aid I can make you the first-aid attendant. A big deal like this should have a doctor."

I said I had a certificate, and wondered if this was just the booze talking or if he meant it, and, reading my thoughts, he said, "Being the doctor gets you two bucks *per diem* more, and driving jeep and not putting it in ditches and muskeg is a buck more. Being my executive assistant means you don't have to work your ass off out there with the mosquitoes and the no-see-ums, to say nothing of the wasps' nest the axemen bring down at least once a week. I think we've got an old first-aid kit lying around, but if you can't find it, buy some aspirin and iodine and plaster next time we go to the store.

"And finally, there are Indians in this country. They wander in and out. All sizes, Big, small, fat, thin, black-eyed, eyes of blue, five feet four, six feet two, some mean, some nice, some well educated at the residential school, so they can come back into this godforsaken country and chip wood for us in the summer and snare rabbits in the winter. Others do better fishing and such and can't put an X on a check. They come in all types, just like the white man, and a hell of a lot I'd trust further than half the guys on this crew. Just don't mess around. Here endeth the lesson."

He unfolded his frame off the rock, got into the jeep, and without looking to see if we'd signed on, he was off like a bat out of hell to the camp whose white tents we could see when we skidded around the next bend.

It was your ordinary camp. A mess tent. A kid was sitting on an overturned lard pail at the door, strumming a guitar. The cook appeared and waved. A thin and very dark man sauntered over, nonchalantly, carrying a magazine. He was introduced to us as Carl. Carl, the mean one. He looked at the boss as if to say, "So, two more. So?" He returned to the first of two sleeping tents, and the boss went to his small tent across the road, slipping a little in his haste because an errant shower had dumped on the place that morning. The bull cook laid aside his guitar as the cook pushed a toe under his rump and heaved him up, heading him for the loaded jeep. He waved us in and as we sat at the long oilcloth table, I spoke to him in French. We chatted for a few minutes and he seemed pleased that he could again communicate; but then, thinking it over later, maybe he didn't seem so pleased. Anyway, we didn't say anything of world-shattering importance.

The boss came in as the cook was laying out cookies and black coffee. I looked down on the shiny tablecloth and somebody had covered a large section with sketches of naked girls. There was a pen lying there and I began shading in certain parts and the boss laughed and said, "The kid does it when he isn't playing that bloody guitar, when he should be scrubbing out the pots and pans and learning things that will ensure him a rich and satisfying old age. Besides, he doesn't know bugger-all about women. Look at the way he's got that one standing. She'd look better down on her knees."

We laughed and as he munched a cookie he said, "You know, the Big Swede is taking a bunch of the gang into town a week from

Saturday. To Frenchie's, last stop. Think we should take the kid? Might learn him something, you know," and he dunked his cookie in the coffee and held it high to the cook and nodded in appreciation. The man in the spotless whites said, "Okay, Charlie, I got ya."

And so, after a journey, we had arrived at the road camp for a summer's work. It was all so predictable. Sleep, work, eat, and then go to town to get drunk and, hopefully, screwed.

Frenchie's—the "In" Place, the Only Place

Oh, and there was the rough and the ruck of camp, so far from other humans that if we had had cats we would have had to import our own tom.

The unending but endurable monotony of it and nothing to complain and curse at except too much rain or too much sun, the stink of the garbage dump behind the tents, the nocturnal bears that rummaged and fought in it, the quality of the food but not the excellence of the preparation, the poker players late in the night arguing about the fall of a bad card in the stud game, the lack of even one indecent woman, the boss's refusal to allow booze to be brought in, and the drudgery of the work—the cutting of line, the fording of streams, the returning to camp after a six-mile tramp, wet and bone-chilled or sunburned and pitted with bites from the swarming mosquitoes.

For two weekends it rained heavily Friday night and Saturday morning. Big Swede, much as he wanted to, dared not take the GMC to town for a Saturday-night piss-up.

On Sunday afternoons the winds pushed the heavy, low clouds off to the east to do damage to hundreds of thousands of square miles of absolutely nothing. By Tuesday the road was bone dry and I would drive the boss to town for groceries, equipment, the mail, and his package of four bottles of Gilbey's gin, brought in by the Monday plane.

On the third Saturday at breakfast Big Swede pounded the table and roared, "Rain or mud, fog or flood, Big Swede rides tonight, and I don't mean maybe. You who wants to get pie-eyed, come, and you who wants his ashes hauled, come too."

The road was dry and the gang knocked off at four. They sluiced off three weeks of grime and, clothed like little gentlemen, ate a cold meal and by five were heading for town. I followed in the jeep with Carter, the transit man, Jerry, and Carl, and we caught the GMC at the hotel.

Carter said, "Lean on that horn," and the signal called the crew over and he said, "No funny stuff, you guys. None. This town doesn't like us anyway. Don't give them a chance to like us worse. I catch any of you patting little boys or goosing pretty girls and I'll hold court at camp tomorrow afternoon. Remember, there's a Norseman flies straight to Lac du Bonnet every morning and there's a nice big bus that goes on to Winnipeg every afternoon."

He said he'd take over the jeep and roared off, and I asked Carl what that was all about.

"Oh, he'll probably go up to the big house and eat some more food and wash it down with the manager's Crown Royal. Or he might be heading over to Loretta's for a little bit of this and a little bit of that."

"Who's Loretta?"

"The worst-kept secret in this bush for forty miles each way. She's one of the teachers. Got that little white house just as you come into town. They'll probably join us later. Let's extend our trapline into this here place and see if the beer is any better than last time."

The gang, with Big Swede directing traffic, had pushed four tables together and the dollar bills began fluttering into the center. The manager began pumping beer, and the little waiter fairly galloped across the twenty feet of floor to load up the tables, tray after tray. The drinking began, and the talk was exclusively about what was being done in camp. Locomotive engineers talk about railroading. Surgeons talk about cutting people open. Writers talk about their rotten publishers. Surveyors and roadbuilders talk about roadbuilding. The learned and earnest discussion of the newest car models would come next, although not a fistful of fingers of them would ever be able to afford one. The evaluation of each man's remarkable sex exploits would be the last item on the agenda, their awesome feats made more awesome by the increasing cargo of beer they took on board.

I was bored right from the start and I looked around and saw that the bull cook was missing. I asked Carl and he said the boss hadn't been able to persuade him to come, and he wasn't about to order him to come. I said, well, the kid would still have his cherry, and Carl looked at me and said, "Oh, I don't know about that."

The 6:30-to-7:30 closing time, by provincial edict, was ignored. The Mountie walked in, talked quietly to the manager, accepted a glass of tomato juice, poured guiltily below the counter. He walked out again. Nobody cared, let alone noticed. An Indian came in and sidled over to a table by the door, and then, oh so carefully, poured each of his ten glasses into a large rubber sack. He poured eight of the next round into the sack, drank two, and skipped out the door. He'd have a woman in the bush behind the hotel.

At 9:30, Big Swede stood up and yelled, "Okay, guys, we're going to Frenchie's. Line up at that bar and buy your boxes of beer. If you're running short Mr. Mawhinney will give it to you on the jawbone. Pay up next time."

By ten we were outside, each with a case, and Big Swede started directing traffic again, and away in a straggling line we went through the dusk toward the lake. At a sign saying "De Place" we went down a wide trail and in a clearing was a large cabin made of logs and strung with about forty sets of Christmas-tree lights, every one winking and blinking red, yellow, blue, or green.

It was a big cabin but this was one big room. Somebody who knew axework had built this. It would take two sticks of dynamite at each corner to break it up.

The place was lit by a dozen heavy-duty lamps and there wasn't even one gloomy corner for some hanky-panky. The tables were heavy, with oiled, rough-hewn planks, and the chairs were the oddest assortment in Christendom. I'd say they were a collection of many years, taken from wrecked miners' houses and prospectors' cabins along the lakeshore. At one end there was an opening in the wall from which issued an unending stream of coffee cups that didn't steam, french fries, and boiled onions, quart-sized bottles of orange and Cola Kik for mix, hamburgers, and venison sandwiches. There was also a piano huddled angrily by itself in the corner, and as I passed, I saw it was a Steinway. How the mighty of the mighty had fallen. I tapped out the first five notes of "God Save the King" and all three keys were jangly out of tune.

But it was the smell that caused your eyes to blink. It was as tangible as the heavy smoke. Mostly grease, sprinkled with the sourness of last week's stale beer and tonight's sweat. One big chunk of gangy atmosphere.

Big Swede, a case of Carling's in each paw, pushed his bow wave through the swarm of people on the floor waiting around for somebody to start up the music but also just gossiping and tilting brown bottles. About twenty of us took over a table. Laronde came over, obviously happy for our trade but just as obviously worried that within his midst, among an alien crowd, was a gang that could, if the spark lit the fuse, wreck his joint. He was a little man, and he tilted his face up to talk to our leader. Big Swede laid a heavy hand on his shoulder and said, "C'mon, Frenchie. It's not that bad and never was. You leave it to Big Swede. Any of these boys want to bust up somebody, make you unhappy, they're going to lick me first," and he snorted. "And anybody who licks me ain't been invented yet."

That was enough. Laronde went away happy.

After cracking off the top of my first beer I looked around. The place was full.

There were miners and their wives and single miners with girls you knew just by looking weren't anybody's wives. There were Indian girls and a few startlingly good-looking breed girls, each with her little cluster of men around her. There were men dressed like trappers and prospectors who looked like bank managers in blue serge. Over in the far corner was the executive dining room, so to speak. In it was the top echelon from the mine. The doctor was there and the woman beside him was more than likely the nurse. I'd bet a dollar that about three of the men were executives of the company, in from Toronto or Cleveland, for some·business and a weekend of fishing. I knew it was the mine table because Mrs. Marwell was there and, when I caught her eye, she waved.

The music started, an accordion, guitar, alto sax, that bitch of a pianner, and some guy who clenched a tin plate between his knees and beat it with two spoons. I think I could discern that they were playing "The Yellow Rose of Texas." Anyway, it wasn't "Jingle Bells." Couples swarmed onto the floor, doing the two-step, the waltz, the jitterbug, and there were two men dancing by themselves, one doing the shuffle-foot and the other foot-stomping.

Jerry said, all he-man-like: "We should get ourselves a woman each. At least, put in a claim on one for later."

I laughed and said, "You kidding? Not for me. You look closely at some of the guys who already have staked their claim. Those guys are big and I am small."

After the first set of three dances the orchestra retired, possibly to reinforce with beer their suspicions that they indeed were musicians. When the second set began, Jerry nipped over to another table and soon glided past with a pretty little Indian. He winked and made a little gesture behind the girl's back, and when I turned around I saw Carl look daggers.

"That your girl?" I asked.

"One of them. Help yourself. They're free tonight. Later, you might pay but not all that much."

About an hour later a waitress walked by and dropped a piece of cardboard in front of me. It was torn from the back of a McDonald's cigarette package. Mrs. Marwell? I had seen her smoking McDonald's on the riverboat.

It read, "Hi, it's me. Wanna dance?"

Carl reached over, swift as a nighthawk taking a bug in the air, and read the cardboard. "If I think that's who it might be, and I'm sure I'm right, then you're not very smart. Carter won't like it, and if you think he won't know, don't be sure."

"Yeah, Carl, you'll tell him, Mr. Sneak-around."

"No, he just walked in with Loretta and they're sitting at the mine table."

"Screw'm," and I walked over as the music started playing another three of the nine tunes they knew, and asked Mrs. M. to dance. She smiled and we went on the floor.

"See," she said. "They didn't even notice. They come up here for business and a little fun, and so far all they've done tonight is talk business."

Either she was twenty-two again or I had bumped myself up to thirty, and we had fun. We stomped and whirled and glided and dipped and carried on like crazy, and when it was over, she said, "That was good. I enjoyed it. Now, back to listening to efficient recovery, cyanide ponds, and how many tons it takes to make a brick of gold. A lot. Bye-bye," and she was gone.

The evening roared on. I grabbed the guitar as the owner sucked up his beer and I stood by the piano, pounded the keys five times with my fist, and the room quietened. I said, "Señors and señoritas, a leetle song from Old Spain," and the only sound you could hear was the hissing of the lamps and the grease spluttering in the kitchen. Apparently this was not done, and not by some government guy off the road gang.

I recklessly let go with a series of high-pitched yips and swung into the song, chording better than I had ever done and making that old geetar stand up and walk around. I was going so fast my fingers tingled, and then I slowed down to a dirge and although I am an amateur flamenco singer I was never as good again as I was that evening. As I finished I threw the guitar twirling into the air and, when I caught it, gave out one thrashing chord.

"Give 'em hell!" yelled Carter. "What's all that dago talk mean? Some guy can't get nowhere with his señorita?"

"No, señor. It is a song that every Spanish mother sings to her child. It is about a little boy who has lost his little dog and is sad."

I stood there, head bowed, the guitar over my shoulder in the pose of a weary soldier awaiting his fate. There was a moment's pause and the place exploded into laughter and applause. I moved back to my table and Carl, inscrutable Carl with eyes like pieces of coal, nodded and said, "Not bad."

I guessed I had made a friend, but did I need him? Menace still surrounded the space he occupied.

I drank more beer, twisted the wrist with a couple of guys, ate some grub that was put before me, paid with money I didn't count, danced with the waitress, who somehow had wound up on my lap, and I was getting higher. Somebody slugged someone on the dance floor and little Laronde waded in with a bottle wrapped in a heavy towel and dropped a guy. Probably the wrong guy, but one man cannot fight with himself. Then somebody was thrown out into the darkness. From a far corner a woman screamed, "Why, you dirty son of a bitch." There was the crunch of fist on bone and the woman screamed louder and Frenchie rushed over and put out that fire.

"The Yellow Rose of Texas" had become big stuff with the orchestra. That's all they were playing now and nobody cared. Everybody danced.

Big Swede came over and ordered, "Pick up your beer. We're going to Rafferty's now. In half an hour this place will be a slaughterhouse."

Our ragged army headed for the door just as the mine party was exercising good judgment, too, and at the door Mrs. Marwell smiled and said, "Thanks again. Where did you learn that Spanish song?"

I laughed and said, "When I was a little boy I lost my dog and became sad and my mother sang it to me."

Outside, Mrs. Marwell's husband said, to nobody in particular, "If one doesn't want to be hanged, he should not stand around on the gallows."

The line formed, Big Swede in the lead. I felt good—like I had drawn four aces and a deuce and discarded the deuce to confuse them and drawn the king of spades. The old lady of fortune was showing she was on my side. We walked, weaved, and wallowed along the road to a wide trail while the crusher at the mine thumped away and "The Yellow Rose of Texas" filtered to us from Frenchie's roadhouse.

The night was black, but the stars were high and bright and Big Swede, his bow wave curling back along the line, took us down the wide trail and soon there were lights and the Swede yelled, "Rooster Town. Rafferty's. Waiting for us."

He steered for a long, low house that maybe once was white and up three steps and onto a porch that used to be one. Two bucks' worth of planking and a handful of spikes would have made it a porch again; all that was needed was a bit of hustle and carpenter's know-how.

The door opened and sound poured out, and a woman, big and heavy, was silhouetted there. She snarled, "You guys again? Ain't you bastards ever gonna finish that road of yours to nowhere?"

"Easy, Mary, we come in the spirit of good will, and we bring supplies," and he held up his beer. "Drink for the hungry masses." It is always surprising what a belly full of beer will do for the eloquence of speech of a man with a limited education.

We filed into the room, a huge room. It seemed to take up most of the house, but there were two doors leading off at each end. The first person I saw was the boss sitting next to his woman, a shy-looking little creature, and he got up and said, "Won't you guys even give us a chance for a short beer? Aw hell, it's a free country, and anyhow we were just leaving. Going up to the big house where the elite meet."

There was a linoleum floor with a flower pattern, a table, a bookcase with glasses in it and, atop, a vase crammed with dead daisies. Last year's. Some chairs. On a wall, paintings of Christ and other biblical scenes and what looked like covers from the *Saturday Evening Post* pinned to the yellowish background.

Half a dozen men and some girls sat around, talking and laughing, drinking and eating fries, the fellows feeling up the girls who wiggled and giggled. They paid no attention to us. I sank into the only easy chair in the place, slung my half-case of beer between my legs, and looked at a sour-faced woman of thirty-five going on fifty sipping out of a glass with something brown in it. She snapped, "No use talking at me. I don't work here; just a visitor. Don't expect nothing at all. See, I'm his doings," and she pointed to a hulk who was leaning over a spindly-legged, wind-up gramophone trying without success to get the hole in the record over the peg on the turntable. We watched and when he succeeded he raised his arms in the victory salute of a boxer. When he got the needle set he stepped back and some cowpoke whined out a tune more or less in the fashion intended by the record manufacturer.

She pointed and added, "He's night-shift boss on Mondays."

I asked what happened to the other days of the week and she said, "There's a Hunkie named Walonski who does that job. My guy's just a flunky up there. Walonski has to get hit by a rock before he gets the job, and then he'll get hit by a rock. That's the way it goes up here. And besides, that's his chair you're sitting in."

"I don't see his name on it."

She said the guy, Craig, didn't have to put his name on any goddammed chair and I said to hell with him and she snorted and said, "Good for you, for all the good it'll do."

I said thanks and reached for a beer and she took an opener from her slacks and said, "Here, have this one. About all anybody in this hole of a place carries in their pockets is about five one-dollar bills, a hankie to stop the blood, and three bottle openers."

When I'd zipped the top off I asked her who was what here and she said, "Over there is Dolly and Silly. Her real name is Priscilla. We call her Silly." She pointed to two young women, both under twenty, with marcelled hair, scarlet lips, and comical but sad smiles painted rosebud fashion. Each was sitting with a big miner, all four piled into a rust-colored chesterfield whose legs had been ripped of upholstery. Obviously this place had some mean cats or humans who liked to chew furniture. Probably both. "Over there is the mother. Mary. Mary is Mary. Not much else to say. I suppose she could make something of herself if she lived somewhere else and wasn't married to the rat."

Mary had marcelled hair too, as unevenly as the two daughters, and I figured they did each other's hair and all were equally inept. She would be a symbol of total despair in a parade of desperates. There was a total lack of style about her, her dress was dirty, and the running shoes she wore had walked many a muddy trail. I felt sorry for her just long enough to hear her rip off a string of obscenities at a tall man who had stumbled against her. When she finished she grabbed his beer bottle and shoved him away when he lunged for it, and rattled off another string of naughty words.

"She's just practicing to be mean," said the lady beside me. "Wait for an hour and she'll really come on stage."

I looked around and figured I'd spotted "the rat." No one could tell his age but he certainly was a tubercular. In the last stages, I thought. He was sprawled in a chair. Others in the room were drunk or getting there, but he was raging drunk. His head lolled and he drooled. He wore a pair of torn pants and no shirt over his Stanfield winter underwear, and the fact that he wore a boot on one foot and a bedroom slipper on the other reduced his chances even further of being *Esquire* magazine's Man of Distinction.

I pointed and asked, "The rat?"

"None other, and up here when we call him that, everybody feels we're giving the real rats, the animals, a clean bill of health. He's got silicosis. Got it here, he says. He worked in the mine and the guys say he was a good fellow and a good worker. Then. Not now. I won't go into it. When the mine offered him a settlement and he wouldn't take it, they said to hell with him. Then they gave him part of his settlement and he moved Mary and the three girls into Rooster Town, to this shack. Everything has been going downhill fast. Everybody used to feel sorry for Dolly and Silly and Connie, but now they only feel sorry for Connie."

"Connie?"

"Yeah, the youngest. The prettiest. Maybe sixteen. She's the only one that has a chance. There she is now, by the kitchen door. She's been cooking fries for these bastards, including me," and she called, "Connie, come over here." The girl hesitated but smiled and the woman said, "She shouldn't be within fifty miles of this place. Can't figure how she hasn't been spoiled, know what I mean? Cooking for these guys in this place. Night after night, and a lot of days. A damned bloody crying shame, and you believe it, mister."

She stood up and walked to the door and spoke to the girl and led her over, her hand firmly clamped on the girl's wrist.

"Connie, sit down your pretty little ass and talk to a real live guy from the bright lights. I don't know his name but he'll probably tell you. He's with Carter out on the survey. Seems like a nice guy. Not like the rest of these bastards. Excuse my French. And I don't think he's drunk," and she shoved the girl into her chair and left, turning and wiggling her fingers and calling, "Toodle-de-do."

She was right. I wasn't drunk. Too much to drink, but it was one of those nights when a barrelful would have been too much but still not enough.

I've always been pretty good at making conversation with females, but at the start this one had me stumped. A black-eyed Susan growing all by its lonesome in this patch of Russian thistle. While every other woman, including Carter's, wore slacks, she wore a dress, sort of a soft brown color, with short sleeves. I guess you'd call it a puffed-up kind of sleeve. Around her neck was a little gold chain necklace with a profile in the cameo. She wore silk stockings and her shoes would be called pumps. Her hair was worn like a cap, glistening black with tight little half-curls, I guess. Her skin was a light brown, natural, not tanned, and I thought, looks like there is a touch of the tarbrush in this one. What stood out about her were two things: the glow of her skin and a kind of serenity. No, she did not belong in this place at all. Not at all.

Definitely about sixteen. Too bad.

What was I going to talk about? We probably had nothing in common and I was not long on meaningless chatter and she didn't look the type. Christ, I thought, maybe that's the one thing we do have in common.

The woman living with the once-a-week shift boss seemed to have been trying to tell me something, but I discarded what I thought she had said and reasoned, if this is a whorehouse and she lives in this whorehouse, is she a whore? If she is, she's the most unwhorelike whore I have ever met.

"Where did you get the lovely dress, Connie?"

"Mrs. Marwell bought it for me when she was in Winnipeg last month."

Things were starting to jump. A smashed glass. A slap from the corner. A good-natured hoot followed by a wild holler. The phonograph blared on: Peter Dawson singing "The Miner's Dream of Home." It had been played twice before and was obviously a favorite.

Another was Jim Ryan's "The Same Old Shillaleagh" and then there was Jim Farrell singing "No Wonder She's a Blushing Bride." I knew them all and they were all awful. People came in from the night and others drifted out. Jesus and the Madonna looked down from their cheap frames on the wall with what I was supposed was compassion. Or maybe disgust at the brawling scene. People danced every which way. The cigarette smoke could be cut with a knife; the beer stink left over from the last weekend was intensified. It looked like any other party in the country after 2:00 A.M.

Anyway, Connie and I had our own little camp in our corner and nobody bothered us except when her father reeled across the room and leaned over as if to slap Connie and she said, quietly and evenly, "Don't, Pa."

He started an oath, stopped, and turned to me and said, "You, I don't like you."

"Pa, this is a friend of mine," and I said, "Never mind it, Connie." I noticed a few people watching, and that tore it. I was bored with all this commotion. "Connie, let's go for a little walk and look at the stars."

She hesitated. Then, shyly, she said, "Well, we could go down the trail to the plane dock. It's quiet there. This sound is awful."

I put a beer in each pocket and we slipped out and as I was closing the door Carl was giving me his small, malicious grin. He made Churchill's V-for-Victory sign. I gave him the finger.

We walked silently down the path and turned left and up a slight rise, with the grumble of the mine machinery always behind us, muted but audible, and she said, "I hate that noise. Even on Christmas Day, which is supposed to be a nice day, you hear it. Everything that is wrong, so awfully wrong, that's what that sound means to me."

I took her hand, diffidently I must admit, and we walked down to the lake and out on the dock and sat on the bench used by plane passengers. I said, "Look up there. Every star is billions of miles away, but they look so close you want to reach out and catch one."

"Oh, Holy Night, the stars are brightly shining,..." And she stopped.

"My favorite carol too, Connie. Do you know, there was once a poor shepherd boy watching his father's herd at night on the hills overlooking Galilee and he said, 'The Heaven's declare the Glory of God, and the Firmament showeth his handiwork.'"

"Who said that?"

"David."

"What's your name? I was afraid to ask."

"Barry."

"I'll call you David."

"How old are you?"

"I'm sixteen."

"I'm twenty-two. Why did your father say he didn't like me?"

"He's a sick man. Here"—she pointed to her chest—"and in his head too. He makes my mother go with miners and guys from the bush. Then he made my sisters do it too. Dolly and Silly. I mean do things in the bedroom. You saw them, acting the way they do. They're not my sisters any more. Neither is my mother. I hate my pa. Really hate him. Soon he'll try and get me to do it. In fact he has tried, but my mother said she'd kill him, and she would. She told me once I was the special one in the family and she wasn't quite sure just how I'd come along. I can't get away from this place right now 'cause I'm only sixteen, but I will. Mrs. Marwell says she will help me."

She paused for long moments and said, "He says that is the only way our family can make a living in the bush. Those D.P. miners coming into the house all the time. Can't speak English and they point and laugh. Make signs with those dirty hands. So, my father makes signs with his hands, and he holds up three fingers and puts out his palm. I hate him and sometimes I hate me. I've got to get out. You know, David, I have never seen a train. I have never seen a city. If I had to point the way Winnipeg is, I wouldn't know. I don't know anything, but when I go away I'll have to know something."

"Where does Mrs. Marwell fit into all this?"

"Oh, didn't I say? I'm her maid, her housekeeper. I look after Monica and Andrew when she's gone. I scrub. I wash. I cook for the kids and make sure Andrew does his lessons. She gives me books to read and she showed me how to put on cosmetics. I can't wear them at home. Pa says it's undecent. Mrs. Marwell and I laugh over that one. Did you see Dolly and Silly tonight? So I wear rouge and lipstick when I'm at the big house. Mrs. Marwell, she and I have fun and I love the kids. She gives me a dollar and a half a day and I tell Pa my pay is a dollar, so he takes that and I've got a lot of fifty-cent pieces hidden away in a secret place.

"I'd like to go to Winnipeg and take a course in hairdressing. I love to do pretty things for people. I'd make money too. But until I got enough to take the course, I'd have to work as a waitress or something."

Oh, what a waif in the big city. What an orphan.

"What would I do? First, maybe work in a home until I know my way about. I've studied on it. Then waitress, like that. Next—Mrs. Marwell says she thinks things will work out—the course in hairdressing and then a nice job and things."

What a waif, what an orphan, what an innocent.

"There is no fun here. I can't stay. There are no boys around here. They leave, or they go underground, and then they aren't boys anymore. They are just like the rest of them. They drink and fight. You're the first nice boy I've met in a long time. Probably ever."

That was a little too much to take and I drained the bottle and tossed it high into the lake and said, "Plop!"

She laughed and said, "Plop" and laughed again and said, "You're awfully funny. No, I can see you don't like being called a boy and you're not, but you're so awfully nice."

I opened the other beer and sipped and the late-rising full moon laid a silver carpet across the lake and the soft breeze died and the hill and the trees absorbed the crusher's thump and I waited for her to go on.

She looked across the lake and said, "A harvest moon."

"Bomber's moon."

"What does that mean?"

"In the war if there was a moon like that, our bombers could go right in on German cities just as if it was day."

"David? How does a girl tell a boy she likes him?"

"Well, usually she doesn't. The boy usually says he likes the girl and then she says she likes him, and they go on from there. I like you."

"I like you, too," and she got up and walked to the end of the dock and waited, and I tossed the nearly full bottle away and she said, "Plop." I walked up to her, put my hands on her waist, and turned her around and kissed her. On both cheeks. So help me God.

As naturally as any woman would, she took my face in her hands and kissed me, the way a man should be kissed. Soft but firm, cool but warm.

"I like you, and I've only known you so short a time. I kissed you because I wanted to, and I didn't even know how to kiss. I never have. The only way I know of kissing is in magazines. That's how dumb I am. Why don't you laugh at the dumb bunny you brought out here? You should, you know. I'm a dumb bunny. But I like you."

She was crying softly.

It shook me. To her, liking was love.

I said, "Connie, I am not laughing at you. That old moon up there is the one who is laughing. He's asking why two people should be standing out here on this dock looking at each other when they could be kissing." I kissed her and some more and she said, "I've gotta get back. Pa will kill me."

Reality.

It took half an hour for the five-minute walk. Every twenty feet we stopped. We got back to her place finally. Christ, was it three-thirty? I told her to wait outside and I went in to reconnoiter. Her mother, not even trying to hide her rage, said my gang had left. There had been a fight. One look around the room showed it. Connie's old man was nowhere in sight. Neither were the two daughters. A man lay on the floor, snoring heavily. Another sprawled in a chair, catching with cupped hand the drops of blood that dripped from his nose. Two others were drunkenly trying to put together a smashed table. The phonograph lay on its side. On the wall, the benign Christ and the Madonna, with her Mona Lisa smile, looked down. Sunday morning in Rooster Town.

I walked out and told Connie it might be best if I took her up to the big house on the hill. Someone would be up and she could sleep there. She said, no, no, that would not be right. She would go in the house. I protested. No use. I felt all joy had left me.

She walked with me down the trail a hundred yards and swung into me, pressing close. She kissed me hard.

"I've been thinking since you were in the house. This was the best time I have ever had. Honest."

She walked away and moments later, from the darkness, came her voice. "You know, David, in another month I'll be seventeen. Goodbye."

I called back, "Not goodbye, Connie. Just so long. Dumb bunny."

I walked past Frenchie's place and it was silent, dark, although the forty strings of Christmas lights were winking all by themselves. At the hotel, Big Swede's truck was gone. I thought of sleeping on the couch in the lobby and then, what the hell, it's a moonlight night and only nineteen miles. I was sober and I was tired, and I just kept going, keeping out of the ruts and the potholes and watching the stars swirling around as their part of the wonderful and complicated machinery of night.

An hour later I heard engine sound behind me and then lights shining and a vehicle grinding along in low gear. It was the jeep and Carter was at the wheel. He stopped.

"Lo, our famous troubador," he said, thickly.

"Knock it off, will you."

"Okay, but get in this thing and drive. I can only see crooked. Where did you take the kid?"

"Down to the seaplane dock. We just talked. How did you know?"

"Sure, sure. I know everything."

I got in and the engine sounded as if somebody had switched all the moving parts around. I asked him what he was using for fuel, pulverized granite and swamp water?

"I don't know. Something's wrong. We'll look at her in camp later. Maybe I'll shoot her, like you do a horse with a broken leg."

Later he said, "That Gallagher's is some place, isn't she?"

"Gallagher's?"

"Hell, I mean Rafferty's. Gallagher's is another cathouse someplace. Maybe in Red Lake. I been in them all. One of the built-in hazards of any business up in this lost-forever country."

He fell asleep, and I nursed that poor old busted-up beaten-down creature the last miles until I came to the spring. I shook him awake and we stuck our faces into the pool below the spring and drank deeply and whoofed and whuffed and shook our heads and combed our hair with our fingers.

As he got behind the wheel he said, "You know, that's the best water in the whole country. Besides, drinking makes me thirsty."

There was false dawn to the east and I said, "Hello, world."

Then he put his head against the steering wheel and said, softly, "Damn it all, I'm too old for all this. Just too damned old."

We drove into the silent camp and the Swede's GMC was there, parked bang smack in the middle of the road.

"Want a nightcap in the tent?"

I told him no, no more for a long time for me, and I headed for the surveyor's tent. I woke at nine-thirty, took a towel and stuff and walked to the lake and shaved in that cold, cold, very cold water and had a good washdown. When I returned the cook called me over.

Now, cooks in camp just do not feed anybody at ten. They work on a very strict meal schedule. But he whipped up a ham and cheese omelet while I looked at the bull cook's drawings of naked women. He had scrubbed away the shadings I had put in. Oh well, some like their women one way and others like them another, and some like to play them three ways from the jack.

When he put the eggs and toast down, he said, "You be dead duck?" I noticed it wasn't his usual statement of fact, but was a question.

I replied, *"C'est probable que vous êtes plus vrai que vous êtes en faux."*

Then I thought, now why did I say that?

6

Farewell to an Old Friend

I knew about Fred Lindsay before I met him, and years later he told me: "We share the common privilege of being friends of each other."

It was in the Cariboo town of Quesnel that the owner of a store told me this story about Fred:

"Back about 1950 he came to town. I think he'd been on a forestry look-out tower for a couple of years watching for fires and writing poetry. Anyway he started this paper and it sure had a lot of guts. I mean, Fred did. If he wasn't lambasting the mayor he was throwing rocks at the premier. He once said, 'I guess I got 'em dodging. Might hit one yet.' Anyway, he was always writing about how dreary Quesnel was and folks was getting pretty mad, and one morning before light, Fred got a pick and shovel and right down the main street out there he dug five holes and planted a fir tree, maybe four feet high, in each hole. Well, after breakfast the mayor came and the provincial police and Fred came along and they said they knew he had done it and they were going to pull them out—and naturally they did. Fred didn't howl, he knew they would, being the way the town was. He just said, 'Okay, you sons of bitches, I showed you a way to beautify this town, and if you don't like it you can rot in this dump.'

"They might have wanted to charge him with something, but they didn't know what... Besides, they were afraid of him."

Well, that is one story the world beyond Quesnel never heard until now, and there are hundreds more like it. It's easy to see why I loved him. I cherish the hours I spent with Fred Lindsay.

Farewell to an Old Friend

Fred Lindsay died several years ago, eighteen months after his good wife, Florence, passed away, one of those unexplained hospital deaths. I know he died of a broken heart. He was my friend for many years and he deserves a place in our history books. There are others cut from much the same cloth, but to me he is The British Columbian. This is his eulogy. He never got one.

Fred was seventy-two when he drew his losing card in Vernon General Hospital on a gray day in March, but he had been around forever. He was ruddy-faced, barrel-chested, tough, profane, an old buzzard. The loss of a leg a few years before had cut down his agility, but he could still go a good lick on his woodpile for a couple of hours.

He had a lot of money—where he got it I do not know—and he spent outrageous sums on man-toys, things he did not need. Example: he bought a gold-dredging outfit, which he would never use, and besides, the placer miners since 1858 had taken all the gold from the river where he lived. Then there was the huge telescope...

Fred spent a lot of money reconstructing the portion of the old Cariboo Road that passed through his property, and he told me: "I like to sit here at dusk. I can hear the miners passing by, heading for the gold fields, swearing at the mules. And I can hear the plod-plod of the animals and the creaking of the harness, and the Fraser rumbling below, and I know, somehow, that I was there with them."

Fred loved an old and decrepit standard black poodle named Gussie and she loved him. She grieved as much as anyone when Fred died.

He loved Indians, and many he helped, giving them work when no other white man would, and he paid them white man's wages. I learned from a friend that Fred was driving on a back street in the Fraser Canyon village of Lytton one day and he passed an Indian, McKenzie, looking very low down. Fred circled the block and came back, got out of his station wagon, and handed McKenzie a twenty-dollar bill. "Here is the twenty you loaned me five years ago," he said. The Indian tracked him down and Fred gave him a cottage, meals, and paid him a good wage, and McKenzie stayed for four years. He'd never seen McKenzie in his life before that day, but this was a chance to help a fellow man. How do I know this? McKenzie told me.

Fred loved to roam, putting his battered station wagons—always station wagons and always full of the most improbable junk—up the most isolated and rugged of old logging and mining roads. He spent several years searching for a deposit of argillite south of Lytton when, if he had read them, the provincial mining reports would have told him that there could never be an argillite deposit there. He had picked up a rumor in some beer parlour. Personally, I think the argillite was an excuse to be on the move.

He started doing man's work when he was eleven, which was not unusual in those days on the frontier. Without going into things chronological, he had been a shoestore apprentice, a blacksmith's helper, and then a blacksmith; he had hustled with his own advertising company, which consisted of hammering posters onto telephone poles. He had seen every kind of logging on the coast and in the Interior. He had done placer mining at Cherryville, and the fact that it was coolie wages for coolie labor didn't bother him one bit. He also prowled around the old Barkerville diggings and in winter he packed 125 pounds of grub on every trip over the Monashee Pass for the miners panning the creeks.

He once ran a don't-give-a-damn weekly newspaper in Quesnel, and he took over a run-down, busted-up tourist set-up on the Fraser Canyon road and built it up until it was an oasis. He didn't give a hoot whether anyone stopped there at night. If he didn't like the cut of a man's jib he would refuse to rent to him.

He loved British Columbia history and he had a large library of the events now long past and he published three books on it. Two of them he wrote at a forestry look-out station far, far back in the woods where the mail and supplies came in twice a month. He told me: "Not once did I see so much as a puff of smoke. Too far away, and I guess even the lightning couldn't find that place." He probably sold as many books as any British Columbian. I have seen him standing at the bus station in Cache Creek, and as the tourists got off Fred would say, "I'm Fred Lindsay. That's my name, and history is my game," and he'd push a book into the hands of the startled American from Texas or New Jersey. "And fortune is fame, and that will be five simoleons." He rarely missed a sale.

He could cook like a wizard, an art he learned in logging camps around the province, and I'll always remember him for his oyster stew. He was a nut on oysters. "They'll do everything for you that you want, and then some more," he'd say. His lamb stews were famous, too, and his Brown Betty was superior to any I've ever tasted since. "Making bread to me is as natural as going for a shit," he said once. For some reason he used an air pistol to perforate the dough when it was rising. Pop. Crank. Pop. Crank. Pop.

He toughed it out on seiners and tugboats in treacherous Hecate Strait with its fifty-foot waves coming in from Japan. He had walked the old Similkameen Trail during the Depression, looking for a day's work in the Okanagan Valley. He found none. He messed around some with bootleggers during Prohibition, and when the provincial police wised up that he was selling beer out of the kitchen of a hotel in Port Alberni where he worked as cook, they mistakenly raided a tea party of the Anglican Church Women's Auxiliary. Whenever he told that story he would laugh until the tears rolled down his weatherbeaten cheeks.

Fred had done some trucking and he ran a successful organic garden—"all you have to do is put plenty of your crap in the ground"—before anyone knew what the term "organic" meant.

He hated government, all governments, any government, all politicians, all bureaucrats: "If they can't find anything more useful to do, then why the hell don't they go out and drown themselves?"

I don't believe he ever robbed a bank.

My idea of a good old time when I was prowling through the Interior searching out stories was to drive up the quiet and narrow mountain-sloped valley to Lumby, a lumbering village where Fred and Flo had settled in retirement in a small white cottage. He had his usual huge garden out back, and flowers growing everywhere. We'd sit at the kitchen table and listen to Radio Moscow and the BBC on his powerful shortwave, twist wrists, tell outrageous lies, and kill off a couple of crocks of Johnny Walker Red Label. Flo would ply me with soup and sandwiches and cake and coffee on the theory that food absorbs alcohol. She thought it would be best if I was sober when I drove off. Fred did most of the talking, free-wheeling and straight-shooting.

This is the story he told me one summer's day. It is pure Fred Lindsay:

"My God, man, there was nothing like it in the world, getting out on your own. I'd been kind of an orphan and when I was just a little kid I lit out for Vancouver. We'll start with Saul Remy. He was once an ox-skinner and then he became a slave-catcher. He was a stout man and he wore a fine suit and had a derby and a watch chain, a great thundering watch hanging on it. He hung around the Red Star Drug Store at the corner of Carrall and Cordova. That was the heart of loggers' country.

"You couldn't get a job anywhere until you went to Saul and he was the most benevolent, kind-hearted, lovable sumbitch that ever lived. Except he was pompous as all-get-out at first. Well, the first time I got a job in the woods I was about thirteen and I had been running errands for F. and F. Henderson and I got fed up and then I got fired. That's what goddam well happened. I walked along the C.P.R. tracks and a fellow with a tugboat skipper's hat came along, a great big fellow with shiny buttons on his uniform, and I asked him where I could get a job.

"He said I'd have to go down to the Red Star Drug Store and see Saul Remy because he did most of the hiring for the camps upcoast. So down I go. I'll never forget him, standing there, king of the castle. I went up, just a kid, and I asked him for a job and my voice went off the end, kind of high.

"He asked, 'Are you a blacksmith?' and I said I sure as hell was, and he said, 'Well, you don't look like a blacksmith.' I was skinny as two matches put together. He told me he couldn't give me the blacksmith's job, but they needed a blacksmith's helper up at The Rock. I stuck out my little pigeon chest and I said yeah, yeah, I'll go to The Rock. I didn't even know what it was, or where it was. I'm telling you now, The Rock was a big logging show over on the island, and old Remy told me to be at the Union steamship dock at six with my turkey.

"I thanked him and walked down the street, asking myself what the hell a turkey was. I stopped a guy coming out of a saloon and told him I could get a job at The Rock if I had a turkey—but I didn't know what a turkey was. He said a turkey was my blankets and my clothes and such, all stuffed into a gunny sack. That was a turkey. I always thought that was pretty nice of that fellow to give me a straight answer, because for all I know I could have been told a turkey was a turkey, and I'd have showed up at the dock with a big bird. Damn it all to hell, I could have been laughed right off the dock.

"I went up to Kitsilano to the house where I lived with some people, and I took two blankets and left them two dollars and a note. I stuffed the blankets and my clothes and some books into a sack and went down to the Union dock. I'm standing there and along comes Saul Remy and he smiles, writes my name in his book, and gives me a piece of paper, and on the boat I go. Simple. He'd made a deal. I'd made a deal. The next time I came to town I'd have to go and see him and pay him his commission. Fine. If I didn't I'd never get a job on the coast again. That's the way it worked. A slave-catcher, but a square guy.

"Now all this is history. Nobody writes about this stuff nowadays. All that la-de-da. Bullshit stuff. This is history.

"I'll never forget that first trip. Never in a million years. Once you left the dock and went through First Narrows it was all timber. Nobody then could have dreamed what it is like today. Trees. Huge. High to the sky.

"And as we went through First Narrows they rang the gut hammer. Bing, bing, and two more bings, bing, bing. I still remember that. Food. I hadn't eaten since breakfast. Everybody headed for the dining room, everybody crowding, rushing. Biggest guys in front. A little guy like me, why, I just went through them like a minnow swimming up some shallows, and there I was standing against a velvet rope and then a guy in a fancy uniform lets the rope down and everybody went in. A rush.

"There was this table with white linen and fanciness at one side and it looked pretty good, so I made a beeline for that, going by the ordinary tables, and in a couple of minutes a bunch of fellows in suits and looking important came in and sat down.

"They kept looking at me and then a flunky came over and asked if I was a company owner or a superintendent. When I said no, he asked if I was going to be a superintendent, and I looked at all of them and I said I was going to The Rock and I was going to be a blacksmith's helper. Proudly. Hell, how did I know I was sitting at the table reserved for camp owners, company directors, executives, superintendents, and high riggers who were the top of the totem pole? I guess that would include government officials—that is, if they could get aboard the ship without being murdered.

"I did not know that then, but I know now, and all the big types were there. There was Jim Shortreed. Old Man Johnson. Johnny Morgan, one of the best high riggers this coast has ever seen. He'd come down thirty feet in a jump, bang, and that whole bloody spar tree would shake. He got knifed, dead, in Seattle. Imagine, 120 feet in four jumps. These guys today are nothings.

"Anyway, I think these high mucky-mucks didn't believe me, and I guess they thought I was the son of the owner of a company, but they seemed kind of scared to talk to me. I guess this had never happened before. First one of them asked me what my father did in this business, what position did he hold, and I said my father was dead or away somewhere. Then somebody asked me where I had learned to be a blacksmith's assistant, and I said by working for the F. and F. Henderson Shoe Company in Vancouver. Well, those big shots finally caught on that I was what I said I was and they almost busted themselves laughing. I didn't realize that the whole dining room had been dead quiet and everybody was listening.

"The big shots let me stay at the table and a steward even brought me a silver ring with a napkin in it. First time I had ever seen one of those things. After dinner I could have owned that ship because the bigshots had kind of adopted me and they took me with them into the saloon bar and we discussed logging and all else very learnedly, although I didn't know a damn thing.

"But that meal. It was the first time I'd been exposed to anything like it. Oyster stew with those funny little crackers. Rare roast beef, potatoes, fancy dessert. The whole shooting match. I was catching on and I watched how these men ate. Like the soup. Not slurp, slurp, like back on that damned stump farm. No. They put their spoon in the bowl this way and move it forward that way and all the time they've got this little finger stuck out. They had learned manners somewhere. Looking round, I saw that the rest of them, all those dumb whistle punks, the chokermen, donkeys, they all ate like they were at a tea party.

"That meal lasted from First Narrows until we were way past the lighthouse, and after my bunch of guys had got pretty tanked up on scotch in the bar we went in and had mug-up. A long table in the dining room piled yea high with cold cuts and potato salad and pickles and cheeses and buttered bread. Big pails of tea, an ocean of coffee, and a lake of soup. You could sit there and eat until you exploded and the cook didn't give a damn. Fifty mug-ups if you wanted. What the hell is wrong with this world today? They don't have things like that anymore.

"Then I went down below. Well, listen, I was just a kid and Saul Remy had give me a stateroom. By myself. Maybe it was his idea of a little joke. Or maybe he thought I might be king of the world someday and he'd keep on the good side of me. I couldn't sleep and I could hear the screw going thump-thump and the salt wind was blowing through that open porthole and me lying there. For a kid of thirteen it was romantic as hell. Going north on my first big job with hopes and dreams. I said to myself I just wasn't a little kid but I was a pirate going out into the Pacific and I'd slaughter anybody who got in my way.

"Well, I woke at five, the dawn, right? We're off Cape Mudge and the wind is blowing clean off Vancouver Island and with the sweet scent of cedar and all the beautiful smells of the forest before the white man ruined it all. There was really no civilization for a long way except an American who had a kind of whorehouse and bootlegging business going on the beach for any loggers or tugboatmen or fishermen who wanted to drop in. Everything else was forest. With the seagulls crying and the waves slapping against the hull and the sun shining through the great trees right down to the chuck—I tell you, it was so damned beautiful I can't really describe it.

"Sixty years later it still grabs me by the heart and I want to cry when I think how wonderful it was that morning. In about an hour I went up to the dining room and had the biggest breakfast I had ever eaten, with four bowls of peaches to polish it off. First time I ever ate peaches. I love 'em still.

"Then we're at Rock Bay and there is an engine on the siding softly going poop-poop-poop and a boxcar and a flatcar and they put a sling down into the hold and up comes a huge pile of groceries and things, and on top of it is a body. Fellow by the name of Paddy O'Reilly. Somebody said he'd been drunk on the Skid Road for three weeks and God knows how he made it back. Somebody else said, 'Good old Paddy, still drunk as a hoot owl.' Two guys picked him up and flung him into the boxcar and we all got in or on the flatcar and away we go up the line.

"It wasn't a bad camp. Clean. That's important. If you've been in some camps I've seen, you could listen in the dead of night and there would be this rustle, rustle, and if it wasn't the cockroaches it would be the mice. When I was running things and that happened, I'd tell the crew to haul their mattresses out and pile 'em, and I'd dump a can of kerosene on them and toss a match. Burn the sons of bitches up. The only way. If the company had said they wouldn't supply new mattresses I'd have quit and taken the damn crew with me. That's what it was like in the old days.

"The job was fine. Fun. It was a life in itself. I worked ten hours a day, but if there was an emergency—some piece of equipment burned out or busted—then I might work twenty hours. The train gang worked to the tides; if there was a high tide at five in the morning and they had a load and something had to be fixed, then I worked all night. I ate like a horse and really began to grow. I put on a lot of weight and I was making fifty-four cents an hours, which was one hell of a lot more than I made a lot of years later during the Depression. That was good money and I saved a lot. Spend it? Where?

"There are some things I remember, like the bull cook coming into the bunkhouse every morning to do the stoves. He'd put in dry kindling and then some dry cedar and sprinkle the coal on top and toss in a match and the whole thing would just explode. The chimneys would start to tremble and you could see the red creeping up the pipe. Then the gang would get out of their fartsacks and stand there, naked, hairy as bears, and hold up their Stanfields, which had been lying on the floor since the night before, sopping wet. You see, it rained a lot in fall and winter, and the steam just used to come roaring out of the long johns, and when they were kind of dry they'd put them on cursing and swearing, and their body heat would finish off the job.

"But one thing I still remember and it still makes me sick. One guy, this big logger with his own bowl as big as a washbasin. At breakfast he'd dump in a gallon of porridge and pour milk over it and then throw in half a dozen fried eggs and a handful of bacon and then chop in about half a dozen big wheatcakes and drown it with a lot of syrup. Then the bastard would dump in a lot of fried potatoes and crown the whole business off with a couple of pieces of apple pie. Then, with a big spoon, he would eat his way to the bottom, slurping and belching all the way, shoving it down that gullet of his. I told him once, me thirteen, that it was a free country and if he want to hog it like that, then not do it near me. I don't think he knew what I was talking about. A trained ape.

"Every Friday, fish. It came in from Yucaltaw Rapids from a guy who had a live tank on his boat—he had cod and salmon and ground fish, you name it—and the two cooks would give it the treatment. I don't know what it is about the Chinese, but they sure know how to do up fish. Always buy fish in a Chinese restaurant. You'll know it will be fresh and done right. Not this salmon you buy today, six months in a warehouse refrigerator and dry as sawdust. On Sunday we had pork. If there were any sheenies in the camp they kept quiet about it on Sundays. The camp had its own pigs and they got big and juicy on the scraps. The Chinese were good on pork too.

"Christmas. Lord Jesus, goddam it to hell. Sorry, sir, if I take your name in vain. The head cook was German, Heinz something, and he laid on a feast for the fellows who didn't catch the Union boat down to Vancouver. A lot stayed just for that day. Christmas to the Kraut was something sacred and weeks before, he'd go to the super, John Hendry, and he'd show him the list and Hendry would okay it and the order would go out.

"The first Christmas I was there, not too many showed up for breakfast because the Union boat had come in and a lot of them had ordered up booze, although it was usually outlawed in camps. Everybody got drunk, but by noon they were in better shape, although some still were half-drunk. They wouldn't let me drink and as I had nothing to do I helped the messhall crew. First we wheeled out two kegs of oysters, beautiful, fat, and delicious, and then we started loading up those tables with everything else. At every table I put out the booze. Every table got three quarts of scotch and about thirty bottles of beer, ale, stout, and when that ran out there would be plenty more. Then we put on the hot food. There was piles of it and at one o'clock I rang that old gut hammer and those hundred and more guys came streaming in. They were all dressed up in their city clothes, shirts, ties, shiny shoes. Oh, fancy, fancy. Christmas, you see.

"The turkeys were roasted, sliced, and fitted back together again. Beautiful. Roast pork and goose and ducks and ham and cold meats and about five kinds of vegetables. Over at a table at one side there was dessert—fruit, puddings, cake, cookies—and if you wanted it, tea and coffee.

"Loggers eat fast, and these timber beasts ate faster, as if it was going out of style, and all the time they were downing those groceries they were swigging scotch and the malts, and when a bottle was dry they'd yell for more. Me and the bull cooks were on the dead run. I kind of felt I deserved a drink during all this, but they wouldn't let me have even a swig of beer. You see, I was the camp mascot in a way. The youngest. If anyone had slipped me a shot he'd hear his ears ring for a week. They were gentlemen that way. Yes sir, you bet.

"Then after all the food was gone we brought in a plum pudding for each table and some of the men just sat and looked at it, their eyes glazing over, too damn stuffed to eat another bite. Then we all sang carols and a chokerman named Dusty Miller recited a long poem about a lost love, and another guy, a chokerman too, he sang a couple of solos. Then, with that business out of the way, they began singing some of the rowdy songs they used to sing in the saloons along Cordova Street, and one I remember had a line in it which went, 'And as she upped her skirt, why, mine went up...'

It went on most of the afternoon, singing and drinking, although nobody got drunk. By that I mean the ones who came in half-drunk didn't get any drunker. They would eat some more, have a couple of drinks, play twist-the-wrist or yank-the-finger, or leg-wrestle and then go for a walk. Alongside the shacks there was a boardwalk, about six feet wide, and here would be all these loggers and the brass in their finest duds just strolling along as if they were on Granville Street in Vancouver where loggers weren't allowed. In their fancy duds and smoking the company's big cigars and talking about logging. Loggers always talk about logging. They don't know anything else. All so bloody civilized you couldn't believe it was happening. Then they'd go back in, have another chunk of Brown Betty and some more of the booze, and smoke another stogie.

"When it got dark the bull cooks brought out gallons of the richest oyster stew I've ever seen, then and now, and platters of brown bread piled high and platters of raw onion rings and pots of hot mustard and the fellows dug in again. When that stew was gone they brought out more until everyone was fat as a stuffed goose. By this time most of them had had it and they staggered off and slept the clock around.

"The next day they'd just mope around with hangovers, wishing they could find a creek full of whiskey. The day after, if it wasn't a Sunday, they would be out on the slopes working harder than any man should work, and for lousy wages and the chance a snag was coming down, called widowmakers, and snuff out their miserable lives. A free trip in a wooden box back to the city. If they had no kin I forget what they did with the body.

"Another thing. They didn't dress up in their fancy duds just at

Christmas. No, every Sunday there they would be strolling up and down the boardwalk acting like civilized men. I guess they had to or they'd have gone bonkers. Deep in the woods, the rails for a road in and out, and there they were acting like bloody toffs, if you'll excuse the expression. Two guys who had beat the hell out of each other in the Saturday-night poker games would be strolling, laughing, and joking and nice as you please.

"I stayed at The Rock three years. I learned an awful lot about life and men, but I decided to get out to see some of the world. Everyone in the camp said it was best, meaning they didn't want me to grow up and be like them. Lost souls, I guess you could say. By that time I was sixteen going on seventeen. I'll never forget those days and the good old B.C. Mills, Timber and Trading Company. They are gone now, bought by some bigger outfit. Always happens—big trout swallows small trout."

And that is Fred Lindsay's story, or rather just one of the dozens he could tell, waving his arms, shouting, whispering, chuckling, and for an audience not of hundreds but of three—myself, Florence, and the bewildered Gussie.

I agreed with my old friend that the life he led for three years at The Rock was as good as any to prepare him for the long road ahead. He came through it with the foundation for becoming a tough gentleman and a rambunctious scholar.

Another insight, and this time it is my anecdote. A year before he died he offered me a 160-acre stump and pasture ranch with house and barn and buildings near Quesnel for $6,000. I said I would buy it. No lawyer, no papers, not even a handshake. Just my word. Then I heard from a mutual friend that he had had an unexpected offer of $10,000 and I told Fred I no longer wanted to buy. He damn well knew what I was up to and insisted I take it. I said no, that was it. But he never sold it. I understand a second cousin in Calgary got it.

The last time I saw him was a couple of months before he died. He was stomping around his little bungalow on that ill-fitting wooden leg, followed everywhere by a very worried Gussie. I had a crock and after a few drinks he admitted he hadn't eaten for two days. He just didn't feel like it anymore. I stewed up a pot of oysters and spuds and onions and got him to eat a big bowl and he said, "You know, it's been a good life, but I won't be around much longer. I'll be seeing Florrie soon."

I didn't go to the funeral. It was held 360 miles away and I hate funerals, but a very old retired Chinese storekeeper from Quesnel later told me: "Big fun'l f' him. Many there."

7

Suds and Sagacity in Saskatchewan Society

Remember the two English ladies on a Canadian tour who stopped at a motel and asked the proprietor, "Where are we?" He replied, "Saskatoon, Saskatchewan." One lady said to the other, "How delightful. They even speak a foreign language."

If I know my human nature, people will say I am taking cheap shots at Saskatchewan in this chapter.

Nope. I like the place. I admire the people for electing in 1944 the world's first government—the CCF—that tried to make a grand and loving social experiment work. Their regiments fought with extreme valor in two world wars, farm boys beside city lads. Some of the world's finest hockey players come from its frozen rinks and run-down arenas. A city like Regina that can consistently produce fine football teams can't be all bad. And there is an awareness of the arts in the province that is translated into solid achievements by writers and artists.

And yet I have always felt that there is a strange process going on in the small and silent villages and towns that are but dots on the map. Okay, if you want a word. I would call it "brutalization," although I use the word cautiously. I believe it is mainly because of the isolation of these places, composed of young people unwilling to leave and retired people too insular to take just one more step into life. It makes a first-time visitor feel that he is an enemy of their way of life until some signal from a self-proclaimed leader in the community judges him okay. I feel it constantly. I do not wish to offend a single man or woman in Saskatchewan, but there it is, and often it is a palpable thing.

*All this aside, there is nothing more exciting than watching the play
of the northern lights crackling across the sky on a bitterly cold night,
and nothing more beautiful than a Saskatchewan sunset seen across a
hundred miles of wheatfields.*

Afternoon in a Prairie Pub

I turned off the highway onto the potholed main street after two hours
of driving through prairie summer heat and monotony. I had ignored
the urge to wheel off at a succession of other small towns until my
throat was parched and the thought of two cold beers was too much.

A prairie town—each one identical to all the others in shape, form,
personality, and purpose—is stultifying to the human condition, as
insistently mean and cheerless as a C-note hit endlessly on a piano by a
spoiled child.

Like the others, it would have the required number of small white
houses with lawns burned brown and behind many of those drawn
blinds there would be a retired farmer and his wife mindlessly watching
television. There would be a widow, waiting to die and sending for
catalogues and writing letters to herself so she would have an excuse to
go daily to the post office in the general store to pick up her own letters,
to bring home the catalogues and junk mail and scan them, and throw
them and her letters away.

This village, which became a town, once had a life, but now the only
reason for its existence is the rigid parade of three elevators—one
white Pool and two strawberry red of the private companies, National
and Searle. These sentinels are the only evidence visible from the
highway three or four miles east or west that there is an organized
existence here on the high plains.

The general store. Once there had been three, but when farmers
bought trucks and cars the new highway was their escape route to the
larger towns, which became cities with a supermarket and a cocktail
lounge, a theater and Chinese restaurants and stores that sold parts for
their machinery and where, because it was there, they could meet

friends and neighbors for many miles in every direction. Also, there was the government liquor store.

So the small villages turned toes up and, to all intents, died.

The general store owner, helped by his family, could not keep up with Weyburn or Portage La Prairie, North Battleford or Brooks, Wetaskawin, Dauphin, Estevan, Yorkton, and others. He dug in and did his best. The store had the post office—without it he might not survive—and as a lucrative sideline he probably had a small bulk oil depot and an old tank truck to deliver fuel around the district. Inside, the store is a curious blend of modern-old, as if he had said to himself, "I'm going put in a line of meat and dairy stuff and get this place going again." He did, but he seemed to stop there, probably with an oh-what-the-hell attitude. Two-day-old Saskatoon newspapers, fruits and vegetables that would have to move soon or even he would have to throw them out. Some women's and girls' clothes and men's work pants and shirts, which were sold only when emergency dictated the purchase. A cooler full of Coke and orange pop and 7-Up, a bunch of magazines, mostly of the field-and-stream variety. The rest of his trade? Canned goods, jars, packages, cartons, boxes, and sacks.

There was a service station with a gravel area in front and two pumps. If the fuel and oil supplier's truck arrived at 3:00 A.M. on a Sunday and the owner wasn't out there with cash on the line, the driver took off and the pumps would go dry. The villagers and farmers cursed, but what could anyone do? It had happened too often. A sign said "Mechanic on Duty," and more likely than not he would be a eighteen-year-old drop-out who had perfected his dubious skills by tinkering with junker Fords and Chevies he had bought for a hundred dollars. He could fix a tire, change oil and plugs, adjust a carburetor, and flush a rad; but, if it was anything complicated, the driver would have to take it "into town." Even those who had lived out most of their lifespan in or near this settlement knew better than to call it a town. Town was where the theater, the supermarket, and the liquor store thrived.

There was a café—not a restaurant—and it would be called Lee's, the Crescent, the Royal, Wong's, or Johnnie's, and the menu would have been revised so often to catch up with rising food costs that it looked like a mess of chicken tracks. If prairie café menus could be classified as collectible, then these would have some value. Bacon and eggs. Who can ruin bacon and eggs? Don't be surprised. Pork chops. The unfailing liver and onions. Chips with gray gooey gravy, a staple in the diet of the Prairie young. Spaghetti, right out of the can to you, four minutes flat. Toast and jam and coffee, $1.50, an outrageous price, but price did not matter because it was an excuse to take up booth space for a half-hour. Stale pies and soggy doughnuts. Cigarettes and cheap cigars and Bic lighters, candy bars and tiny cellophane bags of peanuts for sale inside the glass showcase by the cash register, out of reach of stealthy hands. And over all, as pervasive as the owner's indifference, was the stink of smoking grease, the sound of yearning country-western from the juke box, the sickly institutional green decor, and on the walls—posters of rodeos and fall fairs that had been stuck there two and three years earlier.

There might be a barber shop, a small box-like building attached to a house on the main street and open only Tuesday and Thursday afternoons—never on Saturday because that was when folk drove sixty miles into the town where they could get a bottle of rye, fresh vegetables, and a good steak.

Long ago when the village was born and the big American land companies and the railroad were selling lots and farms as fast as they could list them, the place would have had a bakery. Perhaps it would have been owned by a young widow whose husband had been killed in a runaway and the neighbors kicked into the kitty and helped throw up a little shack, and that put her in business.

When the straining teams were hauling loads from the lumber yard through the muddy ruts to houses being built, there would be talk of putting in sidewalks. About this time a lawyer would arrive and hang out his shingle, and soon there would be a petition circulating to ask the provincial government to build a courthouse. Behind the petition, of course, was the young lawyer. A doctor would have arrived too, and likely as not, he would be elected the first mayor, if the lawyer had not picked off that plum. Or the banker, fresh from the east with orders to grab one more point of usurious interest whenever he could and keep a sharp eye out for foreclosures—he might become mayor. Or the owner of the largest store. For years that small group rotated the mayor's job among themselves, and the townspeople didn't mind. Or understand.

There would be a blacksmith and a bootlegger and a woman who ran a small shop carrying notions and fancies for the ladies and a livery stable with the finest horses for miles around. A newspaper whose editor was also the printer, and the janitor, and on the masthead would be the words: The Finest Little Town in the West—Watch us Grow!

The townspeople said they must have a fairgrounds, a curling rink, a system of wells around town, a lending library, a policeman, a volunteer fire brigade, a bigger school, and they just couldn't put up with having council meetings in the back of A. & C. Smallwood's General Store one damn bit longer.

And so the town grew but as it flourished it was in the process of dying. Roads became better and transportation and communication improved and the boom-and-bust cycles busted more businessmen and farmers than it boomed. Droughts hit, grain prices were low, the First World War took a lot of young men away and if they survived Flanders, the Somme, Passchendaele, and Vimy Ridge, many of them sought more fruitful fields. The Twenties were hard but most survived, and the Dirty Thirties not only took away their income but also their farms, many through the banks but many also to the incessant winds that blew away the precious topsoil and left hardpan. Desert.

So today the ghosts remain, but only an old-timer can recall the building where the doctor set up his shop and where the lawyer opened up across the street. The two empty lots full of rubble over there once were two large stores that burned down. The blacksmith left and the lumberyard went bankrupt. The lady who ran the bakery ran off with a traveling salesman. A succession of proprietors of the newspaper tried and then packed it up. The library never did make it. The policing now is done by the detachment an hour's fast drive down the highway. A heavy snowfall, the worst in thirty years, caved in the curling rink. There hasn't been a town band for forty-five years, and the volunteer fire department ran out of volunteers. The old surveyor's map shows where the hospital and the town park and the courthouse should have been, but those things never did get beyond the talking stage. A fire, driven by a wind from the west, cleaned out one block. Three churches remain, although only the United is active. Once a month a minister comes in from a large town up the highway. Attendance is embarrassing.

But always, there is the hotel. There used to be two but one, the Windsor, named after the huge railway hotel in Montreal, burned down in the big fire of '26. The survivor is prairie architecture. In Tasmania and Tanzania if you spotted it you would know it had been packed board by board and window by window from a Saskatchewan town on its uppers. If Arthur Erickson had been commissioned to design a truly ugly hotel this would be his product, and Ron Woodhall would have discovered it and painted it as a high plains derelict. It is not a derelict—in fact it is the social center—but $750 spent three years ago to put up a new sign and throw on three coats of cheap exterior latex on its silvering boards cannot disguise it for anything but what it is. It is ugly, but it is the best they've got. Nothing can change its essential desperation, a sadsack of a building. Even two boxes of blooming geraniums on either side of the entrance would go a long way as a counterpoint to the dusty, dull windows.

If it had no "Hotel" sign but one reading "Sandra's Boutique" you would not be fooled.

I parked across the street and waited for a green pickup driven by a kid in training for the Indianapolis Speedway to roar by, then entered the bar directly from the entrance. There was no evidence of a lobby, but the liquor law dictated that there be bedrooms, so there must be some upstairs, but when did the last traveler stop, except in the case of an emergency? Only the locals and the outlying farmers and their wives and kids drink here. Die here. Feuds begin or are settled here, deals are made, cars and trucks traded here. A large fan, making a click with every revolution, moves the air around but provides no circulation.

There were perhaps twenty people inside. It was Dodge City. Conversation stopped. The click-click of the fan. Stranger in town. Who is he? Some gunslinger? What the hell does he want around here? In about five seconds they've got his number. The bastard's harmless. Just thirsty.

So I walked carefully to an empty table near a group of six men and one of them with great deliberation slowly moved around in his seat and stared at me. I smiled, shrugged my shoulders, and said "A free country, isn't it?" He grunted. A Blue arrived. I didn't order it. The publican just brought it. Do I look like a beer man?

The bartender was Central European. I'd have bet money on it. I can tell them, just as I can tell when a woman is French Canadian because they all look like the Dionne Quintuplets. He never says much, but he is an observer. He probably knows more about this town than anyone. He probably worked like hell for years to buy this hotel. He probably has a silent partner. He is also making more money than you would believe. His patrons hate him and he hates them. However, if they sneak around the back on a Sunday morning and "borrow" two cases of beer, they like him for one day.

The men at the next table were farmers, easily figured because of their farmer uniforms, but it turned out that the one who gave me the long, hard look was an implement dealer from a town several miles away.

He is a man who likes to hold the floor and he demands respect. He was getting it. He said, "Yuh know," and then took a long swipe at his bottle of beer. Silence. "Yuh know that John Deere rig I had parked by that old shed at my place?" It was not a question, but a statement. "Been there about three months. Got it on a trade-in. Well, that fellow Ripley from over by the river comes in…"

"Had my eye on that, Ed. Thought I'd wait until I seen yeh get hungry," said a farmer.

"Too late, Lloyd. My story. Anyway, I'm asking forty-two for that outfit and I'm ready to let it go for forty. Still a damn good buy. Everything on it but pussy. So Ripley drags along his missus and by God I hate that because women, even if they drive the things all harvest they don't know a damn thing about a combine. Or anything else, when it comes to that. She's poking around while Ripley and I are talking and he says 'thirty-eight' and I says 'forty' and she says 'thirty-five' and he says he'll think about it. She says she doesn't like the color anyway. Damn it all, fellows, the woman doesn't even know John Deere makes all their machines just one color. This goes on for an hour, and Ripley and his missus are saying this is wrong and that is wrong, and I say there it is and and that's my price, 'forty,' and if they don't like it go to town, buy themselves one of those seventy-thousand-dollar jobs. Finally he says 'thirty-eight' again and I say 'split' and he says okay. Okay, so we've got a deal. Then he and the old lady look at each other and smile. We go into the office to sign the papers and so help me, he asks her what account they'll write the check on. Imagine asking that in front of me. He always was an asshole. What checking account? For God sakes, and farmers always bellyaching about living poor and dying rich."

"That deserves a round, Ed," said one and another said, "A good deal, but you let him beat you down that thousand, Ed."

"Beat me down, hell. Irish potatoes to you. I asked the forty when I want forty and he got it for thirty-nine, cash, and when he comes in for parts and repairs he's gonna lose that thousand so fast he won't know what hit him, and it will cost him a lot more. Believe me.

"Well cheers." He lifted his rum and Coke and got up to leave and, as if by signal, the others downed their drinks and followed him out the door. I went out to get a package of smokes from a carton in my car just as the heavy, the implement dealer, was hoisting his obese frame into a gray Cadillac parked beside my car. He lifted a kid of about eight on his knees, and the youngster took the wheel while his father started the car and pushed down the pedal. The youngster wheeled it out into the road and down toward the highway. I watched, and as the car hit the slight bump at the railway tracks it was going a good lick.

I wondered if the boy would live long enough to buy an eighty-six-thousand-dollar computerized, air-conditioned, tape-decked combine. I figure he would. Grow up, work hard, drink a lot, drive dangerously, and watch his father die peacefully with slippers on, sitting in an easy chair, drinking beer and watching a twenty-year-old rerun of "Gunsmoke," a program that will never grow old in the west. Then the outfit would be his.

These big, weather-browned men are the elite of the district, leaving the crumby hotel as if they were knights of yore departing the castle's great hall to do battle with enemies real or imagined. They do not seek power in the form of elected office, but they do have power and they know how to use it.

Their power is in their land, inherited mostly, and if they owe the banker in the city $250,000 on mortgages for more land, then it is the banker's job to worry, not theirs. They remember the Great Depression, but only as boys. Now times are good. Money grows on trees, but their forests are fields totalling two thousand or three thousand acres stretching to the horizon. They know they can grow the world's finest milling wheat and if they get a break from the weather they will do just fine. If one year is a bad roll then there is another year. This is Tomorrow Country. More bankers to talk to, but the land will always be there.

Inside, the shuffle board was going. It was a swift and deadly game with the neat, sharp click of the metal counters punctuating the unintelligible gabble from a black-and-white TV hanging in a corner.

"You stranger?" I looked up and it was the publican and it was not a question but a demand. After all, he has to know everything that is happening in his fiefdom. I said yes, Vancouver.

He thought a moment, meshing the simple reply into the gears of his brain. "Hear there's a lot of mountains out there. No good for place like this." He waddles away. So much for me, my hopes, my dreams, my aspirations, my illusions of glory, and my city by the sea.

The back door opened and in came four huskies, as arrogant in their strength and youth as the farmers were with their experience and land. They were off some construction crew working nearby, and on their yellow hard hats there was the stencilled name of a Regina outfit. They instinctively headed for the table the farmers had left, as if knowing, in that beer parlor, it was the center of power.

"Hey, Fatso, get your ass over here," one yelled and in a few moments the owner arrived with two rum and Cokes and two bottles of Blue. As the two beers arrived they were snatched up and chug-a-lugged and the empties hit the table with the same crash.

"Yah, Shortie, yah lose," jeered one, and Shorty yelled back. "Yah, but only by half a second and that's the head start you had on me."

"You guys damn bums," said the owner as he counted out their change. "More?"

"Sure, Fatso, keep 'em coming. We got a little bending to do." It was the red-faced one with the long sideburns who answered.

I should have been on my way, but a little drama had begun. The two girls who have been playing their professional game of shuffleboard came over—sauntered over—and sat near, not near-near but closer than just near, the four toughies. They ordered screwdrivers.

One of the girls was a stunner. In every small town of thirty or forty houses there is going to be one real beauty, and she was it. Long, blonde hair flowing gently to her waist. A perfect figure. Great legs, but a miniskirt in a place like this? However, there was a question of considerable importance involved here. The beauty's friend was about the same age, say seventeen, and in polite language she was a dog. She did not have one redeeming feature, although—and I'll bet money on it—she was likely a much better person, more kind and considerate and sensitive and intelligent than her beautiful friend. But was she a friend? Why does it happen so often that a beautiful woman will chose a Plain Jane as her companion? Contrast? A foil?

Miss Lovely Legs was chattering and looking nowhere and then she made her move. She called to the bar: "Johnny, can I use your phone?" and he reached behind without looking and swung it over to the bar. Lovely Legs moved around the foursome who sat silent and grave while she dialed a number, waited, looked over at Plain Jane, and then said, "Marge?"

"Look, Marge, Eileen and I are at the hotel and wouldn't it be fun to run into Battleford after you're through and we'll have a few drinks.... Yeah, at the new bar in the hotel there. Then Chinese food. Not in weeks.... Neither have you. Good. I love the stuff. We could leave here at six, be there at seven, and whoopee! All you have to do is get your mom's car. She won't mind. I'll drive if you're nervous. Even stay overnight, maybe.... Marge, you can do that tomorrow night. The party isn't until Saturday. Besides, after two days your hair will look better than after three days. Please, huh? Pre-tee phu-leese.... Oh well, if you can't get the car, then that's it I guess. Another night in this dump.... No, I can't get ours. That old bear of a pop won't let me have it after the last time.... Yeah, that thing with the truck on the way home. Says he'll have no wheels left if I take it to town once more. Okay, but Chinese food would sure go nice.... Okay, Marge, see you at the party Saturday, yeah. Bye."

Now that was an interesting conversation and the young studs took in every blessed and beautiful word from the lovely mouth. Except for one thing. The way she was standing they were blindsided. She had the advantage and I had the view. While she was dialing I saw one finger sneak out and depress the shut-off button on the phone. There had been no two-way conversation, but I was watching a born actress. But there *had* been a dialogue—directed straight at the four young men working out of a strange town, living in company trailers with little or no contact with the local female population, and certainly not one like this smashing creature.

The girl slammed down the phone prettily, in a neat little gesture of disgust and called, "C'mon, Eileen, let's shoot some more. Bring my drink, will you?" and she turned to give her intent audience a head-on view. It was frontal nudity, if some eyes can see through clothes. She walked across the room. She didn't swivel her hips. There was nothing she had to prove.

The four looked at each other and began to talk, not subduing their voices. Speaking their thoughts. These guys in their mid-twenties think they have the world by the tail. Their arrogance is, at times, frightening.

The one with the side-burns said, "Well, what about it? Set it up, it's waiting. Back to camp, clean up, borrow Brad's station wagon, come back here, and hey, hey, Chinese food and drinks and fun. What say?"

One said, "What about the other?"

"A can of worms."

"Let's flip for the blonde one. Two winners get her. Losers the other one."

"Still four against two, no matter which. That's no good. Hey?"

"I'll bet that blonde is the town minkie. Wonder where she's been hiding. Here two weeks and ain't see that one before," added another.

"Why not four on one? Forget the ugly one."

"Yeah, a dog."

"Yeah, but dogs do it too. Haven't ya heard, meatball?"

"She's a stick."

"Maybe a zero, but she might better than the good-looking one. Seems quiet and nice. You gotta watch that kind. I know."

"No, it's the hotsy for me. Or nothing. How about it, Tom? Len?"

"Maybe."

"Naw. Who'd rent a motel to four guys and one girl? The cops would be there in five minutes. Besides, the blonde wouldn't go for that. She just wants food and some drinks and some fun."

"Okay, we'll ask her friend, too, and maybe they've got a couple of others we can take. Say, heh? Maybe that Marge on the phone?"

"Naw."

"Christ, am I the only guy here that wants to get fucked?"

"Aw, forget them. Maybe one of the town guys on the gang can get us invited to that party. Let's go. Five bucks each and we'll haul away a couple of boxes of beer."

They pushed back their chairs and one went to the bar and called into the back room: "Hey, Fatso. Two cases and hurry up. We ain't got all day and Christmas is coming." They paid for the beer and the door slammed. A motor roared and you could hear the sound of the spitting gravel as the car sped away.

I finished my beer, went to the bar, and ordered a half-case to go. Making conversation, I said, "Well, they sure talked themselves out of that one."

Johnny took my money. "Yeah, a bunch of bums."

"Tell Him About the Encyclopedia, Harry"

Another day of driving, another beer parlor, and if this town is fifty miles west of Moose Jaw I still must be in Saskatchewan.

A side door opened, firing a shaft of afternoon sunlight across the gloomy room and one of several guzzlers at a table said, "Right on time. Town don't need any damn clock."

Another called, "The little guy, the walking dictionary."

Laughter. The dozen men and women in the beer parlor must have heard the same sallies, and others equally bad, a hundred times, but indeed, the clock behind the bar did read exactly four o'clock and the character who walked in was, indeed, a small man. He was wearing a very large straw hat, the size of a Mexican bandit's sombrero.

He came to my table and said, "Sir, my table, by Appointment of Her Gracious Majesty the Queen ten years ago, and your rental for the use of, for a year, is one bottle of Blue. Thank you."

I had arrived just moments before the door opened to let in this possibly deranged galoot, so I signaled for two Blues and one of the drinkers called, "He don't own any table, stranger. Buy him a froth but only one. Harry may look like a escapee from a one-elephant, one-clown flea circus, but he's loaded. He holds the first mortgages on the city hall in Moose Jaw and the refinery at Swift Current."

The character had taken his first swig of beer, wiped off his mouth. Now he spoke: "Ignore the rabble, sir, for they are but ignorant farmers, worthy of only a glance and then easily forgotten. They make their penny-ante loot by mining the deep prairie loam God gave us, and they take their pleasures mining the wives and daughters of their best friends. 'Tis a sorry world I was born into, and happier I shall be when I hear Gabriel sound his silver trumpet. I indeed do thank you for the beer, kind sir, and when I walked into this poor place of lost hopes and miserable revelry I immediately said, 'Ah, that fellow there is a writer from Vancouver.'"

There is no point in being amazed or even surprised when you are dealing with what is obviously the town character, so I merely said, "Correct on both counts."

He paused, waiting for me to ask him how he knew what I was, but as I can play it close to the vest with the best of them, I just sipped my beer and let him tip his hand.

"First, I came through the parking lot and saw your car, and as it was the only vehicle I did not recognize, and as it had British Columbia plates, and as there is no excuse for stopping in this town except for a glass of wine, and as the Vancouver area has half the population of British Columbia—then it was perfectly reasonable that you would have come from Vancouver. Right?"

I nodded, sipping again and refusing to play my king to his ace.

"Secondly, and here my approach becomes a little wary, I looked in the back seat and saw an Underwood Five, a truly magnificent example of the typewriter designer's craft and, as no man who claims to be a writer would use a portable or an electric model, I assumed you were a true writer. Furthermore," and he ticked off his third finger, "in the back seat I also saw a quire of writer's paper, two boxes of typewriter ribbons, some carbon paper, pages in a box that appeared to be a manuscript and, in another box, pages that appeared to be duplicates of the pages in the first box. Therefore, sir, you are a writer from Vancouver, and I judge, fairly affluent, judging by your expensive but honest and reliable auto and the cut of your jib. Those expensive casual clothes immediately proclaim you to be a gentlemen and a scholar and it ill behooves you to be seen in the company of such low-life folk of ill repute as do surround you." And he gracefully swept his arm around the room.

The old man had his audience, and a young farmer, still unsure of himself at the table of older men, yelled, "If he's a writer, Harry, he's looking for news. Tell him what it's like to be the town nut. See what he thinks of your encyclopedia and your po-et-ree," laying heavy emphasis on each syllable.

The room laughed and went back to its normal talk of crops and trucks and weather and machinery and the old man put out his hand said, "The name's Harry."

"Barry."

He leaned back in his chair, looked at the ceiling and began, accenting every word with a chop of his hand:

> *Barry meets Harry; why don't you tarry?*
> *Grow old like me and never marry?*
> *But if you do, you surely will*
> *Find life one helluva bitter pill.*

"That's my poetry, or po-et-ree as that arrogant aardvark so ineptly put it."

He leaned back again, did his gazing-at-the-ceiling routine, and, chopping with his hand, intoned:

> *I'm a poet, and don't know it*
> *And haven't got brains to show it.*

I said, "You didn't write that. It's a golden oldie. Been around for a long time. Since Hector was a pup. Right?"

"Right, you elegant elk, a worthy observation but I did not say I wrote it. But the dumbfounded dromedaries who take up valuable space in this saloon think I did, and somehow, even with something as profoundly trivial as that bit of doggerel, I sometimes think I confuse them a smidgeon or more."

"Hey, stranger, he's piling a lot of big words on ya," yelled the young farmer. "Old-timers around here said his mother was once chased down by a dictionary salesman."

"Let joy be unconfined, you roisterous rooster," yelled back my friend of ten minutes. "When the roll is called up yonder, you will not be there."

Enough of this nonsense, I thought, and said, "Harry, where in hell did you get that straw hat? Didn't they stop making them years go when every farmer in the West threw away his pitchfork, got up on a combine he couldn't pay for in a month of Sundays, and started wearing those caps the equipment companies give away free with a fifteen-thousand-dollar order?"

"Correct, and when Jason who ran the hardware and undertaking shop here gave up the ghost about ten years ago, he had a gross on hand. I was talking to him one day and he said, 'Harry, I'll never sell these. Farmers don't consider themselves hicks anymore and these big, dumb straw hats have got hick written all over them.' 'How many you got, Jason?' I asked. He says about a gross, about 144 of them big dumb straw hats. Well, I happen to like straw hats; I think they are the greatest thing invented in the West and the Great Plains since they came up with the snake fence, the Texas Gate, the mould board plow, and the alligator thresher belt. So I tells Jason that if he's going to throw them away I'd appreciate it if they landed in my direction. So to Jason, Jason and I being good friends, and me not wanting to cause any harsh feeling between us before he left for Regina, I said I'd give ten dollars for the lot. He jumped at it and I walked away with the lot, 123 of them, and if anybody had seen me taking them home they'd have thought it was a straw-hat factory with legs. I use one to do my chores, one when I do my housework, one for when I do my writing, and one I wear when I come to town every afternoon for four beers and some intelligent conversation. I got a pile of them left and you're welcome to this one I've got on now. It's been keeping my hair dry for only about three months.

"Don't you think it was about time we discovered if the second Blue is as good as the first?" and he held up his bottle to the bartender. Two more arrived.

"You said you wore another hat when you were writing? I'm happy to meet a kindred spirit high on the windy plains."

"Of Troy," he added. "Well, you could call me the first-grade, blue-chip, white-enameled champion letter-to-the-editor writer of Saskatchewan and all points north, east, and west. I get the *Western Producer*, the *Moose Jaw Times Herald*, the *Regina Leader Post*, the *Winnipeg Free Press*, and the *Financial Post*, and as I am paying top subscription rates for their rags, I think in turn it ill behooves them to reject my missives, especially the detailed and well-reasoned ones describing how the West, the Wheat Board, the province, the country, and the world should be run."

"Do they reject all these missives?"

"By the hundreds, the obdurate orangutangs, and they even reject my letters to the editor berating them for not using my other letters. I have had a few printed, the ones where I say it is a crime against our economy to allow the import of so many Jap cars and trucks. That well has almost run dry now because half the American new car dealers in Canada have bought their wives little sporty Japanese cars.

"You can get the odd other one published, especially if you take a swipe at the immigration of Arabs and fellows from Africa and those Chinese from Hong Kong, but the timing's got to be right. You've got to pick a time when things are tough, like they are now, and those Arabs and Africans and the Chinese are coming in and taking over the dishwashing jobs in Greek restaurants and working the pumps at all-night gas stations and the like. In tough times white Canadians think they should have those jobs. At that time, I say, go get 'em.

"But all in all, as a letter-to-the-editor writer I am the greatest failure since they invented the Ross rifle. The editors won't listen to me; these malignant monkeys in here don't know what I'm talking about—and my goat, Dolorous Daphne, doesn't seem to care, although I have directed more wit and wisdom to her blank eyes than anyone ever has to any other goat in history."

"You live with a goat? I used to drink raw goat's milk because I had stomach trouble. It was expensive and I used to drive forty miles round trip, but it sure was worth it," I said. "Mind if I smoke?"

"You speak of the life-giving qualities of goat's milk and in the same breath you ask if you can partake of the world's most profitable commercial product, one which is guaranteed to kill you dead before you reach the age of ninety-six. But go ahead. Everybody else does. I once thought of starting an Anti-Nicotine League, but then I thought, who am I to spend a lot of money trying to prevent a vice which has a four-hundred-year head start on me? I sometimes send a letter and sign it 'Anti-Nicotine League,' but it never gets printed. Who pays for the biggest ads in the newspapers? The cigarette companies." He leaned back and said, "Think about it," stating it as though he had uttered one of the verities of life.

The young farmer got up and walked to the door to the street and as he went by, he said, "Ask him about his encyclopedia, stranger. It's not for real. Looney."

"Fine, I'll tell him, you corrosive criticizer, I will," Harry answered as the farmer went out the door, laughing. "My friend, it happened this way. I was born in 1902, on May 19. My parents were from England, my father being a clerk sitting on a stool, wielding a quill pen, and fearing the moment Mr. Scrooge walked into the counting house. My mother, before the nuptials, worked in a bakery on the High Street of our town. To make a long story shorter, a man from Canada, a man named Sifton, was chasing his tail all over England in those days a few years before the big war, saying every man and his dog could have 160 acres of land in the Canadian West. It was there for the asking, and if you had a plot twelve feet by fourteen feet as your garden in England, then 160 acres and government help seemed very good. So, hippety-hop-to-the-barber-shop, my father goes down and signs in the big book and comes back and tells Mother the two of them and us five kids are going to the promised land, where you threw your wheat on the ground and looked severely at it and it grew to seventy bushels of No. One Northern in a few weeks. You could also pick apples and pears and peaches off the trees along the bubbling creek that also held more trout than you could eat. You've heard it all. Oft told so many times. So the six of us came, just six because my oldest sister, Bessie, was being courted by a young man and had a job, and she just plain, downright refused to go. That was that. Mother said she was putting on airs and my father disowned her, disowning her from nothing because by the time we got to this place he was cleaned out.

"We took over a soddy that someone had left when they went busted, and as our quarter-section was next to his and he wasn't on it, it was okay to use his sod abode and try to get a crop out of his breaking the first year. Well, it just didn't work. Everybody in the country was going broke. Busted. Gone back to Leeds. Gone to Winnipeg. Dad took my older sister and the other two boys to Winnipeg and got a clerical job, the same as he was doing in Leeds at probably less pay.

"I hung around, working for farmers. Too young for the first war, too old for the second. I worked as a blacksmith's helper, and I got better at it than he was. When cars came in after the war I could repair any make there was. Just give me a broken-down engine and a ball-peen hammer to tap it and I could come up with its ailments. I worked as a machinist for the C.P.R. and the Great Northern. Mostly I worked on cars and trucks and farm machinery, but if you wanted me to fix a wind generator or the pump itself, why, I could make a perfect gasket out of one of the farmer's old boots. If you could show me a John Deere tractor, a Cockshutt, a Massey Harris that I couldn't fix, then that one was made especially just to fool me.

"I'd go visiting a friend and his wife would say, 'Oh, Harry, our separator is broken.' Right there in the milk shed I'd take it apart and if it needed a new piece, I'd go over to the machine shed and make one. If her scissors were broken, I'd fix them, too, and sharpen them into the bargain.

"Nothing I couldn't do. If a town didn't have a blacksmith anymore, gone bust, I could shoe a horse. Two bits a hoof. Ask the price for that nowadays. I've shoed hundreds. In the Depression when everyone was eating sowbelly and washing it down with coffee-barley, or, sorry, barley-coffee, I was making a good living, just going around the country, doing odd jobs with my tools and fixing things in the back of an old truck. I'd go into a town and put up a poster in the hotel, one in the general store, one in the livery barn, the post office, everywhere: Harry Marlow will fix anything, cheapest prices, contact him at hotel. The work flowed in, and I kept prices low, so the word got around. They'd bring a Gruen watch to me, hadn't been running for a year. I'd fix it. One dollar…"

"Do you think the third beer will taste better than the other two?"

"I'm absolutely positive of it," he said, and when they came, he took a long pull and plunged ahead, his keen blue eyes under bushy eyebrows fixed on a point on the wall and again a hand chop to accent every point. "Their truck's got a broken axle and they can't move a foot, but if I can't weld it, I'll yank one out of another in the dump and fix it up. Four dollars. They'd find the money, even if they didn't have it, because I gave them a wonderful bargain and having a truck running meant their farm was working again. I'd say there wasn't a Model A for miles around, fifty, a hundred miles, I didn't know, and they were the easiest to fix because they had only about eight moving parts.

"As for the fancier ones, the kind farmers and town guys bought when times were better before the '29 crash, they were tougher but I fixed 'em all…"

"Okay, okay, I get it. You could fix anything that walked, crawled, or swam," I interjected.

"Precisely, you interrupting interloper. Anything. For two bits. Four bits. A buck. A deuce. Five spot. Sometimes three, maybe five, maybe seven jobs a day. The money rolled in. An all-day job, a tenner, and it was damn well worth it because I was saving them a hundred.

"Why, in depression years I lived like a king. Except I had no queen. Never got married. I lived in the best room in any hotel, $1.50 a night. Ate the best meals the house had, never more than six bits. I bought beer for the town, and the town and country rolled in their cars and trucks and equipment—anything that was busted or wouldn't run— right to the camp I'd set up in the middle of town. Usually some store that was vacant, and there were lots. Pay five bucks for a week to the owner; he's happy. So am I. So is everyone for miles.

"The next war I'm too damned old. The wind stops blowing, the rains come, the price of wheat goes up, everybody's working, but working so hard making big money they don't have time working for the small money like I was. My prices went up and I got a big truck and more equipment and a welding set-up, and I got more and more jobs and hired two kids I trained to do small jobs. For five years, then ten and then fifteen, the jobs and money rolled in..."

I stopped him with an open palm and said, "Look, Harry, can you make this short? It's fascinating but I've got a long way to go before I bed down tonight."

Taking no offense, he laughed—the first time in our conversation. What conversation? I had said hardly a word. "Be back soon as I've patted the one-eyed pup," and he headed to the back of the room, a short, slim figure, erect, sure in his walk. Maybe it was a strut. He came back, passing the table with the farmers and saying, "And a good afternoon to you, gentlemen." He said and and forged on.

"Nature sure has a way of fixing a man up real good," as he patted his flat gut. "Well, I'd been investing my money, and I found a smart young fellow in a brokerage house in Regina, and if he wondered where an old sodbuster was getting this kind of money he didn't ask, but he put me into some real good things. After all, I was paying most of his salary. Farmers don't buy stocks and bonds; they buy machinery they can't afford. One sunny day I said to hell with work. I sold the whole thing for a buck to the two youngsters I'd hired back in the Depression. Gave it to them for one dollar. When we shook hands I handed them two big cee-gars and lit them with their dollar bill and we shook hands again, and that was it. I took only the tools I figured I needed and walked away. Good lads. Grown men when I sold out to them, and loyal. I'd taught them all I knew.

"So I stored everything I had, tools and what-not, with a kind widow lady over in the next township and I flew to Montreal. And I thought, if I have to fly 'round the world on them things I won't survive. So, I went to England on an ocean liner and I tried to track down my kin who had gone back to Leeds after leaving Winnipeg, but I couldn't find them. Saw the things you were supposed to see in London, but I'd seen them all in the travelogues when they had a movie house here. Went to Holland where I had heard my youngest brother had been killed in the war, but couldn't find his grave. Germany was still a mess, but I liked the food. Italy. Didn't like the food or the people. Both the same—kind of sneaky. Thought I'd go to Turkey, so I went to Turkey. An awful lot of poor farmers there. At the Canadian Embassy where I'd gone to get any mail there was, I got talking to a clerk and he said he'd like to introduce me to a Turkish friend who was in the agricultural department. The blithering bloke thought that because I came from Saskatchewan I might be a farmer.

"Anyway, I met his friend and he thought the government might think of hiring me as an agricultural consultant. He seemed to think I needed money, like he was doing me a favor. I could have told him I could probably have bought one of those Turkish battleships out in the harbor. Anyway, he insisted on driving me out into the country to see what I thought of a Turkish community farm. I looked it over and told him there was nothing that could be done until they got rid of the rocks on just this one farm. I told him that farm had more rocks than all the farms in Saskatchewan. He asked me how to get rid of them and I told him. I said, bend down, pick up a rock, throw it in the wagon, then bend down, and pick up another. I said that's the way it's done in Saskatchewan nobody had improved on that method yet. Anyway, we drove back to the city and I thanked him for the buggy ride and, in a couple of days I went to Egypt to see the pyramids.

"The upshot, I can tell you, is that I went around the world and it took me eighteen months and it didn't cost me one-tenth of the interest I was drawing on my bonds and stocks—the way prices were in some of those countries, it was scandalous. So low I don't know how anybody even tried to make a living.

"Two more. For the road. My turn, anyway.

"I came back and I had nothing to do. Absolutely nothing to do. I went to live in the Hotel Saskatchewan for six months and didn't like it because I didn't know anybody. I traveled around a lot but I missed Vancouver and I guess you're going to say I missed a good bet. There's still time. I went to Chicago where I knew I had cousins. I went there, but they didn't like me and I didn't like them. Even trade. I went to California by train and I didn't like Los Angeles and San Francisco, I took one of those eight-day guided tours, but all I found out was about the widow ladies on that tour. When they figured I might have some loot stashed away, they saw something real fine and upstanding in me. So I said bugger the whole thing and came back to this here town, an old bachelor with lots of money and nothing to do, getting old and not even a dog to talk to. Just a goat, a senile slut of a goat.

"I was feeling low-down for a few weeks and then I heard that the schoolhouse a mile from here was being abandoned as the schools were being consolidated. They wanted someone to tear it down and I went to them and said, 'Look, fellows'—and I knew them all—I said, 'There's the school there and it's on two acres someone donated a long time ago. It's got a good well and two big classrooms and if you have it torn down you're going to make a lot less money than the $1,500 I'm offering you for it, lock, stock and barrel, clear title.' They jumped at it. The municipal lawyer had the papers drawn up in a week. I signed them, handed over the certified check, shook hands, and I owned the Crossmore School.

"Well, sir, I went at that school like I was on fire. Painted it. Insulated it. Put in a bathroom with a shower. Fixed the plumbing and made a kitchen. Knocked out half a wall. Put in two bedrooms, living room, dining room, little workshop, cupboards. In two years, and it cost me less than $3,000, I had a perfect little house with an oil furnace and the works. It was about then I saw an ad in the *Western Producer* and I bought Dolorous Daphne for twenty-five dollars, and having that lady goat around and having to milk her, that kept me from gallivanting around the country, doing eighty miles an hour in one of those big Cadillacs. I bought a flock of chickens, too. Didn't need the goat, didn't need the chickens, didn't need the big vegetable garden, didn't need nothing, but now I can live like a king while a family on the next farm could be starving. Do you know, in this township there is not one cow, and only a few lonely chickens. It's just grain, grain, and more grain. They'll regret it. When the next Depression comes, they'll wish they had stuck with some mixed farming."

"Look, Harry," I interrupted again. "What about the encyclopedia business that kid was sniggering at?"

"Snails. I'm up to Snails in *S*. It's like this. When I bought that schoolhouse they had left every rootin'-tootin' thing behind—a lot of books and desks and dust and this nice encyclopedia.

"After going 'round the world and traveling and meeting a lot of people I realized how ignorant I was. Sure, I was smart. I could make money. Plenty. But I was ignorant, naked to a person with education as a naked jay bird is to a cold rain. So I started in on those encyclopedia books. Right at *A*. I didn't read them just for fun. I memorized every word. For six years. Now I'm at Snails. Do you know there are more than eighty thousand kinds of snails? About fifty thousand live in water. They're everywhere. Some are so small you need a microscope to get at them to study and some are two feet across. They say there's not one that doesn't do some good. I can tell you more about snails than you want to know. When I finish *Z* in about a year I'm gonna start on something else. It may not be a college education, but by God, it is an education."

I was flabbergasted. Here was this old gaffer in a straw hat and he was a least seventy and he was memorizing an encyclopedia. Pots of money in the bank and stocks and bonds, and memorizing an encyclopedia. Snails!

He continued, "Apart from my studying and my goat and chickens and garden, I still go out and work and all because of those two young fellows, the ones I sold my business to. Well, they split up—real rouser of a fight. Caused by the wives meddling. Always the same, women! So, instead of one buying the other out, one went to Edmonton to work for wages in a machine shop and the other is teaching at some trade school in Regina. So they both left. So here I am, back hopping around the country, fixing radios, and I know quite a bit about television. Got a kit and can do easy jobs, and the money keeps rolling in. Don't know what to do with it—I sure don't want to give it away and I don't want to quit working because it fills up part of my day. A perilous problem, you might say.

"Like see that big guy behind me, in the khaki shirt and the orange hat? Name is John. Big bad John, but only when he's saucing up. Phoned me yesterday all in a fiery flubber and wanted me to come over right away. He had gearbox trouble on his big tractor, the new one, and he'd be slowed down three or four days until the man came down to look at it. I fixed it up in three hours; just a case of knowing what to do and being patient. Kind of kicking it. So I charged him fifty dollars and saved his bacon.

"He doesn't quibble but for his money he wants some advice. These guys never quit. Now mind, he's farming 2,700 acres. Six hundred and forty his daddy left him and the rest he mortgaged his seamy soul to buy, and he'll never pay it. He lives like an Indian prince. He says he wants me to look at a piece of land. I tell him I don't know much about land, but anyway, he takes me to this chunk, 360 acres, and says it's for sale. I told him this land has always been for sale. Worst land in the district, alkali, marsh, stones, sand. Just real awful stuff. So why does he want it? He decided he'd go to the bank and buy it. It is a bad buy, but no, he wants it. Why? He wants it because he's been feuding for a couple of years with a neighbor and if he buys that 360, he'll have 100 acres more than his neighbor. Now does that make sense? These guys ain't farmers, they're fools. The country is depending on them real hard and they're throwing it away. It does pass all understanding."

He suddenly stood up, thrust out a hand, and said, "Well, it was sure nice talking with you. I do like an interesting talk once in a while. Don't get much of it around here…"

As he headed for the door, the big boss farmer named John yelled, "Keep studying, Harry."

The old man whirled and said evenly, "And you, John, you're gonna fuck up that gearbox once more and I won't be around."

He came back to the table, took off his straw hat, jammed it on my head, and said, "Compliments of Harry Marlow. I'll remember you in my will," and he headed for the door again and was gone.

"Did he tell you about the encyclopedia, the memorizing of it?" called the man named John. "Crazy as hell. Ask Harry about the Crimean War and he'll tell you. Crazy as hell."

I laughed with them and, as I walked to the door, straightening the straw hat, I thought, "Yeah, crazy."

8

Fishermen Come in All Sizes

Men of Canada's west coast fish from million-dollar boats their grandfathers wouldn't believe, for those fishermen of an earlier day set forth in nineteen- and twenty-five-foot buckets powered by fractious and kinky one-lung, stinkpot engines. Or they hand-lined from a rowboat in Johnston Strait at the slack tide, their heavy line wrapped around one leg and a huge spoon dangling far below, daring the big spring salmon to do battle. Today's fishermen still work long, hard hours, but many eat three hot meals a day, shower when the fish have quit, and watch television in boats large enough to cruise to Japan.

Al Johnson remembers the days he spent on his forty-foot troller, far out at sea, days he spent keeping one eye on his lines and the other on the weather. Alone against the elements, a man can't afford even one mistake, for he seldom gets a second chance. When Al finally quit, it wasn't the sea that beat him. It was the overfishing by foreign fleets, the soaring costs, and the peculiar government policies handed down from 2,000 miles away. Like many of his fishing brethren, he still loves the sea.

And then there are other men who set forth in a small boat with a forty-horse kicker hanging on the end, a few cases of beer for ballast, and a willingness to dangle a line over the side in case any fish are hanging around that part of the lake...

"Fish are Funny Creatures"

Al Johnson sits at the table in my cozy dining room on a blustering west-coast afternoon, lights another Craven "A", sips from a bottle of beer, and looks at the waves hammering into the bay. "Southeaster. Forty knots, I'd say. She'll blow out by morning."

I ask him if he misses that kind of weather and he replies, "No, not really, but I guess I've never really thought it out."

Al was nineteen, in 1948, when he took his new forty-foot troller from Port Alice out of Quatsino Sound on the northern end of Vancouver Island and piloted her down to Vancouver for registration. He was thirty-seven when he guided the *Geraldine J.* into the government wharf at Tofino, his home port, tied her up, and walked away.

A long time ago Al Johnson knew he wanted to be a violinist, and at the age of eight he began studying. It was a strange decision for a kid from an isolated mill town where the winds from every direction considered it their duty to blow the tall timber inside out eight months of the year. During the other four months they practiced at it.

In those years a boy's ambition was to be like his father, working in the woods, in the mill, or crewing on the old man's boat and dreaming of owning one himself someday. No, Al Johnson wanted to be a professional musician, and for ten years he studied, mostly in Vancouver, far from family and friends. Then an examiner came out from London and handed him a piece of paper that was his licentiate, awarded by the Royal School of Music.

He laughs ruefully and says, "Just a piece of paper. What's a diploma worth anyway? Not much. I was hired as violinist by the Vancouver Symphony. Just a kid, eighteen, but it was what I wanted to be—a professional violinist. You had to buy your own tuxedo and dry-clean it once a week, and there was the continual practicing and all the rehearsals. I was getting the grand sum of fifty a week, and after deductions, well, there was nothing for me. Okay, it was 1947 and wages were low, but there were guys digging ditches taking home more money than me. There was no chance for outside work then, night clubs, radio work. A chosen few with friends in the CBC got those jobs. Nothing for the rest of us.

"So I said to hell with it. I'll go fishing."

Naturally, he didn't know much about fishing, but in a community where every party begins and ends with the women in the parlor gossiping and the men in the kitchen drinking and talking logging and fishing, a kid had to pick up something that didn't go out the other ear. Besides, they'd beg or borrow rowboats and skiffs or repair a derelict found drifting and go out in the sound and horse around. It wasn't fishing, really, but it was a kind of kindergarten. The sound was full of fish in those days, before the effluent from the pulp mill built up to staggering proportions and killed everything but the dogfish sharks and the sculpins.

In Al's second year of studying violin, his father must have figured what side was up because he decided to build Al and his brother Harold a boat. He was chief sawyer for B.C. Pulp and Paper Company, and he began selecting the very best planks that ran through his saws and sawed them again, fine and straight and true. They were of the best fir, two-by-eights, without a knot in thirty or forty feet.

When Al returned from Vancouver on one summer vacation his father announced that he was building the boat, and it took two years, working after the day's labor and on Sundays, and with help from Al, on vacations.

"She was a beauty. That wonderful planking gave her incredible strength, and in the weather we had, strength means safety. I named her the *Geraldine J.*—Geraldine was the middle name of my mother and my sister. *J* was for Johnson. Half the thousands of boats on this coast are named after some guy's mother, wife, daughter, or sweetie. I think it's only the Japanese boys who don't do it. They're happy with a registry number for a name."

He fished for eighteen years, learning as he went. He was a salmon man, although in '59 he tried for halibut and lost his shirt, and later he made one trip for tuna in the Japanese Current a hundred miles offshore and again had no luck. His territory was as far south as Gray's Harbor in Washington State, off the 365-mile coast of Vancouver Island, in Hecate Strait, a nasty place where the big waves are born perhaps two thousand miles away and can come in fifty or more feet high. In December of '82, a 9,000-ton vessel of the B.C. Ferry Corporation took twelve hours to cross the fifty-five-mile strait in 110-knot winds. Al also fished Dixon Entrance, mean as they come, and off the west coast of the Queen Charlottes, where 15,000-ton freighters proceed with extreme caution. He fished in every weather, usually alone, absolute master of his own fate, from twenty to forty and even sixty miles offshore. He learned that an offshore fisherman alone may survive the first mistake but rarely the same one again.

And then there came that day, eighteen years after he had registered his boat in Vancouver and become an experienced fisherman.

"I was fishing alone off Tofino, about twelve miles out, and it was about one in the afternoon, a beautiful day, and I'd had my gear out for seven hours. I looked in the box and there were two fish in it, a scrawny little Spring with a scar on it, which meant I'd have to take a low grade on it, and there was a tiny Jack Coho, a couple of pounds, worth nothing. I said to myself, 'What the hell am I doing out here? There has to be a better way to make a living.' I went in, tied her up, threw the fish to a couple of kids on the wharf, and walked up to visit my friend, and said, 'Jack, I'm selling my boat.' Jack said he had a buyer and he asked me how much I wanted for it and I said eighteen-five. I asked him who the buyer was and he said he was. He wanted a try at it and, besides, he loved that boat—the best one, I think, on the whole bloody coast. I said, 'Jack, seeing as how it's you, I'll sell it for seventeen and we'll drink the other fifteen hundred,' and I think we did."

That ended his fishing days. The second "to hell with it" decision.

His third career was within sight of the wharf where the *Geraldine J.* lay. He bought a pie-shaped hunk of land on the gravel highway fronting the ocean and opened a drive-in restaurant for the summer trade visiting famed Long Beach.

Those were pretty good days, and he claims to be the first person in the world to sell abalone burgers. Abalone was plentiful then, and the divers brought them in by the basketful. Now the day's, limit is twelve and try and find them. Like so much other marine life on the west coast, it is gone, not worth hunting for, and it is protected by some of the thousand rules and regulations that make a fisherman's life miserable.

"I was buying 350 pounds of raw abalone a week and I made wonderful burgers with them. Two abalones to a bun. I was getting $1.50 each for them and people would travel a long way for them. Today you'd pay $12.00 a burger if you could find one."

The venture folded four years later when the federal government expropriated his land and he and his second wife, Doreen, took their lumps, along with everybody else who had made their homes for years and decades along Canada's most beautiful beach. People still wonder over the absolute stupidity of that expropriation.

For several years, he owned a charter boat, the *Granby*, but the service and meals he provided for forest company groups traveling north was so lavish that there was no money to be made, although he admits they certainly lived well.

They loved it, but "we couldn't afford that love," he laughs.

Now he is doing a bit of bartending, helping friends at odd jobs, and playing for no pay in the Nanaimo Symphony whose many young players scramble to master the simplest works. No regrets. Something will come up. Tomorrow will be better, although he knows he'll never again be sound or quick or strong enough to handle the rough-and-tumble life at sea.

Al says, "There is no place on the salmon grounds today for a young man without capital. Look at it this way. I sold the *Geraldine J.* for seventeen. Jack put radar into her and three years later got twenty-five. Four years after that the outfit sold it to get rid of it when prices kept edging up, for thirty. Now she's at the dock at Tofino and the last price I heard they were asking was one-ninety. She has fifteen-ton capacity and that's a very suitable size.

"You see, like everything else, things went haywire. Everything was going crazy and buyers were fighting to get toward a 'For Sale' sign.

"There are trollers the size of the *Geraldine* that are worth half a million. Half a million! You can't get any kind of halfway decent boat for less than a hundred. If someone wanted to just dayfish, two hours out, five hours fishing, and two hours home, he'd never get anything for less than fifty thousand and he wouldn't be getting much boat. When I started, you could put yourself into business for two, four thousand.

"The big boats today have separate bedrooms for the crew, showers, television, five ship-shore phones and radios, maybe a sauna, a cook, and nets for every kind of salmon and electronic equipment that is extremely sophisticated."

He reaches for a scrapbook, points, and says, "There she is. The best boat, I think, on the coast. Was then, still is. Nearly thirty-five years old and sound. Those planks we sheathed her with make her incredibly strong. Today, they line them inside with plywood."

He recalls, with a shake of his head, that when he switched from a gas engine to a Gardiner diesel a gallon of fuel was seventeen cents. Today it is two dollars. Lead cannonballs are triple in price, so is one-sixteenth steel line. So is every damned thing.

He recalls the Gardiner with affection. A most efficient piece of equipment. He could cruise an hour at eight knots on two gallons. His fuel for the season at seventeen cents was about one-hundred and twenty-five dollars.

"Look at it this way. We weren't greedy in those days. That's the whole difference. If a boat is into a hot spot these days he won't call on the phone to his buddies and say, hey, over here. No. Today, he'll pull in perhaps five hundred Coho on his lines and say to himself, 'I got five hundred and you guys only got thirty and I'm glad.'"

In the old days only the Japanese fishermen, who had been forced out of the fishery in 1942 because of Pearl Harbor, came back and practiced the same kind of tactic, calling to other Japanese boats when they hit a bunch. However, enough of the whites had grown up with the Japanese in the fishing villages and knew enough Japanese to know what "C'mon over here" sounded like.

"Oh, they were good guys and good fishermen, the Japs. I got along fine with them. Remember, we had our own codes and things like that, too, which we'd use."

He understands the small guy who, before dawn, is out with his poles port and starboard like wings moving through the heavenly seas, listening for the dingle-dingle of the bells that mean fish are on. It is the early morning—when the peaks of the range down the spine of Vancouver Island are sharp and clear and dawn is the rosiest, and the sea is flat and a steady breeze is carrying the sweet and pungent land smells to the west—that makes the small fisherman believe he has the best of a poor world. The evening—when he's heading home with a load of iced fish and a good woman is waiting, and the sun is going down toward Japan—is also the best time for the small fisherman. But he also faces the hazard of the massive storms that can roar in with frightening speed—and he must choose to ride it out or run.

Al reminisces about fishing in his day. "It was fun for us. There was no fishing season then. We could fish for salmon any time, anywhere, any day. Today, that's not the way it is. Everything is hacked up into zones to allow so much catchment and so much escapement.

"When we fished, prices were low. I remember once a bunch of the boys got a meeting going and we weren't going to take no twelve cents a pound for red Spring. Some guys were talking about two bits a pound, but I think every one of us was ready to settle for seventeen cents. That's what we decided on and and we got it. So, prices were low but so were expenses. Remember, a good steak was three dollars and fifty cents and a bottle of beer was twenty cents.

"Hell, we just didn't try and get rich. If you made maybe ten or twelve thousand, you quit after that much even if you could have gone on, and you'd say, 'I've got three or four thousand profit and that'll get me through the winter and that's fine with me.'

"We'd lay up for the winter and have a good time. Once Doreen and I moved in with friends at Queen's Cove for the winter. They rented us part of their house and we had a bridge game every week and everybody made home brew, good home brew. When we had the New Year's dance about thirty people showed up and that was about everybody around. We had volleyball games. If somebody got in a skiff and went around to Ahousaht and got a hundred crabs, and a couple of sacks of clams and oysters, and a bunch of abalone, we'd have a big feed. Everybody shared. That was a good winter for everybody, for us.

"You knew everybody around in those days. Everybody. Not like today. You see a face several times now but you don't know him. In those days there was every kind of guy out there. Finns—hard drinkers but good fishermen. Lots of Norwegians. I guess I was the only Swede out there. The Yugoslavs were mostly in big seiners. Indians—they were good fishermen if they got good boats and gear off the companies they fished for. Nice fellows. Sure, Indians drank a lot, but maybe we drank more than them. A lot of them were quitting, though. Going logging, making sure money. You'd pull into a village and there might be sixty families in it and only half a dozen guys were fishing. The rest, all out in the woods making sure money.

"Oh, yes, the Japs. You could say they were diligent. They were out there to fish and not to party."

I tell Al about Noella Wavel, a seventy-eight-year-old friend who fished with a friend for eight years in her thirty-two-foot double-ender troller *Louisiana*. She once showed me her logbook for part of the 1947 season fishing among the hundreds of sounds, inlets, bays, and passages off the west coast of Vancouver Island.

She had no experience, but being a daring soul, she sold her home, furniture, and jewelry to buy the boat and put a new Gray Marine engine in it. The first season did not go well—and none of the other seven did either. The log shows that between March 27 and July 22 they got only $440.20 for their fish at the co-op in Bamfield, hardly enough to pay for the spoons, wire brushes and scrapers, new battery for the radio, lead weights, insurance, paint, rope, plugs, hooks, maps, and a dozen other necessities needed to start fishing, plus food, fuel, and the mortgage on the diesel.

July 10: Ahousaht, out all day, no fish. Sea bad.
Aug. 8: Out at 5 a.m. trolled 11 hours. $23 of fish.
Aug. 17: 232 pounds. Best day.
Sept. 2: Bear Island. Shot seal. Skinned hide. Fried liver.
Sept. 9: Got three quarts oysters. One duck. Bought three quarts venison.
Sept. 14: Lots of fish around.
Oct. 3: Good day. Sold $77.46.

"We moved around too much," she told me, "looking for fish. We should have stayed in one place, but Bruce thought he knew where they would be and they weren't. He was a perfectionist, too. The least thing wrong with the boat, he'd get it repaired. Other fishermen would say, 'To hell with the boat, let's get the fish.'

"But we ate well. We lived on fish, oysters, clams, ducks, geese, venison, and seals."

Al recalls with a smile the fishing villages and camps along the coast: Bull Harbor, Winter Harbor, Ahousaht, Kyuquot, Queen's Cove, Hot Springs, Tofino, Ucluelet, Bamfield, and a host of others, each with its big fish barge and ice and the company store where a fisherman would be sold one bottle of booze while he picked up supplies, steak, hamburger, salt, tea, sugar, all the staples, and also dug into the local gossip. There were also good times with a lot of drinks and some poker when the winds blew outside at sixty knots and inside all was snug.

"I remember sometimes it would blow half the summer and we'd have poker games. Little games, two bits, a half, a dollar on the last raise, and nobody got hurt, really. Anything goes, everything wild. Name your game. Stud, Draw, Seven-Toed Pete, Spit-in-the-Ocean,

Sowsem. Jacks and deuces wild in a seven-card game. A guy could have four aces, losing to five sevens. I've seen pots as high as two thousand dollars. One guy once walked out of a game at Nootka about six thousand bucks in the hole. Bum checks everywhere. Oh, there were some real ones in those days."

When the massive combers from Japan had beaten themselves to death on the rocky shores and cliffs, the trollers headed out to the faraway places on the open sea where a lone man in the cockpit scanned the heaving wastes of water for a concentration of swirling and diving seagulls or the blowing of whales. That would be where the salmon were.

Many a man of secretive nature would fish alone but many used the buddy system, even if the fisherman in the next boat was unknown to him. It was good to have somebody near if something went wrong, a possibility that worried wives and sweethearts ashore far more than it bothered the fishermen.

"Oh yeah, anything could happen. There was danger all around. You were always so busy though, I guess we just didn't think too much about it. If you knew you had a good boat, you worried less. There were a lot of haywire rigs out there at times and those guys should have worried a lot, but they wanted fish."

He remembers some bad times that suddenly appeared out of nowhere. Waves would advance that had no reason for being around, up to fifty feet high. In shallow waters with a tide running against you, that could be skookum trouble.

"In '52 we were coming in off the big bank and this other boat and mine were the last going in. It was a clear night, beautiful, but blowing hard. The fellow in the smaller boat, Harold Snow, was following me closely and I was going slow, taking her easy so he could keep up, and I said to the wife, 'Keep an eye on him. We'll make it, but we'll have to go for Bamfield because nobody tonight is going to make it to Ucluelet.'

"A few minutes later I heard him come on the radio and he said, 'Allan, are you...?'

"At the same time the wife yelled that she couldn't see his running lights anymore. Even in that weather I managed to get turned around and we searched for two hours and found absolutely nothing. There was nothing more we could do and we got into Bamfield at 7:00 A.M. The fleet and the coast guard couldn't get out that day, there was such a gale; but the day after, the whole fleet went out, in long line close together and searched all day. Nothing. That's the way we did it in those days. Everybody dropped everything and went out. Somebody found some of his wreckage later about thirty miles down the coast, near Juan de Fuca.

"You know, if it was a big wave that got him we never even saw it and we were that close. He was there and then he was gone. Wiped out. Just one of those bad things. Those big waves, all by themselves, the power of them is just horrendous. Like taking a sledgehammer to a doll's house. If it had hit us, we'd have been gone, too."

And yet, he says, opening another beer, he is always surprised that more boats are not lost and more men drowned.

I mention a talk I once had with an old fisherman in Port Alberni who said it was awful bad when a fishboat went missing in the days before radio. Nobody knew what had happened, and usually nobody ever did find out. And then most of the fishboats got radio phones and it was worse to listen to a skipper calling for help, pleading for rescue. Often he didn't know his position and nobody could even find him, let alone save him.

"It was like listening to a man die," the old man recalled, and told me of an incident—all tragedy at sea is an "incident" in the government's logbooks—where a man with his wife and two kids, caught by night during a gale, were driven ashore and wedged between rocks while the wind mounted and the waves smashed higher. His radio, amazingly, worked through it all, and a hundred fishermen safe at the dock listened in horror as their buddy reported the little girl had been swept over and was gone. The wife was next and he finally said he could not hang onto the boy any longer. Then he said, "I'm for it." After that silence. The old man added, "Should never have taken the wife out with him. Bad luck. Bad luck for youngsters too."

Al tells me what happened to him one windless but very foggy afternoon back in '62. He and his first wife, Anne, were fishing off Ucluelet, eighteen miles out and at the south end of big bank, where some of the finest salmon fishing in the world is found. They spent their ten-day honeymoon on the bank four years earlier and since then Anne had often been his deckhand and cook. She was in the galley preparing dinner that day, and he was in the wheelhouse, a place he would not normally be at that time of day, when he heard a voice: "Anybody at the south end?"

Al called out he was. The voice of a friend named Joe said there was a big freighter barreling through at ten knots, a ten-thousand tonner, and she had just missed one of the north-end trollers by a dozen feet.

He said, "If I hadn't been in the wheelhouse, I wouldn't have picked up that message. So I stayed up there. Then, out of the portside window I saw her coming. Full bore. Through the banks where the fleet was. No man at the bow watch. No lights. No foghorn sounding. I learned later she was Greek, the *Evginia V*. I'm not surprised about those ships, Greek, Liberian, Panamanian registry. Nothing ever works on those things. I just had time to hit the throttle and move a couple of feet to starboard when she brushed me, taking out all the portside poles and gear and leaving one goddammed mess. Then she was gone in the fog. If I hadn't been able to move sideways those two or three feet, she'd have smashed us into kindling and nobody would have known a thing about it."

He and Anne had stopped smoking but when it was over, leaving the *Geraldine J.* bouncing and sliding about in the wash, she said she was going to find a cigarette and he said he'd have one, too. He never quit smoking again.

"That ended my wife's seafaring days," he laughs, "and I can't say as I blame her. A thing like that is pretty hairy. You just go out again and fish and hope it never happens again."

He and his wife were later divorced.

Al Johnson says he knew the marauding Greek also carried away the net of a gillnetter fishing that night along the blue line, the boundary between the United States and Canada in the Strait of Juan de Fuca.

A pretty good record: one hit, a very near miss, and a near-miss.

He adds that the *Evginia V* knew she was in collision because she sneaked in to Albert Head at Victoria a few hours later and the crew painted away the scratches on the rusty hull caused by the *Geraldine J.*

"I formally protested but her agents denied the ship was ever on the La Prousse Bank, when everyone knows every ship that is on its way to Vancouver Harbor crosses over that bank," and he shrugs. "No way to beat them. But if I had been icing fish in the hold where I should have been, I wouldn't be sitting here talking to you right now."

There have been other scares, some really bad ones, like the time off Cape Scott, one of the wildest places in the world, when he was trapped in a gale blowing more than a hundred miles an hour with mountainous breaking seas. There was the *Geraldine J.* alone out there and without a forward hatch cover, which, he admits, he had stupidly left behind at Kyuquot. Each wave flooded the deck and half the wild North Pacific was pouring into the hold, and when he looks back at himself, trying to steer a course for survival and checking the pump in the hold, he says, "I thought I was a goner, but I was so busy I really didn't have time to give it sufficient consideration."

After these perilously close near-misses, I ask, didn't he ever think of fishing the protected inlets? Or packing it up and let the other guy go on until the final drop of the ball on the roulette wheel, wiping him out with an obituary in the *Vancouver Sun* saying, "Lost at Sea."

Never, until the bleak reality that afternoon out on the La Prousse Bank when he looked in the box and saw those two pathetic fish.

After eighteen years of fishing, surely he would know about fish. No, he doesn't and he doesn't think the marine biologists with their degrees and floating and shore laboratories know much either. As for the faceless bureaucrats in the Department of Fisheries in Ottawa, who have never been hit in the face by a ton of icy water, they know nothing.

Al Johnson does know you have to be out there eighteen miles offshore at the break of dawn with your gear out because ten thousand years of experience have taught fishermen that fish do not feed at night but at first light. Then—music to the troller's ears—the dingle-dingle, the constant ringing of the bell as the beautiful silvery Coho and the deep-bellied Springs move up on the flashing spoons and lures and hit hard. They do the same an hour before the sun goes down and they come up on the steel lines and are flipped off and the lead cannonball sends the gear down thirty fathoms again. And on the starboard side, the gurdies whine as another set of lines comes up, often with four or five Coho on each line, kicking and slapping away their lives.

"If they're there and you've got the right depth you should get them. If they're coming in fast, you're working the lines like a madman and you're scraping them and cleaning them and chilling the buggers and later you fill up the body cavities with salt and stack them away. It is a fifteen-hour day or more. Day after day, but you're catching fish. You don't sit there and play a fish like a salmon fisherman in a sports boat. This is not a sport. It's called making a living."

But what does he know about fish? He smiles and says, "Fish are funny creatures."

No, I won't let him off the hook.

"Okay, let's see. They're supposed to be in this place, but they're not, and everybody's crying. I say to a buddy we should go up off the west coast of the Charlottes. He says why? I say, just a hunch. So we grub and ice up and take off. Everybody has said we're crazy and we'll never get in a day's fishing because of those gawdawful storms coming down from the Gulf of Alaska. So, our two boats get up there and there's glorious fishing. We're not supposed to be up there and the fish aren't either, but there we are and there they are. It's a hunch with me, but what is it to those fish?

"Sometimes we'd just hang around out there, doing a little fixing of this and that and lying around in the sun and watching those big waves go by and eating big meals. I once had a deckhand with me named Jimmie Fraser and I'd cooked a chicken with gravy, brussels sprouts, mashed potatoes, salad and wine. We're eating and there's a shout and an old Norwegian, a highliner, is saying he's into Cohoes and he's bringing them in five or six to a line. I yell back that we're having dinner and I'll get at it when we've finished.

"Old Knutson went into Ucluelet with that story and nobody believed I'd done such a thing."

He says there is no such thing as a quick, easy buck, and there never will be. A fisherman's investment is enormous when the size of boat and gear is considered, but it doesn't stop many from buying a boat and getting in, no matter how little their experience.

"They usually have no experience, unless you consider sports fishing as experience. But I know doctors, musicians, lawyers, writers, salesmen, and every type of businessman who wants to get away from land and give it a try. One day a guy who's made his pile will say to his wife, 'C'mon, lets quit this and go fishing.' And often she'll be happy to go. Same with everybody. And boy, do they make mistakes. But everybody does. There was never a day in eighteen years out there that I didn't learn something. By doing something wrong and figuring out what it was. You learn, too, from the old-timers.

"I knew only one man who was utterly and everlastingly a hopeless fisherman. That man would go out with the rest of us and we'd come back with forty or fifty fish each. Good ones, too. He might have two or three and most often he was skunked. Nobody to this day has figured out how. Somebody once asked him if he was fishing without lures or spoons and he said, 'No, I don't think so,' and checked his lines just to be sure. He was a floating and walking wonder. We've never figured him out.

"And then there was an old guy, tough as leather, and he'd fished all his life. His boat was filthy, full of grease inside and out. That's a no-no, absolutely.

"He never used clean gloves like the rest of us did and his lures and spoons were black with rust and muck. But he'd go out with us on the first tack in the morning, and before you know it he'd have six hundred pounds of red Spring and the best one of us could do would be two bites, maybe fifty pounds. You couldn't beat the guy. He'd get them.

"One time I wasn't catching any fish, and he came alongside and checked everything and said everything was fine. He told me to stop and then start my motor and he listened. 'That's it,' he said. 'Go back in right now and start filing the leading edge of your prop. Just the tiniest bit off. It's setting up a kind of hum and it's going down your lines and scaring the fish.' I did and next day I was catching as many fish as anybody else. That old bugger was a fisherman."

I tell him about fishermen I have known who have trolled buddy-buddy only eighty feet apart, same lines, same lures, same speed, same depth, and in two hours one boat will bring in fifty salmon and the other a big fat zero. What's this thing about some men having strong chemical smell on their hands which the fish dislike?

"An old wives' tale. Some believe it though. I've never seen any evidence to that. Know why? Because the guy who was skunked one day will pull in fifty fish the next day. All I can say is that fish are funny creatures."

So are fishermen. Like Al Johnson. He tells of the day before halibut season opened, his hooks brought in about fifty of the flat, almost round, clammy, white fish with the one eye that wandered around until it joined the other eye, making one large eye. He didn't dare ice one of them down because the fisheries boat was skulking about, and it broke his heart to throw them back, dead. Next day he figured on several hundred bucks in the bank pulling out fifty more halibut.

He laughs. "Not a one. I couldn't catch one if my bloody life depended on it. If there is a god of the fish he was doing a lot of talking that morning. I could have iced down those fifty the day before, but if I'd got nailed, I'd likely have had my boat confiscated. Which is just as stupid as it is with salmon. I'll bring up maybe twenty undersized Coho. I can't help if they're on my lines. So while the seiners are bringing up thousands of dead small Coho, I'm cleaning and packing just one box of them for my friends for cooking or canning. Free. Not selling them. They're dead, of course, but I'm supposed to throw them back, and if I get caught giving them to my friends I could lose my boat, my life's investment. Fisheries regulations just never did make one damn bit of sense."

And there he is, in the warm house, flexing his left hand to supple up his fingers for fingering the expensive violin he is now playing for free in the Nanaimo Symphony. It's something to do. Jobs are scarce as halibut on opening day. But does he regret leaving fishing?

"No regrets. Not a one. I had a damn good eighteen years of it. I got in when I was a kid and I met a whole gang of wonderful guys who will always be my friends. I was out there at dawn, just where I wanted to be, looking at that sunrise and knowing I'd hear the dingle-dingle any moment. I'd be there at sunset watching the sun go down and the seagulls flying and maybe a few whales going by.

"I didn't make much money, but I made as much as I wanted to. Don't kid yourself, fishermen bitch a lot, but they live real good and they're doing just what they want to do. At least they did. Now, of course, a lot of hungry dog-eat-dog enters into it, but that's the way the industry wants it. Keep 'em greedy. It's not the fishermen who get rich; you could say it is the packing companies. Everybody is still at the mercy of them, although they're better now.

"I want to say this. It's the independence. You are your own boss. If you're day-fishing and have a hangover or it's blowing outside, you just roll over and say, to hell with it. So you go out tomorrow, the next day. In an office or factory you've got to have a damned good excuse not to be there.

"When we're in Tofino or Ucluelet or Bamfield and we're working on the boat or hanging around, smelling of grease and fish and covered in scales and with three days' beard, you see the tourists, the men, coming down in their expensive sports clothes and they look at us. Their eyes are hungry. You could say desperate. Everyone is thinking, 'I wish I was him and just go out there and tell the whole wide world to go piss up a rope.' If you can't see it in their faces, you can sure hear it in their questions. They want to know where you go, what do you do. It's kind of running away to sea as a cabin boy, which they probably dreamed of as a kid.

"It's then I say, 'I've got it pretty good and it was so for eighteen good years.'"

Then he says, "When they'd come down to the wharf I'd answer all their questions but I never told them one certain thing. If we were out on the bank for ten days I'd eat nothing but the best meat I could find. Beef, pork, chicken. I could have lived free out there, eating fish. I didn't tell them that if there were twenty-eight meals served on that trip, only one was ever salmon. Couldn't stand it. They're in and around and on top of you every day and you get to hate the sight of them. Yep, fish are funny creatures."

So are men.

A Boozy Day on Jackfish Lake

I could hear John yelling when I reached for the door latch of the main house overlooking Jackfish Lake, yelling at Felicia to get the breakfast going because damn it all, it was 7:30 and the day wouldn't last forever.

It was a domestic argument, so I backed off and looked out over the lake, the sun polishing the surface, a beaver making a widening V as he went about his business, and the lunatic call of a loon coming from the shadows where the huge pines hung over the water. The sky was blue and a few cumulus clouds grazing toward the east like sheep in a meadow made the morning perfect.

I opened the door and now John was on the phone, yelling, "Goddam it, what you mean you can't guide us? You promised. You said when Broadfoot got here you'd be ready and he's just walked in the door.... Yeah, last night. In the shore cabin. Yeah, we had a few. Yeah, you might say the evening was fine and full of the sounds of conviviality.... Yeah, and now you're telling me that you can't take us. Yeah, you're bloody right. A piss-poor show.

"Oh, Helge. You know he doesn't guide. He fishes. Sure he's the best man on Jackfish, the whole country, but he's hell-and-gone up at the far end. Twelve miles. By the time you get up there with that stinkpot of yours and we get out of here it'll be eleven o'clock.

"What do you mean last night you told him? You're as nutty as Helge. You know that, don't you? Those reefs, the narrows. He said he'd be at the landing at eight? Okay. Knowing him, that means ten o'clock and he'll be feeling no pain. Eight for sure? Okay, we'll be there."

John turned to me as I filled a coffee mug at the stove and sat down at the kitchen table.

"Helge Christenson will be our guide. A crazy Icelander. Only commercial fisherman on Jackfish. Makes big money and talks hard times. He's got a shack that you got to see to believe. Plywood painted a dumb white, a tin roof, a table, chairs, a cot, his nets flung in a corner, gas cans all over, and on the wall are dozens, hundreds of magazine cartoons and magazine covers that he's pasted there with a kind of glue made out of flour. He's got an insane dog named Thumper. That's the name of that rabbit in the Walt Disney movie. Want to go number one or number two? Just go into the bush thirty feet from his door, but watch your step. A good man, knows Jackfish better than anyone. The landing in thirty minutes so, Felicia, will you please get the lead out?" And then John ran out of gas.

I asked who was on the phone and he said, "Don," and went on checking out rods, tackle, and gear and throwing canned goods into a sack.

"Who's Don?"

"Just a guy. Works for a small newspaper in Manitoba and gets fired the first of June every year and comes over here and camps out on the point for three months. Different broad every time. Always talking about writing the Great Canadian Novel. He wants to meet you. Talk to you about that novel of his. Didn't you write one? He thinks you did."

"Tried, tried two, but they didn't work out. A bright high-school kid could have done better."

"Well, don't disappoint him. Nice guy. Fishes and drinks all summer and comes over here a lot."

By 7:45 we'd eaten breakfast, and loaded everything into the pickup and when we were done I asked, "Aren't we forgetting some things?"

John looked at me and said, "Hats? No. Sunglasses? No. Christ! The booze!" He ran to the toolshed and yarded out the three cases of beer that I'd bought on my way in last night, plus a bottle of Smirnoff vodka, which he waved, and said, "For Helge. Drinks it like water. This is his pay. Don't offer money, he'd be insulted."

In the truck John said, "Tear open one of those cases and there's a cranker in the glove compartment. Let's have one on the road," and I pulled out two warm beers, opened them, and handed one to him as the foam cascaded down my hand. We reached the highway, drove down it for half a mile, turned right and passed a car coming at us with Illinois plates and John said, "Those Americans! I guess this is one part of Canada they can't fish out, but they'll die trying."

Hitting the big lake, we passed a scattering of small winter ice-fishing shacks, a run-down café, gas drums stacked in a row, a dock, a couple of houses, a workshop, a toilet with an "Out of Order" sign hanging on the door. John said, "Welcome to Jackfish Lake, where the big ones jump into your boat, so eager are they to see you."

Don was waiting, and we shook hands. He said, "Helge's back at the dock. Got in half an hour ago. Gabbing. That means another half-hour. Sit down. Have a beer. They're warm but they are wet and have a certain alcoholic content. Meet my friend," and he pointed to a towsled head sticking out of a little orange tent. That tent could have been good for only one thing. He didn't mention her name—a local girl, probably.

Suddenly there was a roar and a fourteen-foot aluminum lapstrake with a big kicker came skidding around the point. The man at the helm killed the motor just twenty feet from shore and gentled the craft sideways against the rocks, just kissing them. This man could handle a battleship.

John made the introductions. Helge was a medium-sized man but very heavy in the shoulders and chest, like a Siwash Indian who spends most of his life paddling a canoe. He was shy, soft-spoken, his face weathered to a brown as richly deep as a Florsheim shoe. His eyes crinkled. His hands were rough and scarred and one finger on his left hand was only half there. He wore rubber boots, Levis, a heavy flannel shirt. He wore no hat and his hair was blond. A real ghoulie. I grew up with them in Winnipeg and I'll travel down the road with an Icelander any day of the week. I also noticed a mickey of Lemon Hart rum sticking out of his back pocket, and as we stored our gear I saw a dead soldier lying in the bottom of the boat.

He saw my look and picked the bottle up and tossed it away. "If you don't start early, you're going to finish too late and miss all the fun. If you run out of that," pointing to our cases, "I've got another up front."

We cast off, moving slowly, the powerhouse on the rear of the boat muttering, using up only one-tenth of its rpm's. Helge and I talked, casually, the talk of two men who take a liking to each other but know they will never see each other again.

I asked if he was a relative of the senator, a public figure with the same name, and he replied, "Cousin. Second, I think. We don't exactly run in the same social circles."

Ten minutes passed and we just dawdled along, and then he called to John up front to hook up the live minnows and he pushed the throttle. There was that deafening roar again and we took off. The shore flew by and he yelled in my ear, "You know timber wolves pull down moose along here in the winter and the Trans-Canada Highway is only a quarter of a mile beyond those trees."

We throttled down to a slow trot and against the shore there was a small red and white cruiser. Helge said, "Americans." I was beginning to get the impression that Americans weren't too popular around this neck of the woods, although they must bring a lot of money in the tourist season. About half the cars on the streets of Kenora had Illinois, Wisconsin, and Minnesota licenses. As if reading my mind, Helge said, "Some okay. I get along with them."

"I could say some things, but I won't," yelled John. "Barry, catch." I turned just as an open bottle of beer came flipping at me. This was going to be quite a day.

Helge cut the motor to trolling speed and we dropped our lines over the starboard and puttered back and forth for half an hour until Helge said, "To hell with nothing. Last winter I caught a dozen ten-pounders through the ice right along here. All in one set. You should have seen them. All same size. Brothers and sisters, I reckon. We'll fool around further up, around some other reefs and by the narrows, and if nothing's doing by noon we'll go up to my place."

Rum bottle number two had disappeared, flung in a high arc out into deeper water, and number three had appeared and was taking a beating. So was our case of beer. We stopped at one reef, no luck, and then another, and as we lazed along Helge gave a long dissertation on the controversial question of mercury poisoning and the effects on the fish and the Indians who lived off them and who were dying. His opinion was that all those scientists who said the mercury was poison had it all wrong. It was not coming from mine waste. He said that every rock in this country had some mercury, and some, just a little bit, leached into the water every year. All this talk of pollution and of people dying from mercury poisoning was a lot of baloney.

"I know what I'm talking about," he said, concluding the debate in which he was the only speaker. "It's just nature working," he added as the clincher.

John caught a walleye, small, no fight, and he said, "I'll keep him anyway. Mount him as a trophy." Half an hour later I caught another, smaller, with less fight, and John said scornfully, "A snagger." We were about two hundred feet from two men trolling in a canoe and as soon as we moved along they paddled over to the exact spot I'd boated my lunker.

"Americans. They'll do it every time. See somebody hook into something and they move over. Right there in half a minute. Do you call that bad manners or just plain stupidity. Or dumb greed?"

Helge yelled, "Reel in, screw this part of the country. The big trout saw your visitor from Vancouver coming and they won't show their snouts, thinking he'll be comparing them with salmon. It's 11:30 so we'll head for the shack."

Suddenly we were away in a great swooping turn, a curve as graceful as any artist's free-form line. I thought, if you've got to drown, let it be this way, in a country so beautiful that God must have thought twice before he allowed the human race into it. Incredible speed. Was Helge a rum runner? I thought he must have a jet engine hidden somewhere and the Evinrude engine was just to fool the game warden. Shoreline cliffs flashed by. Islands dropped astern fast. Ducks barely skittered out of the way. Helge tapped my shoulder and pointed and there, far away, a white dot against the green background, the home of the only fisherman on this large lake.

The dot grew closer and became a dwelling, and thirty feet from shore Helge cut the motor and the boat settled and then glided up a ramp. We stepped onto the land and a white mongrel sporting black spots came racing down the path and was all over us.

"Skunk," I said, holding my nose.

"Yeah, the bugger seems to like them and there's been one under the shack for a month. Having babies, I guess. Thumper tangles with her once in a while. Never learns, but maybe he likes the smell. I'm used to it now. Kind of nice after awhile."

I picked up our foodsack and John shouldered a case of Molson's and walked toward civilization. Helge said he never locked the door because some idiot might come along and kick it in and then he'd have to fix it. Anyway, he said he was so far from the fishing camp that not too many people knew he was here.

We entered the castle. It was as John had described it, even to the cartoons, and one could spend a good hour just walking around looking at them. I did for a couple of minutes and saw that mine host had a rare sense of humor. Most were from *The New Yorker*. Helge went into a rambling account of how he had bought ten acres of this land from a pulp and paper company. I think I lost him halfway through, but give a good man a good story to tell and he doesn't really mind.

"What's for lunch?"

"A drink first and then we'll think about it. I got nothing left here, so I guess lunch is what you've got in that sack."

We sat down at the kitchen table facing windows that looked down the long bay to the lake. Helge talked about other lakes he'd hiked into, lakes he claimed had not been visited by man for many years and were seen only by passengers in jet airliners 35,000 feet up. He said there were cabins way back in there with all kinds of stuff in them—traps, furniture made with axes and saws, dishes, cutlery, tools, old books—which he someday meant to take out and use to start his own museum. A man of a thousand ideas.

John got the little gas stove hissing and opened up two cans of Spam and two of beans. Soon he had two pots boiling furiously. As he ladled out the lunch on dirty plates he said, "Damn it, Helge, don't you ever wash these dishes?" The reply was, "Eventually, but these things take some considering."

Finished, John said, "I cooked the grub, so you can wash up, Broadfoot," and I replied, "You don't cook Spam and beans. You just put it on the burner and walk around for a little while until it all heats up."

I lost the argument and took a pail and went down to the lake, heated up the water, and tackled a midden of crockery and thrift-shop cutlery. I was having a sloshing good time of it when Helge came over with a dish towel and we polished off the job. Helge said, "You can throw that dishwater over the pooch. Time he had a wash."

We sat down again and John said "Get the news. Let's hear who Trudeau is screwing today."

"Battery's dead."

"God, why don't you get a new one when you're in town picking up your booze? You've got lots of money."

"Keep forgetting."

"You don't forget your booze, but everything else. Forget your head if it wasn't glued on."

Banter, nothing serious. Talk among friends.

Then it happened. It always does. There is a formula for letting a guy down easy when he suggests that he might make the subject of a good book. I told Helge that hundreds of writers and nonwriters across the country were doing books on other people or themselves, and they didn't have a chance in the world because the market was full to the top with "I Am a Canadian Pioneer" stories.

He took it in good grace, nodding gravely, but that didn't stop him from entertaining us with an outline of his life. He had done it all, from working in the harvest fields as a kid at a dollar a day, winter fishing on Lake Winnipeg, and cutting ice for a cold-storage firm, to driving a truck, working on oil rigs, railroading, doing a hitch in the army, working in a wet coal mine in Alberta. One marriage, lots of girls, a good life, a grim life, and now he was commercial fishing on a large lake. And there was much more.

Helge stopped and said, "Boat coming." We looked and saw a boat a long way off and Helge hadn't even been looking out the window. I asked him how he knew.

"I heard it. Don's boat." He returned to polish up the story of his life, and then he added, "Guess you're right about you writing a book on me; but if I write my own book it will be a book I really like. I don't care if its only got one reader as long as that reader is me." Wonderful!

It was Don and we watched him make the same skimming stop on the ramp. When he came up, lugging a box of beer, Helge was arguing that a 1966 Pontiac he had bought for $250 last year would be worth $2,500 as a vintage car in two years.

"Rusting away," said John. "Give you $100."

Don who had caught the drift of the conversation, said, "Worth $50 at the most."

After a few more drinks it was decided that the two boats would go south, into another lake, a long one with only one house on it, owned by an American family from Cleveland who were very snooty and rich and had "Keep Out! This Means You!" and "Beware Of The Dog!" signs along the beach. As Helge described it, his face got hard and he said, "They don't keep me out. I am the only one in the country for eight months of the year and if they got a dog up there today, it is going to be one sorry fellow with half its ribs kicked in."

I got into Don's boat and John and Helge roared away first and since we couldn't keep up we didn't try. We had trouble following because the connecting stream between the two lakes was a creek only ten feet wide, but we finally found it. Far ahead, as we emerged, Helge was wheeling and dealing and doing cartwheels with his boat and I could imagine John screaming at him. With all the shenanigans up ahead we caught up and cruised into the yellow sand beach thirty minutes later.

Through the pines I could see a cottage. Some cottage! Some house! Some mansion!

We lay on the beach, just yakking, and Helge now was working on our gift bottle of vodka and his stories kept us laughing. Then he pulled the same trick—"Boat's coming"—and, sure enough, far away there was a boat coming fast. "Owners," Helge said.

Somebody said we should shove off but Helge said, "Remember what I said about the dog. That applies just as easily to men," and when the small cruiser grounded a few feet from us he lifted a hand and said, "Welcome." The rum and scotch and vodka were definitely at work. The men sensed it, I guess, and one just grunted. Or was it because there were four of us and two of them?

The men struggled to lift from the stern a large and heavy cylinder of propane and were getting nowhere fast. Helge rolled over, heaved himself up, waded into the lake, and told the two Americans to handle the front end of the cylinder. He casually lifted his end and it was done, easy.

"That Helge," said John admiringly. "He could sit down and chat with Hitler."

Helge moved down the beach with the two men after picking up his quart of vodka and they sat on the steps leading to the house talking. Yes, he could talk to Hitler.

That was a signal for us, and we began moving gear from Helge's boat to Don's. "Wind her up. He'll be here the rest of the day," John said. As we headed home I waved to our guide and he lazily waved back. I said to John: "What will he do?"

"How should I know? Get invited for dinner. Go to sleep on the beach. Hit a floating log and drown. Go home and feed the stinking dog."

As on most fishing trips, the return was an anticlimax. The trip home was slow, livened up only once when John, waving his beer bottle, gave a five-minute harangue about how stupid it was to go on a serious trip with a bunch of drunks.

Two hours after leaving the beach we were at the dock and after unloading our gear and persuading Don that it was not a good idea to come for supper, we went home.

In the kitchen John said, "Anything doing?" and Felicia said, "Nothing. Just a carful of Americans, Wisconsin, wanting to rent one of the boats. I sent them across the lake."

"Good. Don't the bastards know we own our own country and our own boats? Our country may be for hire, but my goddammed boats aren't."

"Any luck?"

"Yeah. Two. But there were so big we couldn't get them in the boat and we didn't have enough gas to tow them. Any other smart questions?"

Felicia replied, "A typical day. No fish and both drunk as farts."

Dinner was pork chops, fried potatoes, stewed tomatoes, and cake, and when it was finished, Felicia cooed, "Best lake-trout feast I've had in a long time."

John's look at her was murderous and I cut in and wondered what Helge would be doing; would he make out?

John said, "That bastard is a survivor. If there was another ice age tomorrow, he'd be the only person left alive."

9

Two Tales of One City

Remember the hippies, the flower children? Some called them part of a protest against the Establishment; some exceeded reason and called it a revolution. Maybe it all began with Beatlemania or the voice of millionaire Bob Dylan telling the kids to hit the streets. Viet Nam certainly added fuel to the flame. Perhaps it was all a vast and cynical media event. Whatever it was, whatever caused it, psychologists, sociologists, and every other kind of "ologist" had a grand time selling articles to national magazines explaining the phenomenon. I doubt if they understood the hippies any more than the parents of the rebellious youths who read the articles. As a reporter in Vancouver, I had a chance to observe the "movement" and I walked among the kids and talked to them, but I can't explain it.

What remains today? Different hair styles for men and health-food stores and restaurants. Some far-out, flamboyant clothes and funny first names given to so many children born during that era. The peace and conservation groups and Women's Lib. An incredible rise in the amount of pot smoked and hard drugs taken. And a deeper distrust of all things political.

On the other side of town—millions of miles away from Kitsilano—was Skid Road and the Indian girls who, driven there by the same society that spawned the gentle hippies, met violence, degradation, and death. Where were all the "ologists" and social workers and welfare workers to help those lost souls? They were too busy analyzing the flower children to try to understand the other problem. Sick, destitute, and drunken Indians were old hat. Nothing new there. But the Second

223

Children's Crusade was different. That *was interesting.*

One tale has ended. Nobody in the other tale really counts, so who listens, who cares? Just another sad story that has no ending...

Where Did All the Flowers Go?

Eric leaned back in his Barcalounger, his head against the black leather, his arms flat on the sides and adapted what he called his Abraham Lincoln pose, staring into space.

"Do you mind if I start at the end of it all rather than at the beginning and how I got involved and what I did?"

I said certainly. It was his story.

We were sitting in his penthouse, seven stories up, looking through a thirty-foot expanse of glass to the blue waters of English Bay and the low mountains of West Vancouver. A dozen sails were floating across the sea and my friend said, "This is all about nothing, but when those hundreds of kids, hell, maybe two or three thousand, who knows, were down on Fourth Avenue, I would sit here and watch them down there on the street in all their sweltering, bitchified squalor and their crazy ideas. Sitting there in bunches talking, and half not knowing what they were talking about. They called it rapping, a term they picked up from a Negro militant in the States who was causing havoc right and left. Actually they knew very little more than I did about the American hippie movement. Everything that came up here was in a sanitized, martinized, buggered-up-wise version."

Eric was a tall man, six-foot-one and heavy in the chest. He had been a star in college football. At about thirty-five years of age he realized that the things he was importing and selling so successfully were not all that great.

He sold half his business, and let his new partner run it. He got down to the business of inventing things people really needed. Four of his ideas came up big and he sold the patents, picking up a share of the profits, and now here he was, sitting in a chair custom-made for him by the finest Roman manufacturer, remembering the late sixties when he was involved with the flower children, when Vancouver's Fourth Avenue was the center of Canada's revolt-of-youth movement.

"I'll start at the ending," he said again. "The daughter of an old friend of ours came out to Vancouver to look around and her mother asked if she could stay with us. We said of course. Lori was only fifteen and we wouldn't have let her live anywhere else. She was staying in Vancouver only four days, so Marj or I took her around the first day and showed her the sights—you know: Stanley Park, the suspension bridge, Chinatown, the U.B.C. campus, and so on—all the things a bright and lively kid of fifteen didn't want to see. I sensed this. What probably gave me a clue was when we took her to Gastown, the famous Gastown"—he chuckled and I knew he had money invested in some renovated buildings—"and she was completely turned off. After walking through the awful shops and poking into some of those restaurants and arcades, her word for it was something like 'gross' or 'sleazy' or maybe 'yucky.' It's hard to keep up with their vocabulary.

"The second day I asked her what she would like to see next, and she said Fourth Avenue. Fourth Avenue and hundreds of flower children, just two blocks up, and it never occurred to me to go there. That's how out of touch I was with her generation.

"Fine, I told her. 'We'll go right now.' I want you to get the picture. There I was in tailored slacks, Italian loafers, and a white cashmere turtleneck, smoking this pipe. Lori, as sweet of face as a violet, was wearing the fifteen-year-old female version of my outfit. Top of the line. Lord, did we stick out! No matter to her. She was absolutely fascinated. That's not the word: she was *enthralled*. The kids of her age and up to twenty-five or more, lying around, smoking, drinking wine, talking, talking, reading, and making love up to a point. I had always driven along Cornwall, not Fourth, so this was the first time I had seen this, even though it had been going on for two years. Why this six-block stretch of Fourth Avenue? One look could tell you. It was a decayed area, one step from dying. A few vigorous businesses, but the rest of it was tumble-down. Little restaurants had been taken over and goosed up with purple paint and streamers and gimcracks on the walls, selling health food. A store had underground papers from all over North America and, right in the open, pipes to smoke pot and hash. Girls in long skirts and faded sweaters out of some maiden aunt's trunk in the attic. The men in faded and torn jeans, old sweaters or T-shirts.

Both sexes wore sandals. If you didn't wear sandals, you didn't belong. If you didn't look bored and world-weary, you didn't belong either. Slouch. Drag along. Lean against store windows. Look wise and nod gently to the crazy, whining, high-pitched excuse for music that was blasting out from a loudspeaker five feet over their heads.

"Another thing struck me. The street—and it is a wide one, as you well know—it was jammed with cars. Not the cars you'd expect there would be, the cars owned by these kids. No. They rejected cars, as I found out, as they rejected anything. Anything but money," and he laughed his Great Dane bark, one like you'd expect from a big man.

"Yes, everything but money. These gawkers were the burghers of the lower mainland, the middle and upper middle class and their big cars were moving slowly, in both directions. They were gawking. This was a new entertainment in town. Hippy watching. I could just hear some West Vancouver matron, after the liqueurs at the Hyatt Regency: why don't we drive over to Fourth Avenue and look at the hippy kids? God, who ever pinned 'flower children' on them? If they were flowers they were the kind that grew forlornly at the side of back-country roads.

"Well, as I said, Lori was enthralled. I realized then this is why she had wanted to visit us. She was beside herself when we got back here and she asked if she could go back on her own the next day. I was a little dubious but after all, what really could go wrong? As it happened, nothing. She apparently had a glorious day, didn't smoke pot when it was offered to her because she was still too new to it all, and she met some people and they took her to an organic restaurant. Naturally she paid the bill, and admitted she had lent one fellow five dollars. Okay, it was her money. She was hooked and next morning there was a bit of a scene when I told her it was time to get ready to go to the airport and she said she didn't want to go. She wanted to see her new friends again. Uncle-like, I put my foot down and said her parents expected her back on that Air Canada flight.

"At the airport, she said, 'Uncle Eric, I'm coming back next summer as soon as school is out and I'm going to take off my bra and wear sandals and spend the whole summer here. My friends say I can stay at their house.' Well, that was in late July, as you know, of the year the hippie movement had arched toward the sun and the next summer it went down fast. Even the year before Lori visited, the LSD and other bad drugs were being moved in. The hucksters, the rip-off artists, the con men, men and women, boys and girls, streetwise, amoral and immoral, donning hippie costume to pretend they were flower children too and the whole thing began to sour in a hurry. The kids were destroying themselves. That's where I come into the picture.

"Anyway, in fall and winter and next spring the ones who hadn't gone back to their nice homes, the summertime hippies,the ones who stayed, had a very hard time of it. Cold. Hungry. Some starving. Some with battered minds. Cut off by their families, nowhere to go. No trade, no work ethic. How can you walk into a business office in a granny skirt and sandals in November and fill out an application for a filing job? The youths were too emaciated or spaced out to do any manual labor, which was all that was available to them. The situation was bleak. Their little macrame-and-leatherwork acts were old hat now. Just in two long summers. I knew the situation very well by this time, because I was spending a lot of time with them."

Eric heaved his large frame out of the easy chair and said, "All this remembering and talking has made my whistle dry. How about a drink? Scotch?"

"Water, no ice."

He came back with the glasses.

"No more than three days after Lori had gone home, the phone call came."

"What phone call?"

"It was just after dinner, and I was sitting where I am now and the phone rang. The woman said she was phoning from Brockville, Ontario. A very good friend of ours had suggested she call me. I'd never heard of her. Would I listen to her story? Certainly. Her sixteen-year-old son had run away from home. You know how mothers are with an only child. He had shown a bit of rebellion as boys that age always will. One Friday night she and her husband—a doctor—had gone out for dinner and then on to a party, and she had just assumed the boy had gone to bed. When he hadn't come downstairs by ten next morning she was worried and went up to his room. The bed had not been slept in, and on it was an expensive bottle of wine with a card tied to the neck. Maybe the bottle was his way of saying, 'Mom, you and Dad are drinking too much.' The note said he was tired of the small town and he was going away. She phoned the police immediately and the constable told her there was really nothing they could do, the boy probably had a twelve- or fourteen-hour head start on any search. As an afterthought he suggested that the boy and a friend might have taken off for Vancouver. That was the first thing she had ever heard about the scene here. For three weeks she went through hell, and then, yes, the cop was right. She got a collect phone call from here and the boy said he was doing fine, had lots of new friends, and she wasn't to worry.

"Peggy—that's her name—wanted to know if I could help. Playing detective was something new to me, but after my recent experience with Lori on Fourth Avenue, it was the kind of coincidence I couldn't ignore. I found out everything I could about the boy from Peggy—more I think, than she really wanted to tell me. Her son sounded like a real nice kid. I wrote everything down and I said I'd phone back if I found out anything.

"Next afternoon I put on some old jeans and a shirt and sallied forth. I started talking to the kids and found them so-so to meet. Nice kids, but wary at first. I had to convince them that I wasn't a private detective when I told them I was looking for someone. I bought them their damned herbal tea and wheatgerm muffins in those little cafés with the weird music playing. Some tried to hit me for a few bucks, but I said no, I wasn't going that route, and they'd look at my clothes and shrug and probably think I reminded them of their fathers. I soon realized that they didn't think of themselves as flower children, probably because they didn't watch television or hadn't read that absolutely ridiculous cover story of *Time* magazine, which was supposed to be the definitive essay on the whole movement. I had read it, and after just three or four days with them, I could see that that article was the all-time piece of crock. These were just kids, some thrilled, some apprehensive, some scared. The hard-core ones were out on the street, too busy hustling to bother with most of their childish conversation.

"The kids told me to put notices on the bulletin boards. Damn things were everywhere. Someone wanted to share a pad. Did anyone want two puppies? Typewriter for sale, cheap. Learn yoga, lessons Saturday, reasonable. Lost, strayed, or stolen, six string Suzuki, at party on weekend, somewhere in West End. '67 Chev Fordor, for sale, no license. Cheap. That kind of thing. Typical of any bulletin board. A kid from Toronto, a tough but likable streetwise little bugger, said to put up a card saying, 'Jeff, from Brockville. Money arrived.' and put my phone number. He said not to use the full name because that would embarrass him with his friends.

"It worked. I got a phone call the very next afternoon after I had paid my streetwise friend from TO to put up cards on every bulletin board he knew. The kid did a good job and I paid him ten bucks and waited for him to ask for more. When he didn't I gave him another five and made a friend for life. Anyway the voice said he was 'Jeff from Brockville' and just in case this caller knew my Jeff and was impersonating him to get the money, I asked him what his mother's name was. He had it right. We arranged to meet next afternoon at two-thirty in the Alcazar Pub, across from the bus station.

"I went in and it was a zoo. Every hippie type in town must have been there. They might not have money, but they sure were using money to pay for all that beer. You could get high just breathing the air. I sat down at a small table and in about two minutes this kid comes over. He swaggered. Large kid. If a kid of sixteen can look mean, this one was. I can spot a polecat at fifty yards. He sat down and reached for one of my beers. Didn't say hi, hello, or anything, but his attitude spelled out 'screw you.' I asked a few questions to make damned sure he was Peggy's son and he started talking. Trying to impress me. He'd hitchhiked to Alaska and down to Mexico and spent some time in Vancouver. In four weeks, the time since he'd left home? He didn't know I had his background. He claimed he'd made some money hustling. Hell, he didn't know what hustling was. In short, the kid was mean and a liar. His mother's description of him certainly didn't jibe with my quick opinion of him.

"He asked me how I'd found him and I said *he* had phoned me. Oh, yeah, right. I laid out everything that his mother had told me, and I asked him if he was okay and he said sure, man, sure. Everything was 'sure, man, sure.'

"He finally came out with it and asked for the money. I told him there would be money and a job for the rest of the summer if he phoned his mother collect and said he was coming home. The way Peggy and I had arranged it, if I found him I'd buy him a bus ticket to Brockville and give him twenty dollars for food and she'd pay me back. He could hang around Vancouver or go home. It was up to him.

"The little bastard stood up and sneered, 'Thanks for the beer,' and swaggered back to his gang. A minute later I heard some of them laugh.

"That night I phoned Peggy and told her I'd found her son, skipping the gory details. I said she could send him money for a bus or train and food, but there was no guarantee that he wouldn't spend it on booze or pot. I said the Missing Persons Bureau could pick him up and ship him back to Ontario, but there was no guarantee he wouldn't get off at Chilliwack and hitch back to Vancouver and be in the Alcazar that afternoon and spend all his food money by closing time.

"I also told her I'd already phoned the Missing Persons Bureau and a nice sergeant had told me they already had about seven hundred missing persons on file with more coming in every day.

"She sniffled a little and her husband, the doctor, came on the phone. I gave it to him straight and he said, 'Christ, leave him there then. He'll come back the end of August. He pulled the same stunt last year.' Well, that was a nice little tidbit of information I hadn't gotten out of his mother. Anyway, I washed my hands of this snot-nose, but I still was fascinated by these kids and that's how I got into the most fascinating two months of my life.

"I had bushels of time on my hands. Marj was taking off to Europe with a girlfriend for a month and my boat had been stove in by a drunk at the marina, so I said, what the hell, I'll hang around with those kids down there and maybe I'll learn something and help them. I didn't put myself in the role of a do-gooder because I could sense the mistrust that various agencies had built up by sending in do-gooders with sincere smiles and a notebook to mark up how many souls they had saved.

"Strangely—but maybe not—the kids trusted the cops. The police chief had made it a policy to send men and women into the Kitsilano area who could relate to the kids and could understand their problems. If a kid was in deep trouble—sick, abused, or suffering from malnutrition—and didn't have the sense to seek out help, the police would guide him to it. I got to know all those people and they were fine, they really cared.

"But when it came to the drug pushers on Chemical Alley they could be tough, and I do mean tough. Chemical Alley? Oh, just one short side block where a lot of the dope and peyote and LSD and other hallucinatory stuff was sold. That was the kid's name for the place. They had a name for everything. They called me 'Rich Eric.' They'd ask 'Hey, Rich Eric, how many millions did you count today?' All in fun.

"But they had some funny ideas. War, for instance. The 'Ban the Bomb' business was going on, of course, and some of the girls wore T-shirts with 'Ban the Bomb' across the chest. If they were well endowed, so to speak, the word 'Ban' would be sticking out of the right breast and 'Bomb' on the left. It had an interesting effect. All the male eye would see was 'Ban' and 'Bomb.'

"They seemed to concentrate on the Pacific war; their knowledge of Hitler and England's long, lonely fight was skimpy. All they knew about the war with Japan was Hiroshima, and half of them probably couldn't find Japan on a globe. They said the Americans destroyed a whole city. I asked, did they realize that Hiroshima—hell, they, couldn't even pronounce it right—did they know it was an industrial city making armaments and therefore a legitimate military target? Had they heard about the Rape of Nanking? Blank stares No, dammit, the A-bomb was the symbol of all that was wrong with Western society.

"I spent dozens and dozens of hours with them, a revolving group of maybe a hundred, on the street, in restaurants, in this very living room, and my one conclusion was that they were totally unprepared for life, the results of a very unsound educational system.

"As I got to know them better and they trusted me more, I'd invite a dozen or so for a chat and some grub. Nothing special. Two pounds of weiners and a bunch of buns, half-packs of Pepsi, and I even went so far as to stock up on their herbal tea. By the way they conducted themselves here, it was obvious that all but a few came from good homes, even wealthy ones. Not one or two, but several girls quickly identified the English bone china cups I served tea in. You don't get that coming out of hell's kitchen. They had taste and admired the paintings and the antique furniture. You know, I don't think I met one who came from a farm or a rural area, although some came from small towns. A lot were from good areas, like Westmount in Montreal, Toronto's Rosedale, Mount Royal in Calgary, or Shaughnessy here. Oh sure, some were just in it for a lark, an experience, but others were deadly serious.

"Despite their being city kids their dream was to set up a commune in some nice valley in the Kootenays or the Okanagan or the Gulf Islands. They'd live together in a house they'd fix up or in a log cabin they'd build. They'd have barns with a couple of cows and goats. For some reason they were surefire on goats. They'd dig a well. My God, those kids digging a well! They'd generate their own electricity and there would be love flowing like a Niagara and the girls would work around the commune and the boys would work the fields and get daywork in the district.

"I asked them where they'd get the money to buy the land. I told them nobody was giving away land anymore, and if they had some money, the owner would double the down payment because he'd figure he'd get the place back within a year. Had they heard of Thoreau and Walden Pond? Some had. Most hadn't. My God, the bible of the back-to-the-land and living free and off nature. No, their bible was a bimonthly publication from the States called *The Mother Earth News*, and, if you stacked every issue until it was ten feet high, you'd have a ten-foot-tall pile of bullshit.

"They'd sit around on this floor here and be giggling and drinking Pepsi and munching hotdogs just like any bunch of teenagers. Then they'd earnestly and learnedly parrot back all the useless junk they'd memorized from *The Mother Earth News*. They were going to keep bees and butcher and smoke their own hogs every fall and make cherry and plum wine and build a windmill to get power. They'd buy a fifty-dollar wreck of a truck and get it humming again and make goat's cheese and sell it and sell honey and breed fish in a pond they'd dig out of a marsh and soon build a Frank Lloyd Wright house or maybe just the biggest Manchurian yurt in captivity. They'd build a big ferro-concrete boat and half the commune would go to Tahiti one year and the other half the next. They'd have a huge garden and grow tomatoes and beans all winter in a cellophane greenhouse, and sell pickled quail's eggs and keep geese and sell ducks, down comforters, and breed and sell dogs and rabbits and worms. How the hell do you breed worms? They'd make jewelry and sell it and peddle fresh corn and pumpkins from roadside stands. They'd grow their marijuana and sell what they didn't use down in Vancouver.

"Perhaps you've caught something in what I've just said? One word. That word is 'sell.' I don't think I've ever heard of youngsters whose minds were so solidly concentrated on money. Why? Because they had mainly come from good homes where money was always something to be taken for granted. Now, they had very little of the stuff, and it dominated their thinking.

"Strangely, yes strangely, they did not talk much about drugs. The hippie generation has always been presented in the media as being dominated by drugs. I certainly didn't find that to be so. I know, I know, most or all them smoked pot, but they were quite fearful of any hallucinogenic drug. All they had to do was look around on Fourth and see those who had dropped acid. Those kids with their minds wasted were tragic. One kid used to pick empty match folders out of the gutter and try to sell them to straight people on the street. He told them the folders were rocket tickets to Mars.

"I remember one time I had a dozen up here and one girl caught me in the kitchen and asked if she could have a shower. Her name was Darlene. They all had those kind of names in that time. Debbie, Janis, Suzanne, Dawn, Karen. What ever happened to the good old biblical names like Sarah, Ruth, Mary? There are three bathrooms, so I said sure. Thank God Marj wasn't around! Anyway, she came out ten minutes later shiny and bright as a new penny. By the time they left every one of those kids had had a shower. They loved it. Thank God this bloody apartment house has a hot-water boiler as big as an atomic submarine.

"But back to the commune bit, which seems to be the main thing we recall when we think of the hippies. To my knowledge not one of all those street kids ever went to a commune and to my knowledge not one commune was ever successful.

"Oh yes, they had communes of a sort, all through Kitsilano and in the West End. One couple would rent an old house and another six or eight would pour in. They'd scrounge, beg, steal furniture, and cups and plates and cutlery and frying pans, and they'd get their greens from the supermarket garbage bins at night, throw-away stuff, but still good. They'd stock up on the organic junk that the health-food stores would rip them off on. I'd ask if they were aware that the organic carrots and spuds they were eating raw had been grown in soil heavily fertilized with cow and pig shit? They'd laugh. I'd ask how they could tell that a carrot or a spud had been grown organically anyway, except for the sign in the natural-food store.

"I was in a few of these houses. Most, I think, may have been condemned by the city. In one the toilet plumbing—one toilet for a dozen people—hadn't worked for days, but they used it anyway. Fill it up, and pressure the weakest one in the house to dump it. Probably on a scruffy patch of veggies they were growing in the back yard. Honestly, the houses were filthy. I think that the kids deliberately broke all the rules they were required to observe at home. Another protest.

"These house communes cracked up too. Probably because of the

Joanne-hates-Zeke-and-Grant-wants-to-sleep-with-Joanne-so-who-does Zeke-sleep-with? routine.

"They were intelligent, no doubt of that, but they just did not have the smarts. Some were getting it, some never would."

While Eric was refilling our glasses I asked, "Why did the whole thing fade out so quickly?"

When he returned, he said, "Well, my theory is this. When those who I've just said finally got the smarts looked around, they said, 'What the hell am I doing in this situation, wearing these ratty clothes, not getting enough to eat, being cold, sick, shacking up with that dumb dame in the sandals, long skirt, bomber jacket, poor complexion from eating the wrong food, stringy hair, and both of us looking like losers?' Or words to that effect. Anyway, the smarts went back to Winnipeg, Toronto, Boston, wherever, and the not-so-smarts didn't have the brains to carry on. Something like that. Maybe the smarts told themselves that this was something they believed in, but it was never going to work in a thousand years, so to hell with it. So now they're lawyers carrying fancy leather briefcases or teachers striking for higher pay for less teaching. Or maybe union leaders keeping kids like they once were out of the apprenticeship plan. The girls? Mammas, maybe. Secretary to the sales manager? Nurse maybe. Hell, maybe even whores. They sure had plenty of practice on Fourth Avenue.

"There is evidence around that its side effects are still with us, but I don't know. When somebody like you asks me what happened to the hippie movement, to the flower children I counselled and fed and showered, I always say, 'In the end, the flowers fell into the mud.'"

"Eric," I said, "earlier you told me about Lori who wanted to see Fourth Avenue and that got you started on it. What happened to her?"

He roared with laughter, slapping the chair's arm hard, and said, "That's the whole story right there. I phoned her next April and told her just what I've told you, shorter, of course, and a bit more gory."

"And?"

"She thanked me and that summer she got a job as a supervisor at a playground. That fall she went to university, graduated, got a job in the provincial department of recreation, or whatever, married a geologist, now has a kid of her own and plays golf in summer and bridge in winter. Just like all the other girls who *did* spend a summer on Fourth Avenue."

"So Many of My People Die..."

I was staring at my Underwood, thinking that if a thing was not worth doing, it was not worth doing well. The article I was working on, I decided, was not worth doing although when I had done the interview it had seemed like a good idea. I was glad when the phone rang.

"Hi!"

I would have recognized that voice if I had picked up a field telephone in a water-filled shellhole in no man's land in 1917. It was Gerry, a guy I had known for a long time although we had seen each other only two or three times a year lately, and usually by chance.

"Look, you still doing that book, the one you told me about?" and before I could answer he carried on: "Well, I was up to Lytton yesterday and I pulled in to a gas station on the highway and this Indian asked me I was going into Vancouver and was there a ride? I said, sure, and all the way down she sure gave me an earful. Apparently she's a kind of roving missionary or a perambulating social worker or something like that. Interesting as hell."

I broke in; "Gerry, you picking up squaws? At your age? For shame. Dangerous too, if you don't know it."

"Naw, not this one. This one's what you might call kind of special. Not too young, not too old. Fifty, maybe? She talks like she's been pretty well educated and she knows one hell of a lot about things. You could say she was a pretty neat lady. Anyhoo, old boy, it wasn't until we were about the Port Mann Bridge when I mentioned you and the book you were writing about people..."

"About people and places and peregrinations," I interjected.

"Exactly, kid. Well, she's got a lot to say—not about herself, but about the people she works with, Indians, kids on the Skid Road, the things she does to help them, that sort of thing. You might get some good stuff. Hell, I know you would. Want to try?"

I said sure. What was her name and phone number?

"I think she said it was 'Mark' or 'Marv.' Something like that. Anyways, short, starting with an *M*. No phone number. Seems she travels a lot, here and on the prairies, and she always stays with friends. Anyway, she seems to have an unofficial office in the Royal when she's in town. She'd like to talk to you and says she may be there for ten minutes or two hours, just depending. I can't see the harm of you going over there tomorrow, about 11:00 A.M. Ask the bartender if he knows a lady named Mark. Somebody there should know."

"What's she look like?"

"Indian. West Coast, she said. Color like an oversmoked sockeye. Kind of husky. Blouse, one of those shiny blue rain jackets. Black slacks. A black purse. Smokes a lot."

"Hell, that could fit two dozen down there. They all dress like that. Well, I'll try. Might be worth something."

"Take care, guy, and don't get scalped."

The Royal is on Vancouver's East Hastings and is part of the notorious Skid Road. Inside, it is neat and quiet, rather dim, a place like a club to many old men who are waiting out their lives sitting alone or in twos or threes, talking quietly among themselves. Yugoslav fishermen, Finnish loggers, Germans, Dutch, Scots, a lone Chinese, an old, old man who comes in, drinks two drafts, and leaves on his own schedule, never talking to anyone. There is much talk of the old days and, as in many hotels around, probably more fish are caught, more gold found, and more timber felled than occurred in any ten years in B.C. There also is the businessman slipping in for a pair of quick beers and the unemployed and those on welfare counting the money they can afford to spend that day, plus a few wise hookers who know it is too early to ply their trade and foolish young ones who feel they might be lucky enough to turn a trick before noon.

There are also Indians. Many of the men and youths are in cowboy boots; they slouch, hands in pockets, and wear their cheap black hats blocked Chilcotin cowboy style. They are usually from the west coast of the island and wouldn't know how to saddle a horse if they could catch one. An aged couple, loaded with parcels and brown bags with 'Army & Navy' printed in blue letters on the sides, come in for a couple of beers, probably off their fishboat docked at the foot of Campbell Avenue and more than likely much more affluent than their garb indicates. Young girls, alone or in pairs, come through the swinging doors from Hastings Street and look furtively left and right for a friend who might buy them a drink to start off their day, a day that has no meaning or reality anymore.

Time really has little meaning for most of them here. Nobody is doing anything and nobody is going anywhere. It is quiet except for the clicking of balls on the small pool table at the rear, the low hum of conversation, and the voice of the bartender saying, "Okay, four up." There will be no fights in here, in contrast to other pubs around. If one did start, the huge waiter, working the Royal until fishing starts, would cover sixty feet in six strides and that would be it!

A patrol comes in, as they do several times a day. Police. Big men. Young. Hats square on their heads, signifying absolutely no nonsense. Two-way radio, cuffs, billy, gun, neat, purposeful, two very tough guys who know that one mistake can mean their own deaths. Fresh information on Skid Road activity since the end of their last shift has been programmed into their minds and they search the room, every corner, while looking straight ahead. They make the circuit without speaking to anyone except the waiter.

I ask the waiter if he knows anyone here, an Indian woman, maybe fifty, called 'Mark' or 'Marv.' He says no, and I look at my watch, ten minutes to twelve. Maybe she's gone. I'll give her twenty-five minutes more. The waiter came back, saying, "There was an Indian lady in here earlier looking for a guy who might be you. You Barry?" She told him she'd be back, and I asked him to be on the lookout for her. About ten minutes later I could see him pointing me out to a woman, Indian, windbreaker, black slacks, black purse.

She came over, smiling, and stuck out her hand. "I'm Mary," and I wonder how Gerry could have missed her name. We moved to another table away from the bar and I asked her if she wanted a beer. No, but she'd like a tomato juice. She asked me what exactly I did and I told her, briefly. She seemed amazed, asking, "You say you can make a living that way?" I shrugged and changed the subject, asking her if she usually came to the Royal when she was in town.

"Usually you'll see me in the tougher hotels, the places where everybody is mean. Mean drunks, mean junkies, mean hookers, mean pimps, mean everybody. I kind of use this place as a little office sometimes. There won't be anyone to disturb us. I just got in yesterday with your friend and was out in Richmond for the night, so people won't know I'm in town yet. So, what do we talk about? Something for a book, he said. Lots of books have been written about Indians, but I never saw one of them do any good. People still look at us and say, 'Ah well, just another dumb Indian.'"

I asked her about herself and she said she had been born on a gillnetter coming into Port Alberni from the Broken Islands where there was a fish camp. That was forty-seven years ago, she said. Three years later a seiner going up the canal had swamped the boat her father was running and he drowned. It was Depression times and her father had been more than lucky to get on a white man's boat. The gillnetter overloaded although they did not even know if they could sell the catch. An Indian in the water, and they are notorious for being unable to swim. She shrugged as if to say 'the same old story.' Her mother left her to the nuns and went to Vancouver with a white man. The nuns put her through grade ten, all the while extracting about ten hours of kitchen and laundry-room time out of her, seven days a week. However, she could thank them for their beneficence. Unlike almost all Indian girls, she had a good education and knew table manners.

In the late forties she went to Vancouver and stayed with a family she had known in Port Alberni and for three years it was summers traveling with other girls in the back of beat-up trucks, following the fruit harvests through the State of Washington and up into the Okanagan, and the rest of the year working as a flunky in a succession of gyppo logging outfits up and down the coast.

"In oh, about 1953, I got married to this breed from Rupert. We lived on his boat and for three years I never got rid of the smell of fish and gas and booze. In that last year I had my little girl, born just like I'd been, on the boat, and the women from the other boats delivered her and gave me clothes and things. It was no good, though. I gave the little girl to my sister who wanted her and could look after her and give her things, little nice things, that I couldn't. This guy, he used to hit me around and I was sometimes sorry I didn't push him over the side when nobody was looking and gaff him through the throat," and she made a vicious swipe as though striking a flopping salmon.

An Indian came up to the table, grinning foolishly, drunk at noon, and she said, "Go away. You'll probably be dead tomorrow," and she made a gesture I had often seen among West Coast Indians. The right arm extended halfway and the hand, palm out, makes an arc. Done the way Mary did it, the gesture meant 'Go, I am in command here and I've made my decision.' A sign of authority by a person in control.

"Sorry," and I said there was absolutely no need to be. She said he was from Ahousaht and she had known him for years. There was no hope for him and she wanted to spend all her time with the younger ones for whom there *was* hope.

She tapped her glass and said, "You understand, white people think so many Indians are alcoholics. They may be, but not in the white man's way. It is hard to describe. The older Indians drink because of the despair they have. The young ones drink because they see their parents doing it, and when they've been out in the white man's world, then they get despair too. An Indian's whole life is despair.

"I think alcoholism is in their head. You give two Indians two or three glasses of whiskey, two-ounce shots, and then give one fellow more and more shots, and he gets drunk. You give the other guy just water and coloring, and he thinks it's rye, and he gets just as drunk as his friend. Kind of like it's in the head, you know.

"So many of my people die of the results of alcohol, like getting stabbed to death or they're hit by a truck as they cross the highway or they fall in the chuck and drown or sleep out in the bush and get pneumonia and they're gone. But they don't seem to die of booze the way a white man does.

"I got to stop the young boys and girls from starting in the first place. My God, that's hard. Tell an Indian kid he can't have beer like his friends and he's going to get that beer any way he can and, by God, that kid is going to drink as much of it as he can.

"I was talking about men and boys, getting hit by a truck or stabbed to death, that sort of thing; but I am more concerned, my work really is among the girls. So many die, oh, so sad, because when they come to town from the reserves, their villages, they just can't cope. A coroner here in Vancouver said once that when one of our girls comes to Vancouver she soon finds she has nowhere to go but to the Skid Road, and the day she steps over that line she signs her own death warrant."

"Prostitution?"

"Yes, that's it, right down the line. They have no money and they hang around and a white guy comes along and the girls—they are not angels and I've never said they were—but when a white man comes along with money in his pocket and buys them whiskey or wine and takes them to a room, they are lost. Gone. They get drunk, they do what they do, they are punched or strangled or thrown out of a window. Anyway, they die. They may be there one day and the next they are not and nobody wonders why. Where did they go?

"I know a social worker for the city and she told me they don't bother too much about Indian girls and I asked her why? She said something about the girls being wards of the federal government and I said no, they are not. When they are on their reserves, yes, they are; but in this city, in Kamloops, Prince George, Williams Lake, Calgary, Regina, Winnipeg, no, they are off the reserve and they should be helped like any other person who's in trouble. She was very nice about it, but she said our girls don't come forward and say they are in trouble, they need help. Their background, you see, teaches them to distrust these people. It is too bad, but they know that if they go they will be sent back to their village and the reason they left the village is because they didn't like it, or they were kicked out of it, or were afraid to be there. It is like that Catch-22 situation."

Mary paused and to prompt her I asked, "Who does this to these girls?"

"The white man. Always. Never a native. If one of our guys sees a young girl in trouble he might see me on the street and say, 'Mary, a kid from Tofino, she's hanging out at the Balmoral and you better look her up. See what's happening.' No, it is the white guys who are it. They take her to a beer parlor and get her drunk and then drunker and if they buy her a meal she is lucky. But usually they just take her to one of these hotels around here and do what they do and then kick her out, out the window, down the stairs. The boss doesn't care. Half these hotels, not this one, should be shut down. The girl, she may ask for money and maybe she gets it, but so often, so often, she wants somebody to talk kind to her. These girls are not stupid, you know. They are uneducated. In a world where education means everything, even if it is a piece of paper saying they are educated but they just went through eight or ten grades learning nothing, those people are ahead of our people. Look"—and she rapped the table sharply with her glass, signaling to the waiter for another tomato juice—"Look, our girl will know how to run a fishboat, caulk it, mend a net, clean fish, smoke it, can it, dig clams, trap a marten, otter, skin it, tan it, look after the younger brothers and sisters like a mother, fix an axe cut with things she finds in the bush, shoot a rifle and kill seals that eat the salmon, all these things. She may not know how to run an electric can opener, which is all the city girls her age know how to do."

A burly type, six feet and two hundred pounds, stopped at the table and said, "Mary! Back again, ho ho. Protecting all the tarbrush girls still?"

Mary laughed and said, "Mike, you get along, you're blocking the view," and he laughed and reached into his shirt pocket and dropped a twenty on the table and said, "Get on with your good works."

When he left, she said, "That Mike. Used to be a faller at Camp Five and now he's running cat up Rivers Inlet somewhere. He's a good guy, a good white man. That's the way I can operate. The good white guys give me money. They know I'm not going to spend it on booze or put it away for my old age. I'm going to use it on my girls, help them. That's all I can do. Tell them where to go, and how to go.

"That Mike. Running cat, he makes maybe $250 for a long day. Board and room, maybe five a day. Company flies him in and out. He's got money, so if he wants a girl he goes to the Hotel Vancouver or any of them and orders one for the night. He's down here on Skid Road because he likes it here, his friends are here, and if he wants to fight he can find a fight here easily."

I said, "Mary, you were telling me about your life. I think you got as far as kicking out your husband."

"Not much to tell. I cooked for about six years in logging camps, around the island, along the Skeena, a couple more years in the Charlottes. I was a good cook, a good camp cook. Not a restaurant cook. In camp the most important person is the cook. Logging is logging, so a good cook makes the difference. The boss gets good men. Pick and choose, like. Once in the Charlottes the superintendent wasn't filling out my weekly grub list as I'd marked it, and I went and I said I was quitting, and he said, "Okay, Mary, see Figures in the morning. You're too aggressive for a Siwash." That night I went to every table at dinner and told them I was quitting because the super wasn't filling out the grub list like I'd made it and I wouldn't feed them on the junk he was ordering. Next morning I went to see Figures, the bookkeeper, and there was about thirty guys there too. Figures asked what was up and a faller said that the superintendent was cutting back on their groceries and that I had packed my duffel. The guy said to hold everything and ran for the boss and when he came—because thirty guys walking down the trail would wreck his operation and cost him his job—he told me, 'Mary, please don't quit,' and I said, 'Nerts. I want my money.'

"The big faller said, 'Super, what's her money?'

"'Just over $300 clear, end of the month,' I said, and this big guy threw his hat on the ground and jumped on it and said, 'Super, Mary from right now gets $600 a month clear, and if Vancouver won't okay it, then I'll take it out of your pay. She gets it, we stay, and no goddammed cribbing on our food list. You don't, this camp walks out. Half of us can go to Crown Zee and the other half to M & B. Take your choice.'"

Mary said, "The fool had no choice. I stayed and although there were only about ninety guys in that camp, the other six thousand loggers on this coast know about that story. They know what I'm doing now with my girls. Like Mike there, he knows the story and about the girls. That's why he drops off a bit of money. They know I'm honest. A lot more than a few of them have wrecked native girls, and if it is guilt, then it is guilt. Those guys are great, the best, tops in my book.

"I went to Calgary and got a job cooking. This time in a restaurant. You don't see many logging shows on McLeod Trail. I was walking home from work late one night and there is this little bundle of clothes in the gutter. You say clothes don't cry? No, this was a girl, about seventeen, off the reserve at Gleichen and she had been raped and beaten up by some guy. A white guy. I took her to the little apartment I had and put her into a tub of hot water and cleaned her up and fed her boiled eggs and toast and tea, and she told me about the life she was living. A few months' work, stoop labor, in the beet fields at Taber. They worked by the acre and it was up to the farmer to decide what they had earned. It was awful. They were working for just about nothing. She stayed with me for two weeks and I took her to the restaurant and I said to Mr. Michelson, I said, "Mr. Michelson, this is my friend Stella and if you want me to stay on this grill, you're going to give her a job at two bucks an hour. He couldn't say much, and she worked like a horse, never stopping, and even Michelson, Jew that he was, was impressed and said he would give her two dollars and fifty cents an hour if she stayed. But no, when she had about $250 and clothes of mine that I'd remade and new shoes and was well fed, she said thanks, Mary, but she was going out on her own. That was fine as I like to live alone anyway, and I said give me a phone call at work if you need me, but she said no, she'd go her way and get a nice job in some other restaurant and find a room and everything would be okay. She was such a pretty little thing and so smart and quick, and I figured she'd make it."

Just then, an Indian girl about twenty, hair everywhere, face bloated, jacket scuffed and dirty, stopped at the table and hesitantly said, "Mary?" The waiter was bearing down on us with his six-yard strides and Mary put up her hand, palm up, that West Coast gesture saying "Keep out of this, I'm in control" and he stopped and shrugged and left.

The girl said, "Mary, Joseph said he saw you coming in here. I'm in trouble. My father will kill me."

Mary said, "Josie, sit down. Don't cry," as the girl was weeping. "Tell your friend Mary about it," and when the girl pointed, she said, "Josie, this fellow's okay. Just say what happened. Don't cry."

I went to the bar and got a glass of tomato juice and talked with the barkeep for a couple of minutes and he shook his head and said, "That Mary. What a nice old lady. All the stray cats and kicked dogs, she looks after them. She gives this place a good feeling when she walks through that door."

I walked back and the girl had gone, so Mary took the tomato juice, saying, "She wouldn't have drunk it anyway."

She said the girl had told her she'd been picked up by a man in the Ovaltine Café and he'd bought her a hamburger and coffee and when she'd drunk half of it he'd filled up the cup with rum. He told her he was taking her to his room and when she said no, he began talking dirty to her and then he kicked her leg hard. She started to cry and he leaned across the table and punched her in the mouth. The girl said she grabbed the glass off the table and broke it in half and shoved it in his face and ran out of the place.

"I told her this guy wouldn't report it to the copshop. They never do. I guess she knew that, but she was afraid he'd find her on the street and beat her up. That's why she went to Joseph and he told her he'd seen me coming in here and that's why she came. I gave her two dollars and my cigarettes and told her go to the Savoy and have something to eat and I'd meet her there in half an hour."

"Do you think she will?"

"Yes, I think so. Then again, maybe she won't."

"What will you do if she is there?"

"I don't know. Everyone is different, but they're all the same in one way. They want some kind words. A bit of kindness. You know, they are so lost. So vulnerable. Maybe I can get somebody in the social welfare to look after her. I don't know. They've been saying for years that I'm a nuisance down there, but I keep coming back for my girls.

Maybe she will let me phone her father. I've met him. He's a good man and he's got a troller. That makes him wealthy. If she says fine, I'll phone him. Do you want to hear about her?

"Okay. She came to this town about a year ago. Her father, who has some pull, got her a job with the Vancouver Public Library. She has a good education and is smart and they put her behind a desk in the library, sorting cards or something like that. She is not trained as a librarian, but anyway I never did think that job was worth four years of college, or however much it is. So one day, there she is. I'd call her the library's token Indian. You know, hire an Indian to show how liberal and broadminded you are. Bullshit. Excuse my Siwash. So, this woman comes in and you can see her turning up her nose when she sees the kid. She must have been a mean one. You know, husband a top executive with some lumber company. Takes his secretary to a hotel room at noon and puts on his expense account that he'd taken some visiting executive to lunch at a French restaurant. Kids spoiled rotten and going bad. Big house in Kerrisdale. She makes some nasty remarks about what time is the next powwow and gets nastier and maybe she had one too many martinis for lunch at the country club. She goes to see the head librarian and gives her hell, saying how come my daughter did not find a nice, cozy job like that Indian has? The truth probably is that daughter wouldn't take a job if it was handed to her on a silver platter. I don't know what happened after that and neither does Josie, but some pressure must have been put on and yes, you guessed it, she was fired. No, not fired. That's too crude. She was told the budget had been cut or something.

"She tried to find another job but no luck, and her savings ran out and she wouldn't phone her father, so what's next? Skid Road. Where she knows people from the island. Friends. People to say hello to."

I said I found it hard to believe that one woman could get a girl fired, and even if she could, why would she? Why would she?

Mary said, "I don't know this woman but if you put her in a man's clothing you would find her down her on the Skid Road. Do you know what she'd be doing? Right. She'd be picking up these girls and abusing them. Getting them drunk. Punching them. Hurting them. White guys do it their way. She doit her way. End of story."

"Mary," I said, "let's go back. You were talking about this girl in Calgary. Stella, I think you said. What happened? You seemed upset when you were talking."

"I'm always upset, but she changed my life. Okay. She moved out and two night later, just two nights, I get a call from the matron in the city jail. Yep, she's there. Drunken and beaten up. My God, she couldn't have gotten across Centre Street that night before she fell among thieves. I told the matron to hold her until 1:00 A.M. when I got off and I picked her up. Stella was half sober. Her money was gone. She was sick and beat up. She wouldn't know the real meaning of the word, but she felt contempt for herself. I took her in again and I said, what will I do? Mary, what will you do? I couldn't send her back to Gleichen where those Blackfoot braves had turned the town into a hellhole. I didn't think I could get her a decent job, but Mr. Michelson probably would take her back as scrubber and dishwasher. She did it good but she didn't like it, so she'd probably leave again. Mary, what do you do? There I am, at three in the morning, drinking tea and Stella is washed, fed and in bed and probably dreaming bad dreams. What did I do? I prayed. I prayed like I had never prayed before. I think the spririt entered me and told me to walk in the world and help the young girls of my people.

"The next night I asked Mr. Michelson if I could get on the day shift, and after a lot of humming and saying, well, we'll see, and me saying, no, I want to know now. He put me on days. When I went on the new shift the next week I started going downtown at night. I didn't start here, like some people think. I started in Calgary. If I saw a girl who looked like she was in trouble, drunk, hurt, sad, I'd talk to her. I had my wages money and a lot I had saved when I was in the camps. My husband had died, that no-good guy, and left me money. I got $3,000 after they sold his fishboat. The band buried him. So, I'd help these girls and I'd talk to the Salvation Army major and they helped a lot when they could. The mission too. I went to the city and a snotty little clerk asked me who the president was of my organization and the names of the members of the board of directors. I said it was just me, helping girls who didn't trust themselves no more. He practically threw me out of the office. That's how dumb I was.

"I'd go to the library on Saturday morning and read up on things about Indians, things I didn't know. Boy, did I get an eyeful. Then I read that in Saskatchewan more than 90 percent of the women in jails were Indians or half breed and I said, Mary, that place needs you. So I went to Regina, and good references from Mr. Michelson got me a job cooking and I did the same thing. Helping girls who didn't know how to help themselves. Then one fellow at the Salvation Army told me about Main Street in Winnipeg and I went there and it was very bad. Very, very bad. I worked there and got a bit known and the cops would say, Mary, there's a girl in such and such a café and maybe you should go and see her. So I would. I'd try to help her. Get her a room. Get some food into her. Take her to the free clinic. It is amazing how many of these girls have some venereal disease. Ulcers, too. At that age. You do what you can. I'm known to people who can help. I go here, there and there's always a job for a good cook. If I can't find that I'll wash dishes. I once worked in an egg-candling plant. I travel by bus or somebody knows somebody who is going my way in their car. I don't stay in Vancouver much in the winter. Winter is the worst time for everybody in those prairie cities. Oh, it is so cold. I am scared of winters. But I go."

The two patrolmen came in again, an indomitable two-man Roman phalanx, and as they came to the table they both nodded and passed on.

"I'd say that is a compliment, Mary."

She laughed, a good strong laugh.

"Oh, such good boys. I think they go through a lot before the chief decides who to put on. Strong, hard, but undertstanding too."

"Mary, just what are you accomplishing?" I asked.

She paused, drummed her fingers on the table, looked at the opposite wall, and you could imagine her throwing my question in the air and slamming it as it came down, the way one whacks a tennis ball.

"About one-tenth of what I want to do. You know, it is very hard. My worst enemies, you know, are not really the bad white guys and their money and their fists. The girls themselves. Once they pass a certain point, have done so many things, they don't want to be helped anymore. Maybe some call me a busybody, but I try to help these kids. I pray to Our Holy Mother I can help them. I pray hard, and I know she listens. But the girls, do they listen? It is frustrating. Sometimes when I am praying I am crying. Nobody wants to help. 'Oh, she's just an Indian,' people say. 'She puts the money into her own pocket.' I don't. I've fed girls when I am hungry myself. My boys, I call them, like Mike the logger, they help. They understand. But others don't and I will not, will not, will not beg. If I won the lottery I would live in a tent and spend the money helping my people.

"Oh, I suppose I should listen to what other people say and forget this, but I can't. My heart won't let me. But I help a girl one night, two nights, for a week, and what do I know she's up to when I don't see her again?"

She was weeping softly.

When she stopped, I said, "Mary, what about the girl that was in here? The one who worked in the library."

She replied, "Josie. I'm going to see her now. At the restaurant. If she's there I'll feel a little bit of hope. If she is in the beer parlor next door and some guy is buying drinks, then I won't have any hope. She won't come with me to get help. When I went to Winnipeg four months ago she was bad. Now she is worse. I think she has crossed over that line..."

10

Ah! When Sweet Hopes Come True

"There's no people like show people," but they are not all alike. The major difference between Laurie and Lillian is that Laurie always refers to her future as "my career," while Lillian speaks of her work as her life.

Laurie the singer is young and talented and very ambitious, and her capacity for hard work is, I find, terrifying. Lillian the actress is a gifted performer who has seen it all, done it all, and, with a candor that is refreshing, she says she is happy to accept what life chooses to hand her and do the very best with it.

Laurie is going for it, reaching for the top, and she believes enough in herself to feel that she'll make it. The life of an entertainer is all she wants, all she ever wanted even as a child. Lillian, also as a child, wanted to be an actress and she chose to remain in Canada, even if it limited her opportunities. Applause is music to her ears because she knows she has reached her audience. The quiet that falls over the room as Laurie approaches the stage is what she needs to make her sing her heart out.

Both are my friends, and if they knew each other I know they would like each other very much.

"All I Ever Wanted To Do Was Sing"

It was after her first show Thursday night in the large, noisy, smoky neighborhood pub, Piper's Inn, Nanaimo, and she was relaxing in the owner's upstairs suite, sipping a 7-Up, wiggling her toes and looking at the first question I lobbed.

Who is Laurie Thain?

She waited for it to reach its apex, hanging there for the split of a split of a second and as it slid she swung: "Well, I was born in Terrace in northern British…"

I held out my hand, palm first, and said, "Look, we're friends and this is not a big interview for *Variety*, so let's get to that later. Just friends talking."

"Okay, but nobody has asked me that question. I mean that way. Sure, let's get on with it."

Okay, twenty-seven years old, and yes, born in Terrace in Northern British Columbia, five foot nothing and packing around about ten pounds more than Weight Watchers would approve, and she wears what you'd call a pert face with a short nose that does a little zip upward. She has pageboy hair styling and gray eyes, somehow just the eyes you'd associate with the name. She's a singer. Western. Folk. Ballads. She's been at the game professionally for more than four years and is the only female singer of her type in Canada. She moves around, covering ground. Constantly. A one-gal act. A tough-minded but also sensitive lady traveling alone on the roughest entertainment circuit of all. Not even a cat for company. Her caravan is an '80 Firenza with 110,000 kilometers on the clock and her worldly goods—clothes, books, typewriter, guitar, sound equipment, and a host of other things—are stowed here and there with what seems abandon but is actually practiced precision. When she drives off into the night after the last show, she could be heading for an engagement three hundred miles away, through the mountains, across the prairies, and the springs of her auto are bent down.

Her turf is mainly Alberta and British Columbia, the tough neighborhood pubs, the downtown clubs, and some of the most elegant rooms in the multi-million-dollar hotels in the big cities. She takes them all in stride. A cautious first night to size the place up, as a batter studies a new pitcher, and then she plays them with the expertise that comes from a thousand nights on the road.

Before the Piper's, she had done a charity telethon in Vancouver, along with Diahann Carroll, Shari Lewis, Pat Boone, and Canadian luminaries like Juliette. They got paid well but Laurie Thain did a freebie, an insult to Canadian talent by the promoters—and that probably frosted her because of her fine list of credentials. But the telethon, her fourth, gave her lots of exposure and that is the name of the game, although it is not the bottom line. The bottom line is still big money. That will come later. No pay is the punishment for daring to be a Canadian.

"It was fun. Everybody, friendly, loose, laughing. Jokes, you know. We're not a bunch of entertainers competing; we're singers goofing around. Nobody talked down to me, and why should they? If they make money at these things, fine. They know more about how it's done. I will too, soon.

"I'll tell you a story. I was talking to Shari Lewis, a very big star and a wonderful person, and Diahann Carroll, all Mrs. Feathers and Gold Lamé, comes up and butts in to talk to Shari, and Shari turns back to me and we keep talking. Then Diahann Carroll, what a beautiful dame, says, 'I don't believe we've met,' and puts out her hand.

"'Right. I'm Laurie Thain, B.C. singer.' She says, 'A what?' I say, 'A B.C singer. British Columbia. That's the province you're in now.' She says, 'Listen, I heard you warming up tonight and you sing beautifully. You're not a B.C. singer,' she says, 'you're a singer.' I'm not sure what she meant."

I said, "Simple. She's one of the top singers anywhere and she was saying, 'I accept you.'"

"Yeah, yeah! Hey, yeah! She accepts me. Definitely. They all accept me," and you could almost feel her heart doing a little jig of joy.

"Let me put it this way," I added. "What she said was that she was accepting you as a professional. It is something you should think about. Hard. When I go to a writers' conference there might be ninety-nine writers there from Canada and the U.S. I look for writers I can talk to, whom I accept. It is snobbery on my part to a degree, but it is also my professionalism. In her way, she's telling you to think, act, and be more professional."

"Yeah, sure, I see," and she got up to get another 7-Up from the fridge. She sat down again and saluted with the can and said, "This is about all I drink. Booze has killed more musicians and entertainers than drugs. If my doctor told me to cut out chocolate, I'd be sad; but if he told me never to have another drink again I wouldn't care. As for smoking, I just don't. Even the secondhand smoke hurts my throat, and anyway, that is worse than fresh smoke. But people come to watch me and they drink and smoke. It's all part of their fun and they're paying me. You know, it still gets me that I get paid for singing because it is all I ever wanted to do anyway."

I asked, "What was your big break? When did you hear that loud click in your head that told you that singing as a career was for you?"

She smiled and said, "There never was a click."

Laurie looked at her watch and said we'd have to go downstairs for her eleven o'clock show.

"Into the fray?"

"Sometimes. Maybe tonight. Never can tell."

She threaded her way through the tables, stepped up on the small stage, smiled a funny smile, not a hello smile but a "Hi, I'm glad you're still here and I'm here" smile. The talk was loud and she was going to have trouble getting to the back of the room because her voice doesn't have the power to bounce into the corners, but you find later that she has no intention of doing so anyway. She's no screamer.

Trouble came fast. A ruffian of about twenty-five staggered up, more than half smashed, and plunked down on the stage, and the front of the room quieted.

"You the singer?"

"Yes, sir, I'm the singer."

"Kinda little. Well, you better be bloody good because I'm not going to listen to a bunch of crap."

She paused a moment, thinking it out.

"He turned the speaker around so it was pointing at me. Now when I set up I'll spend as much as two hours getting the sound right. It has to be right. So, by doing what he did he sure got my attention fast. He was trying to wreck my performance. I told him so. Part of the audience was listening by now. I wasn't going to sing one note until he put that speaker right back. A voice called, 'Forget that asshole. Play "Lay Down, Sally."' There was some whistling and hooting and this guy knows he's the target. The audience hadn't done a whole lot of listening during the first show, but they're getting angry now. At this guy. He's boxed in between me and the audience. He's beginning to feel ashamed and humiliated, but still I can see he's bitter about something and wants attention. That's the only thing any heckler wants. I say, 'Hey, mister, you want to hear that one, "Lay Down, Sally?"' Naturally he says no. What else can he say? Well, he says, 'Play one of your songs,' and I smile at him because I am flattered. I tell him I will if he'll turn the speaker around, and he did. Then I sang the song to him and he was on my side for the rest of the show. You see, I had rescued him from his stupidity and the hostility of the audience. The audience was also on my side because they thought I was mighty cool in the way I handled it. That's positive thinking. You develop that, psychology in a way, when you've seen a lot and heard a lot."

No two audiences are the same, but any audience outside of an elegant dinner lounge is hard to handle. A rowdy town like Prince George will have a tough crowd on Thursday night, in from the bush and loaded for bear. The next night, quiet. They're paying attention from the first group of songs, as she shows off her voice and what she can do, and she grabs them.

"At times it is a terrific responsibility, you know. Sometimes I don't think I can handle it. A couple comes in and he's as old as my dad. I'll bet they have never been to this type of room before. Somebody told them that they would like me, so they came. They don't drink much and they just stare and I get nervous. Then after the first show they come up and say, 'Thank you very much. We had a lovely evening.' It always gets to me. How do you handle that? What the hell, who am I to stand there and sing when they are expecting too much? I don't know."

But she wants to get back to the Prince George Thursday Gang. Anywhere can be P.G. She doesn't know why Thursday is a tough night, but it is. When things go from roar to uproar she'll pretend to strum the guitar and will smilingly mouth the words. Parts of the room will realize the singing has stopped and they'll start yelling, "Hey, lady, no mike," and "Hey, you, no sound, no sound."

She'll yell, "What do you varmints care anyway? You weren't listening," and again she'll pretend to sing and play and someone will yell, "C'mon, lady, we're listening to you. You just don't know because you can't hear over the drunks."

Just a trick, but often just enough to get it moving as she wants it. Every entertainer wants attention. Otherwise they die.

"Sometimes I'll say to them, 'Hey, you out there, I'm doing everything right tonight and you're doing everything wrong. I'll have to get the manager to book in a new audience tomorrow night.'"

Isn't that too subtle? Yeah, she concedes, but she likes to make them try and think at times. People don't want to get too much involved with their brains while drinking.

She sips her pop and says, "You know, I don't want to play to a room full of rowdies and drunks, but in this business you take what walks in the door. Some towns, that's all they seem to have. They're roaring around. Look, they are the kind of people who say, 'Let's go to the pub and have a good time.' They don't go to the pub for a bad time. But a good time for that kind of audience is profanity, dirty jokes and lots of them. Of course you can get laughs with dirty jokes. Low class. But you can be funny and entertaining and express yourself without being crude. Being crude is cheating.

"Western and country fans are the worst kind, and those in Alberta are by far the worst. They're like a bunch of spoiled children. They have no respect for what is being provided and they don't want a singer. They want a clown. Lots of comedy, lots of dirty stuff. If they were decent people they would give me the dignity I require, by listening to me."

A series of nights with a crowd like that bashes the ego, bruises the sensitivities but you've still got to get up there for four hours and sing, sing, sing, smile, smile, smile.

The worst nights are when she is down. The audience quickly picks up her distress signals. Their antennae are in good working order. She might have had a narrow miss against a eighteen-wheel freight truck on a mountain pass and hasn't quite recovered her nerve yet. A vital registered letter containing a contract hasn't arrived. She might have the flu. The last wage check has bounced—disaster. Her car might need extensive repairs.

"Not too long ago I felt very down. After four years of the hardest work anyone can do, I was about ready to quit. The main reason was, I have sunk every penny into making a single record and I wasn't getting any feedback from the disc jockeys on its air play. Everything in my future was riding on that record. Down, down. Why go on? But the next day I got a wonderful report on how good the record was doing and then I could go out there and really work. The audience feels it and everything was just fine again. But that was close. Your highs are high, but your downs are down, down, down."

If it had been down and out for the count, where would it have been next?

Not Terrace. That world is far behind her, but that's where it all began. A small city west of Prince George, heavy on logging and lumber but light on culture and sophistication, but yet not a Saturday-night fight town. Her father and his brother had a construction company and her mother had been a schoolteacher. There was an older brother, a younger sister, a normal childhood. It was not a musical family. Her mother had a fine voice but limited herself to singing tunes from *Oklahoma!* and *South Pacific* while she did the housework. Her brother and sister might have something going for them but they didn't care. Her father had an old violin and a repertoire of three tunes.

"I can see it now. Everybody in the living room and there would be Dad scratching away on his three tunes: 'Life in the Finland Woods,' 'Old Joe Clark,' and 'The Bear Went Over the Mountain.' Scratching them out," The memory set off a sustained fit of laughter, soprano, then shifting into a cackle.

Her brother had a guitar but since he was righthanded and Laurie a southpaw, she played it backward and upside down and didn't seem to be getting anywhere until she told her father she just had to have her own guitar. He plucked a Gibson's electronic out of the window of a secondhand store for $125 and low and behold, it was the fluke of the litter and had a million-dollar sound. It took time but she got an armlock on its personality and started to make creditable sounds. Talent was pretty thin in Terrace and by shopping around she was able to pick up a few dollars playing for May Day teas, a telethon, dinner parties, and service club bashes. She got to be known far and wide up and down the valley for her renditions of "Over the Rainbow" and "My Favorite Things." She wrote the school song at graduation and that fall went off to the University of Victoria for a year of physical education training. She switched to the University of British Columbia the next year and took her guitar along.

"I said to myself, 'Oh well, I'll try the big town but they'll tune me out.' Surprisingly, I was able to get a few dates now and then and they didn't turn me off. They liked me."

By the third year she decided that she would probably never teach physical education—supervising the girl's volleyball team, as she put it—but she'd rather die than let the folks at home think she was a quitter. Besides, a degree from U.B.C. was light baggage to carry around and might be useful later. So she picked up the degree.

Then she went back to Terrace, worked a bit with kids, and did some figuring.

"You know, when I play those tapes I made back then, I think they are awful. Just awful. But when I got back home after university I thought they were pretty good and I thought I was Miss Wonderful.

"Boy, did I have dreams. I couldn't wait until everybody was out of the house and I could stand up in front of the big mirror and pretend I was on 'The Tommy Hunter Show.' CBC TV, national, out of Toronto. I'd mime away and I couldn't even play the guitar any good.

"And, then, you know, going ahead a bit, I was on 'The Tommy Hunter Show,' and it was the loneliest time of my life. I couldn't believe it. These are professionals? Reading their cue-cards and everything. Those shows are taped, naturally, and I sang and everything went bang-bang, razzle-dazzle. I was good but nobody said I was good or bad. I went back to my hotel and I thought, 'Laurie, you're in Toronto and you just finished taping "The Tommy Hunter Show." Wow! This is the big time? Aaagh!

"So I said, 'All right, you said you always wanted to do "The Tommy Hunter Show." Well, you've done it. This is the big time, the biggest there is in Canada, and you're nowhere. Obviously your goals are nowhere.' So I had to go back to Terrace and reorganize myself."

She did some shows and people said she was good and some urged her to try out for the du Maurier Search for Stars, a cigarette company promotion held every year in Toronto to find new talent in Canada. Resolutely, she took her savings of $350 from the bank and flew to Toronto, not with high hopes but with a sense that if you're going to start, you've got to start in Toronto. She wasn't good enough, but she did break into the top forty-five and won $500. Back in Terrace again, she rehearsed and worked at writing songs and did more jobs here and there until it was du Maurier time again. This time she hit the target. She was selected to be the anchor singer on one of the three TV shows produced for CBC TV that went national, and her take-home pay was a very satisfying $2,000. More important though, she had had national exposure, but just as important, big names in Canadian entertainment told her they liked her voice and her style.

She went home again—to what? Well, people who hadn't given her the time of day now wanted an hour of it just to chat, when all she wanted to do was get on to the store and buy a carton of milk.

Laurie Thain looked at the town, and after the excitement of Toronto she knew she couldn't stay any longer. The house she had grown up in now looked so small. She had been brought up in a happy and protected family and she had thought they were rich. Now, she knew they were a long way from that. Everything was locking into place. She had to move on.

"You say Terrace is not much more than a railroad station on the C.N.R. line between Prince George and Prince Rupert," she said to me rather defensively. "That is true, I guess, but I'm not like some entertainers and deny my old hometown. The people were good to me in those days and I was given a lot of opportunities and a lot of support. Sure, when I got back from Toronto the second time I got even more support, but those were people who had seen their little gal from Terrace, British Columbia, on national TV. But everybody was so happy for me."

She admitted that the du Maurier show was the big break in a career that had really not started, and it made her make the big decision. She was going to go down the road despite all the trouble that lay ahead, trouble she really didn't have a clue about. She thought she knew how to survive, but something told her she had to design the ideal system for herself and make that work. She had so much to learn. She didn't even know what an arrangement was. She didn't know about agents or how they worked. She didn't know how to get an engagement, a booking. What was a contract? Did she need a lawyer? An accountant? A manager?

Getting a week or two in Red Deer and Cranbrook or Nanaimo was different from walking into the Terrace Hotel and signing up for a week in the dining lounge. She didn't know rates of scale, how much to charge, or more important, how much to accept. She knew enough to know that if she signed up with a big agency she would immediately be a has-been, just another singer in the stable. She wanted to be her own boss. The singer and her audience. Nothing between them.

It all came slowly. Equipment had to be purchased. She cherished the old Gibson but it wasn't good enough. She scraped together all she had and was smart enough to take good advice and buy two speakers at the rock-bottom price of $650 and a public address head for $900 and a $1,200 guitar for $800, and one wonders if she didn't use her little-girl-lost act in that deal. Beside the $30,000 or $60,000 worth of equipment some singers have, her stuff looked pretty ragtag and bobtail.

She smiled and said, "Sure, sure, you can have that much in equipment, but if you don't have the music inside you before you step up to the mike, then all the gadgets and gizmos are not worth much. That stuff might make you sound better, but it's not going to make you better. There's just me up there before the audience, without all this other stuff intruding."

She got moving around and people liked her, and management liked her attitude. Other entertainment people liked her and in a business with more backbiting and bitching per square yard than any other, that was a blue-chip asset. Somebody would hear her sing and would speak or write to another friend in the business and she kept moving on to other dates, and in a couple of years the bigger shots began to come. A month at the Château Lacombe in Edmonton. Another month at the Palliser in Calgary. The Chelsea, home of Country and Western in downtown Toronto, booked her for a month, on the recommendation of Billy O'Connor, the former TV star who had heard her on du Maurier. The pay had risen to $650, to $700 and up a week with room thrown in.

She incorporated her own company, Pure Pacific, to manufacture and distribute the records and albums she hoped to make. She scraped up $7,000 and friends kicked in another $2,000 in interest-free loans and she made a single, Laurie Thain, with "Lady, You're Gonna Lose Him" and "I Can't Believe I'm Leaving," a 45 rpm designed mainly for radio station consumption.

She knew she had to go first class—"all the way because there is no other way." An old friend in Toronto did the arrangements for both of her songs and his name on the label meant a great deal. She chose Century 21, a highly respected recording company in Winnipeg. Behind her she had a piano, guitar, steel drums, bass, and four good men on strings plus a three-voice vocal on her side. This just is not done in Canada, and it is never even dreamed of being done by a kid with a guitar from the boonies. But she did it! Two damn good songs, a fine voice, and a sound as professional as can be had in Canada.

After a slow start the record caught on and "Lady, You're Gonna Lose Him" had all the makings of a disc jockey's favorite, maybe because she gave it her best personal shot. None of this long-range bombardment from New York, Nashville, and L.A. No strident phone calls to musical directors. No hoopla. No high-powered tours where the famous entertainer does the radio station a great big favor by condescending to walk in the door and talk five minutes to a disc jockey. She went face to face with the men and women who chose the records for airtime. A small station in Vernon in the Okanagan Valley would be treated exactly the same as the powerful C and W Vancouver station CKWX.

She'd go into a radio station and ask the musical director to play it. "Please sir, just to let me know what you think. I need some feedback." He'd play it and yell, "This is Canadian? You're kidding! This is Canadian, made in Canada? Wow! Hey Joe, c'mon in here and listen to this. It's Canadian."

Their reaction, Laurie thinks, is entirely understandable because she feels that far too many Canadian entertainers who record are sloppy. They think they can get points in the Canadian content ruling just because they are Canadian.

"There are people who record in their basement or garage," she says with contempt, "and they expect radio stations to play it. To cover itself on the Canadian rule a station might play that schlock once. Then it is gone. A bad voice and a bad sound make a radio station sound bad. Simple as that."

Laurie knows just how important radio people are to her career, and while her name might register with only 2 percent of listeners when her record is played, it is 2 percent she otherwise would not have got. Two plus two plus two begins to add up. When she's passing through a town and hasn't met the station personnel, she'll stop if at all possible. She asks to see the musical director if there is one, or the top disc jockey. She often wonders if it is not her little-girl look as she stands at the counter that causes the receptionist, probably five years younger than she is, to take pity and get her in. Little girl, hah! Tough little girl.

"I've never once been turned down from an interview, and once they've talked to me and heard my record, they give me air talk-time and play the record I gave them and I've made friends in another town."

There is also a bit of flimflam involved because she believes that in many cases the disc jockey on the small stations might be the only person in town who wanted the job. Most are young and inexperienced, and often all they know about the big world of entertainment is what they read in the trade magazines they buy out of their meager salaries. They form their opinions from these hot-shot magazines and really don't have a clue as to how the music scene relates to their station's listeners. She waltzes in, happy, smiling, confident, and they think, gosh, here's a gal who is out there doing big things and she's got this record and it has a big sound and it is just great.

"I act country and I look country, but I don't think country and I don't feel country." She knows better than anyone that she is a product, packaged, and her job is to sell her talent.

She is the only female singer in Canada with her lifestyle. She is a nomad. A wandering troubador. Since her parents' divorce, she occasionally visits her father on the Sechelt Peninsula, north of Vancouver, where he is a commercial fisherman. Her mother lives in Mission, forty miles east of Vancouver, and she has a room in her house for Laurie when she's around. Her mother's address and phone number is on Laurie Thain's business card and that is the only tangible sign of permanence she has. There is also a family in Vancouver who have a room set aside for her when she's in town. That's it.

She's here, she's there, the red Firenza hitting the highways and byways in every season, the wonky alternator still not replaced although she knows it will one day out-wonk itself and leave her with a big headache in a small town that has no Dodge dealership.

In late fall, winter, early spring, those B.C. and Alberta highways can be murder, and that is when she is often afraid. There are long runs, often at night, between Red Deer and Jasper or Prince George and Cranbrook. And there are high winds, drifting snow, blizzards, glare ice, black ice, and sudden squalls. And worse, drunken drivers, fools and truckers on high beam, wandering cattle and jumping deer, and "every corner is trying to kill you."

Here's a typical first day on the road. It is four-thirty one Sunday afternoon and she has driven into a small Interior city three hundred long, long miles from Vancouver. She is tired and her gaze is blurry as she pulls in at the motel-pub-entertainment complex. She asks the clerk if she can have the key to the lounge. He'll try and find it. She starts lugging her suitcases and garment bags and boxes to the room that is awaiting her.

"Motels are just fine with me," she says. "They are geared for efficiency. You know where everything is. Clothes closet here. Bathroom there. Desk that way, bed by the window. It only takes me about half an hour to set up my little camp. Then I go to the desk and get the key and open up the lounge and I walk around it for about fifteen minutes getting the feel of it, even if I've played it before. I also get the smell of it, the booze and smoke of Saturday night in an Interior town. Then if I can't find someone to help me with my equipment, I lug it in to the lounge myself and I start setting up. I could do it in the morning but no, I want to do it now. I'm in a new town and I'm on a high. I fiddle and I fuss. I change things around and I test. Maybe an hour and a half goes by. Then when I know I have the right sound I can climb down the ladder a bit."

She usually gets her meals free but often just eats around the town. Juice, toast, jam, and coffee in the morning. She's a meat-and-potatoes gal at dinner. She's also conscious of a small weight problem and vows this time she's going to get some exercise. She never does. After dinner she takes her guitar and goes to the dark and silent lounge and rehearses for an hour, songs she's sung a hundred times because she claims she's never sung one song exactly the same twice.

Then she goes back to her room and she might write some letters— "I'm an avid letter writer"—and maybe do some accounting and business work and make a friendly phone call to the local station. If she has any friends in town she phones them and thinks about getting her hair done and finding a laundromat. On working days there are also four hours of entertaining to be squeezed in.

I laughed and asked how many hours in the day she'd like to have. She said, "If there were thirty hours that would suit me fine. I can't remember recently when I've said, 'Oh, what am I going to do today?'"

I could see she was thinking deeply and she said, "I can handle it now. In the future I might not be able to. I might have to hire a piano player with a voice if I moved up into doing just the big rooms in big cities. But he has to be the right guy. No second rater and no girl, any time. This is the Laurie Thain Show and I am The Girl!"

When she says "The Girl!" her voice always becomes tight and hard. Emphatic.

"A strong manager, that would be great; one who understands the work, the job; me and my music. Think of all the pressure he could take off me. I'd have more time for everything. Not just the big things but the little things. It's work, work, work, but that's the road I have chosen. I can't remember when I watched a TV movie. When I hit the bed I am asleep in ten seconds. I don't even wiggle. In the morning I get up and go feeling life around me again, about ten-thirty.

"You know, everybody likes me except chambermaids. They're always waiting around about eleven for me to clear out of the room so they can make it up. A while back I had to get up at eight-thirty and the chambermaid in the hall said, 'Oh, its only nine o'clock, dearie. What did you do, wet the bed?'

"I felt like saying, 'Look, you turkey, where were you at 3:00 A.M. when I was doing some paperwork and planning for today and trying to keep this show on the road?' Aw, well."

On the road, that endless road, she does some fraternizing with her audiences between and after shows, but only for a short time. People want to buy her drinks, but that is a no-no. Her lifestyle is so different they almost seem to consider her a freak. A tiny girl with a big guitar roaming the backwoods all by her lonesome. If she strikes up a rapport with a couple or a foursome she might accept a meal with them, usually Chinese. However, it seldom works out because they cannot understand her, and seem to expect her to say and do strange things, whereas actually she is as Canadian and down-to-earth as a prairie grain elevator. So, rather than endure the embarrassment of the inevitable slow-stop conversation with the five Chinese dishes still to come, she gracefully declines. The last thing she wants to do is hurt anyone's feelings, but hell, that's the way it is.

Laurie Thain held up her hand like a traffic cop and said, "And no emotional involvement. If I find a nice, intelligent, interesting guy and he's interested in my music and me, I might go for a coffee after work, or lunch the next day. But it is only sometimes okay, and mostly not okay."

Her eye is always on the future. Another TV show. A telethon, a big one. More songs to be finished or begun. More jottings in her notebook of life, which she hopes one day will become a book. Put away money for that new record. Pay off some debts. Do this, do that, and don't fall flat. Maybe the States and big money.

Tonight is the last night, Saturday, at The Piper's. Tomorrow she'll pack and head for Fairmont Hot Springs for two weeks, a long and grinding run through four ranges of mountains over bad December roads and "winter is out to kill you."

This is a good crowd, young, under thirty, reasonably quiet, beer drinkers one and all. She moves through the tables and mounts the stage, dressed in a fresh white shirt and blue soft velvet slacks. To many she is just another singer moving around, covering ground, singing somebody else's sound. The regulars know better and they begin clapping when she starts off with "Lady, You're Gonna Lose Him." She'll sing it as her sign-off number too. It means a lot to her. It could mean the big time. Then I notice she's gone into her Chicken Dance. It is one of the dances of the Blackfoot Indians. Hers consists of a little hitch of the right shoulder and she gives a little "yip." Then the left shoulder, and "yip." The little hitches are hard to spot and the "yips" are only heard within her own heart, and she doesn't realize she is doing this little dance, but it lends an endearing quality to her performance.

"That Applause—and You're Hooked!"

I had phoned Lillian two days before and asked if I could visit, just two hours of her time. She laughed and said time was something she had a lot of these days. She wasn't exactly suspicious, but people who have been in and out of the public eye for thirty years are a bit wary, and I almost detected a slight shift in the main gear in her brain that indicated, 'Easy Lillian, what does he want?'

Answering her question before it was asked, I said, "I want to talk to you about your career. About what an actress is and what makes her tick…"

She interrupted with another laugh and said, "You mean what makes an actress go on being an actress in these the most rotten of times?" Her voice was low and husky, yet smooth and assured, and I could not determine if she was onstage, projecting the woman who is ready to help a writer but somehow hesitant to open up her deepest thoughts.

I explained as best I could that I wanted her to tell the young ones coming up in her difficult and curious trade just what it was like a long time ago and what they could expect now. She said okay, and two mornings later I was parked outside her ground-floor apartment on Oriel Way. There was nobody home when I rang, so I just waited, looking around at this two-storey, low-rental, government-subsidized complex. The yellow-stained stucco walls needed painting; the grass was brown from lack of watering and scuffed bare in many spots from the hard running of children at play. The whole area was monotonous to one's eye, even debilitating, if one were presumptuous enough to believe he had a soul. In her window two geraniums flared, scarlet splotches of challenge to this rather drab world.

Then I saw her coming up the walk, lugging a brown bag, and as I went to meet her she called, "Hi, sorry. I went to the liquor store on Fraser because I thought you might like a spot of gin."

We hadn't seen each other for, oh, maybe six or seven years, and she laughed and said, "I guess you think I've grown older and you think I'm thinking that you have grown older. Well, we have! No way to stop it that I know, so relax and enjoy it. Here, take this bag and I'll find the key to this dump."

Inside, she hung up her coat and took the bag and went into the tiny kitchen and called, "Gin? If so, what with?"

I said no thanks, so Lillian put on water for coffee and came back. "Well, this is it, subsidized rental living and the rooms are small, but enough for us. I've only got my last boy, he's fifteen, with me now, and when he's gone I'll be banging around here like I was in a castle. I'm looking forward to it. So what have you been doing? Last night I could hardly sleep a wink, wondering what I should tell you, what kind of questions you will ask." And this woman with the golden hair shot through with white, a serene face, the bluest of eyes, and a full, matronly figure reached out and patted an overflowing box and laughed again, nervously. "I even got out all the clippings and photos and theater programs and all that sort of thing—stuff I haven't looked at in years. I'll show them to you later."

"No, Lillian, I'd like to see them now. Sort of gives me an idea where to start, although I usually just start at the beginning and go until the end."

"Okay. Here, this is one my father took of me when I was eight or nine, and I guess it was my first time on the stage. I think it was in some church basement. Some children's play but I can't remember what it was. That costume, I don't know whether the seamstress was making it for an elf, a sugar plum fairy, or a character out of *Winnie the Pooh*. For all I know, it was from the play the year before and they had just taken a few stitches here and a few tucks there and, yipes, a new costume. They did things like that in those days. It was in the Depression.

"These are jumbled up. This one is a review from the *Vancouver Sun*. It was a very good play by a local playwright named Perry. I don't know what happened to him, but he had plenty of talent. Everybody worked very hard on the production, and the audience just adored it and it looked like word of mouth would extend the two-week run or put us out touring the province. Then this theater critic went back to his office and wrote this review"—she waved it savagely—"he murdered us. It amounted almost to libel. I didn't think that was possible in Vancouver theater and the funny thing, if it is funny, is that this critic knew absolutely nothing about theater. He'd probably review *South Pacific* and decide it was a fine musical, but only after he'd read the reviews in the *New York Times*. Anyway, he went to Toronto where his lack of talent and understanding of playwrights, directors, and actors would be appreciated. Oh, we have to live with those kind of people. They are not really critics at all. Just little men with very big egos."

She dropped it on the floor and said, "I'm damned if I know why I even kept that one."

"Now here's one when I played the lead in *Born Yesterday*. Billy Dawn one of my favorite roles. A lot of what was in it is relevant today, you know. Profiteering. Big bad business. Crooked politicians. Cartels. It had a lot to say although most people treated it only as comedy."

I told her my favorite line was when Billy and Harry, the junk tycoon, had had a vicious fight and they faced each other across a double staircase and Billy Dawn said softly, "Harry, do me a favor..."

Lillian interrupted and yelled, "Harry, drop dead!" with as much malicious pleasure as Judy Holliday had used in her role as Billy in the Broadway musical and the Hollywood film.

"Now this little mimeographed sheet, it goes back a long way. It was the program for *Waiting for Lefty*. Everyone who came through the Depression must have seen that one. It toured everywhere, everyone saw it," and in a harsh and bitter voice, and pounding her fist on her knee, she screamed, "Strike! Strike! Strike!"

Those three words took me back to an evening in an unknown year in the Dirty Thirties when my father took me to a play in the gymnasium of Riverview United Church. A small group played *Waiting for Lefty*, vehicle of protest and at the time the expression of the sorrow and hate that the working man had for powers over which he had absolutely no control. It was a small stage, perhaps twenty feet wide by twelve feet deep, and although the actors tended to mill about finding space, they conveyed all the frustrations of those terrible years, and I remember that the cry "Strike! Strike! Strike!" electrified that predominantly middle-class audience who had expected to see just another evening's entertainment.

"John Garfield toured the United States in that one. His real name was Julius Garfinkle. He was a fine actor. Years later Senator Joe McCarthy and his gang went digging and they must have dug deep because they came up with his name as being the lead in that play and because it was anti-monopoly, pro-union, and maybe pro-Communism to a degree, they hunted him down. McCarthy ruined his career with his phoney accusations—that play was such a long time ago, but he ruined Garfield. They found him dead in a New York apartment. Suicide, many suspected, even though the papers called it a heart attack. I never knew him, of course, but I loved him.

"Here's a photograph. Dear me, is that me? When I was twenty-one or so, I'd say. Here, a lot of time has passed," and she handed me the picture while she went for the coffee. I was looking at one of the most beautiful young women I had ever seen. It was a three-quarter profile of Lillian, without makeup, posed against a black velvet cushion.

She came back and I said, "We'll start from here," and when I handed back the photo I said, "Great face."

"Great photographer," and she laughed.

"Okay, a bit of me first. When I was little my dad was away a lot and my mother would take me to the movies. They were dirt cheap in those days. A dime or so. I remember them all, but the one that sticks in my mind was *Tugboat Annie*. I don't know why, except my father worked on the tugs and Marie Dressler played the role of Tugboat Annie and I just thought she was the most wonderful actress in the world. That film and a hundred others, good or bad, were memories that will live forever in my mind. And we also went to the legitimate theater, touring companies. They'd come through Vancouver on a circuit. It was then that I decided I would be an actress."

She looked at the years-old picture again and said, "Other than that, you could say I was just another kid and then a teenager growing up. I was active in high-school theatricals and I began working at being an actress in my teens. I got small parts in radio and in the few productions going on around and about, but nothing exciting.

"Then I got on with Everyman Theatre. Sydney Risk was the director, and a wonderful one. We did all sorts of exciting things there and learned to play every kind of part. As I remember, the pay was thirty-five dollars a month. How we did it I don't know, but we managed. Just a bunch of crazy, hopeful kids.

"There was CBC radio, too, and that was a godsend. We were doing a half-hour drama a week, and it was the same in the late fifties with television. When we weren't working at acting we got odd jobs here and there. We didn't starve. Two of my odd jobs, as I call them, were working as a flunky in a logging camp and a desk clerk at the YMCA. Such diversity!

"Thankfully, with plenty of work and because I was not about to rush off and try myself in some strange place, I got a reputation for reliability and also, I am not ashamed to admit it, I was a good radio actress and a good television actress."

"I remember you in Paul St. Pierre's 'Cariboo Country' in the old days. That was a damn good series and you were first class in it."

Lillian said, "Oh, 'Cariboo Country.' What a wonderful time we all had doing that. Paul had written such wonderful scripts and we had such good actors in it; we all loved the series and Paul had such a real feel for those people in the Cariboo."

I said, "Remember that one he wrote where the little Indian girl, about ten, who had been shoved into the school to bring the number up to eight pupils because there were only seven white kids in the district and, without her, they wouldn't have local school?"

She said, "'The Education of Phyllisteen.'"

"Remember when the school inspector smelled a rat about what was going on and he went to the school and sat down next to Phyllisteen and asked her if she could read. He was very kindly but she was scared stiff and, of course, she hadn't been taught to read in that school or any school—but somehow she had picked it up just by sitting there, ignored, week after week. She opened a book on her desk. Poetry. He pointed to a verse and she began to recite:

> *What better way for man to die*
> *When facing hopeless odds*
> *Than for the ashes of his fathers*
> *And the temples of their gods.*

"The school inspector told Phyllisteen that if she remembered those words and lived by what they said, she had nothing to worry about."

Lillian said, "I'll bet there wasn't a dry eye in all of Canada when the viewers saw that. Paul is such a beautiful writer. That is one play I wish I had been in. Or was I? One forgets. So many roles, so many productions. No, I wasn't.

"I went on and on, working fairly regular. I got married, had three children, got divorced. I got good parts in radio, mainly. I didn't have to audition because I have a very good reputation and a director would phone and say, 'Lillian, I've got just the part for you. C'mon down and see me,' or better still, some young actor would say to a director, 'I'd like to play this part but I think the cast would feel better if Lillian plays the lead. Nowadays, of course, I have to audition like all the rest. Times have changed and there are so many good actors and actresses on the West Coast and the competition can be fierce."

Can an actress make a living in Vancouver?

She thought for a few moments. "Yes, if you work consistently. Like last year, I made more money than I had in a long, long time. It didn't come to $10,000 and that's good money for an actress if she decides to stay on the West Coast. I can live on that because I live here and I only have one son left at home."

I asked what makes an actress.

"The first time you're up there and you know you've done a good job and know your peers will respect you for your performance, and you hear that loud burst of applause when you've finished a scene. At one time I trained and became a qualified secretary, and I could work in an office now if I really had to—but I would detest it. You're hooked, of course, just like I was hooked as a kid when I saw *Tugboat Annie*, and you go on and get hooked and hooked again. You say to yourself, how many people in the world are really doing a job they really want to do?

"Also, we live in a world that sets us apart. Some childlike thing. The need for approval. Fantasizing, maybe. The need to express yourself. The need to, ah, I really can't put it. It is is not the need for money, because that moment when the applause blasts at you, that's when you're really locked into your profession. You think then of all the other jobs you had to do for money, and you say, 'What's money? I belong here.'"

I told her I had heard a great deal about acting schools. What about them: can someone be taught to be a top-line actress?

"No. I've never been to an acting school. I believe you can teach people about their craft. Voice projection, movements, learning to sing a bit, or dance—that sort of thing. It all helps, oh yes. But as for talent, the same as a writer, you can't teach someone to be a good actor. It is a talent, it's a gift. I think acting schools—and they are popular—it's a delusion on the part of the people going to them. They say, I've been to an acting school, so I'm an actor.

"However, at an acting school a fine director can teach you something very important: Learn your lines! Get your moves down pat!

"If the director of an acting school has a very good attitude, then acting school helps. So many boys and girls dream of becoming a star and that's nonsense. They don't realize what hard work it is. A good director is very careful about weeding people out, in six months or a year. He tells a student, 'Forget it! The profession is overcrowded, it's insecure, and you're not going to make it.' Then, the kid can either say he or she is going to make it and to hell with the director or they can say, okay, I tried. I think that is where acting school can be important: weeding out those who are good but not good enough, or not good at all.

"I consider responsibility a very important part of being an actress. I mean my responsibility to my audience. The audience pays ten bucks to watch me give everything I've got to a role. I cannot stand actors who goof around, fool around on stage, doing their little funnies, their little in-jokes. That's not an actor's job."

I asked her what it means to be a star.

"'Star' is only a word. A star is only for one play, and you've got a small part in the next one, probably as a character. Let's take Chekhov's *The Three Sisters.*The first time I played it I was thirty-three and I played Mascha, and that is considered a plum role for an actress. She is romantic, passionate, and beautiful. I played her and I played her well. The next time I was in the same play I was cast as the eighty-three-year-old peasant servant. It wasn't a big role at all but I loved it. A so-called star the first time, a character part the next time. Playing a small role like that, you don't get any recognition, but I still felt it was great to be playing probably one of the oldest women in any play. Playing a bit part—that golden old lady—doesn't diminish me in my mind.

"A glamorous beauty, once her looks begin to fade, loses that thing she must project. But an actress can go on as long as she's happy and as long as she's healthy. She will still get good parts. And, more important, she'll be doing something she loves to do."

Lillian poured herself a gin and tonic and brought me coffee and I asked, "Do actors resent a producer bringing in people from New York or the West End to play the lead in a Vancouver production?"

She said, "If a producer or a director knows that an actor or actress can do a better job that anyone local can, and if that person is available, then he should try and bring him in. He may not succeed, but I think he should try. I have worked with some of the finest actors from the United States and England here in Vancouver and I never resented them. I usually found them to be fine people and great actors, and I was grateful to work with them because anybody can learn a lot from people like that. There should be no resentment. After all, while the producer is trying to present the best play he can, he also has to make money on that play or there would be no theater. But if a producer brings in a person who may be a huge success but is wrong for that particular play, and therefore he is just in the game to make a lot of money and to hell with the quality, then actors will resent that person. Human nature, isn't it?

"Another thing. I once did an important radio drama with Dame Peggy Ashcroft, who is one of the biggest names in the theater in the world, and it was a treat. Charming, about seventy, a great lady. But what made us so proud, the Vancouver people in the cast, was that we could keep up with her and she told us so. I thought, if she says this, we must be good. But what does the big time theater world think of Vancouver? Well..."

"Back to critics?"

"Okay. As I said, I don't have much use for them. I certainly would if I knew they were honest and sincere and knew something about the theater. Once I went to help Kate Reid in a play being put together in Chicago. I forget the name but it was a good play. Kate is one of North America's finest actresses, but because she chooses to work mostly out of Toronto she is hardly known in the States. There were rewrites, as there always are, and the cast, a good one, worked very hard. It was a good play and the Chicago critics loved it. It went to New York and one man, just one man, Clive Barnes, killed it. One review, dead. One man or any four men should not have this power and in New York, the drama and comedy and musical center of the world, with supposedly the most sophisticated audiences in the world, these men can lead them blindly into a theater for months and months to see a lightweight Neil Simon play, or close the doors to the theater after a couple of performances. A play can run with bad reviews in London for quite awhile, but not in New York.

"Oh, I can't talk about critics. I can only be my own critic.

"Another thing, too many reviewers—and that's what they are, not critics—will beg, borrow, or steal witticisms, clever phrases, or lines from somewhere else and put them in their reviews. Just to show the readers how clever they are. They ignore the play itself. If some scene or act doesn't work, they shouldn't just say it doesn't work; they shouldn't write that it doesn't work—because! If they could tell *why* it doesn't work, I would call them critics instead of reviewers."

It was noon and the children from the nearby school were shouting as they ran across the grass to their homes for lunch and she said, "I love the sound of children shouting. It's so innocent, so nice, so real. I've always regretted that playwrights never put those kind of children in their plays. Of course, you can't have kids stealing all the scenes, can you?" and she grinned.

"Some things I should say. Almost all of the theater groups, work-shops, museums, symphonies—well, almost everything is dependent upon grants, no matter which government gives out the money. That money, the amount given each year, is disappearing. I don't think the money should be in the hands of the politicians, and you can say it is not. It's in the hands of Canada Council and boards and so on. No, in the long run, it is the politicians who control it. And what is a politician? A person who has power and will go to any length to retain it. What do the arts reflect? They reflect the soul of Canada. Not factories, mines, or farmland or freeways or dams. The arts, and the politicians are strangling the arts and that makes me very sad. God knows, I'm not trying to sound highbrow. That's the last thing I am. But it is a rotten shame that what is so important to all of us is in the hands of these grubby little men called politicians.

"And when it is announced that a Hollywood film company is coming to B.C. or Alberta to make a film, everybody cheers. Whoop-dee-doo! Another boost in the film industry. So, the company comes up and hires Canadian technicians, bit players, extras, and the like. Our scale is $138 a day, which may sound good, but remember, we work maybe only four or five days on every film. They bring up their own stars who are paid fantastic sums, just fantastic. We don't get sixty-five-dollar-a-day hotel accommodation with gourmet meals and limousines. We sleep in our own beds, eat a catered noon meal, and drive our cars to and from the set. They pay us in Canadian dollars, so they make 20 percent or so on top of that. The independents love Canada. Great scenery. Good studios. Very good technicians and a large pool of excellent acting talent, so good that Mr. Stabler, who produced the "Huckleberry Finn" TV series, told me he was amazed at the excellence of Canadian actors.

"I said, 'Okay, Mr.Stabler, you who created "Gunsmoke" and other top shows, why don't you come forth with a few bucks to give us a living wage?' He just smiled. He knew what he was doing. Give the peasants a bowl of rice a day. Yes, he just smiled. And he'll be back. I know that. Oh, I get so mad!

"Take our finest actors. Take Christopher Plummer. First rate. He made it big. How many Americans know he is a Canadian?"

"How many Canadians know is he a Canadian? How many care?" I countered.

"And the newspapers! Ooooh! A kid like Deanna Durbin from Winnipeg can be taken down to Los Angeles when she is two by her parents and then she becomes a huge success as a child singing star. She had been down there for forty-five years now, but everytime she does something the papers call her 'Winnipeg's own Deanna Durbin.' She is no more Winnipeg's own than I am Moscow's own.

"Me? If I got a chance to play a role in a Broadway play or in Toronto, if the play was a good one and if the part was good and the money was good, sure, sure I'd go. But, you see, money doesn't mean all that much if you can play good roles here and then you go to New York or Toronto and play one good role and then all you get is lousy ones.

"Another thing, I've got nothing against dinner theater. It is entertainment—but it is certainly not theater. First, they deal in musicals and that is not theater. They condense three hours into forty minutes, just the best songs, maybe four actors, and forget about any plot. But if people go to that, have a nice dinner, a few drinks, and enjoy a musical, such as it is, maybe that will get them into the habit of going to real theater. I've no objection, really. At least four actors are getting jobs and two or three boys are working as technicians. That kind of theater is really an outing, a celebration, and who am I to not wish them a good time.

"And to go back to what I was saying about politicians, I read that more people watch the arts—theater, ballet, symphony—everything the arts entails, professional and amateur—than those who watch sporting events. I found that amazing..."

"I find it astonishing..."

"Well, apparently it is true and when I thought about it, yes, it would be true. So, they've built a huge covered stadium in Vancouver. Government money, every penny of it. How much? Tens of millions of dollars, maybe a hundred million. Who will use this thing? A soccer team that is privately owned and the B.C. Lions. No one else. Maybe two or three high-school track meets a year. Just think the good for Canada if even half that money was spread across the country to make the arts happy and healthy for years. Remember, I said the arts was Canada's soul. The politicians seem to think Canada's soul is a covered stadium with teams of big men kicking a ball around."

Okay, I said, "What does all this add up to?"

"When someone asks me why I am an actress or what I feel about the theater, I would like to express it in eloquent terms. I'm afraid I am not able to do that, but I came across a wonderful statement by a very fine American actress and I'd like to read it."

Lillian found the quotation in a coffee-table book, scanned it quickly, and then began to read in that perfect voice, as though it were the most important speech she had in the most important role she had ever had, and this was it:

> *To constantly take yourself to the centre of all pain, joy and despair, looking into and experiencing raw, the public bleeding, expressing your secrets unashamedly, is both the curse and the blessing of the actor or artist. It forces you to deal every day with insanity, tamper with your own psyche and enter a world beyond your control. For this commitment, society should be grateful. A true and visionary actor or actress can expose the best and the worst in us. And if we are able to accept this perception we can make the next step toward enlightenment.*

But a crazy thing happened. We had been talking into the tape recorder for sixty minutes. Exactly 3,600 seconds. But we needed 3,601 seconds to finish and we didn't get it because the tape clicked off, omitting the word "enlightenment." On the cassette, I printed: "Last word is 'enlightenment.'"

We looked at each other and laughed, and Lillian said, "Perhaps your machine is trying to tell us something."

"That there is no enlightenment in the arts, or from the arts?"

"Yes, that's what I was thinking but I know the tape is wrong. It's just a machine. The arts are here," and she put her hand on her heart. "Here is where enlightenment comes from."

11

Daughter of Joy

*A lot of Deborah Kerr with a delightful dash of Judy Holliday, and
though she is a lady of the night, I knew she was a lady.*

*She said, "The difference between a lady and a tramp is that so
many of these ladies don't know they are tramps, but the tramp knows
she is not a lady."*

*I'm not sure I know what she meant, but obviously she did, and I
feel that she was making a significant contribution to our folklore.*

*Dare we hope she got her millionaire mate, or at the very least her
high-class boutique?*

I know this: you'll never see her on the street…

Daughter of Joy

It was no big deal. A cold and drizzly morning and her squiffy
Triumph was tilted on its cute bottom over a ditch and she was
standing by it, a damsel in distress.

I had caught the 7:00 A.M. *Queen of Oak Bay* at Sidney after
overnighting rather boisterously with old newspaper friends, and just
made the ferry, the last car on before it pulled away for Tswwassen on
the mainland. I seem forever to be fated to either be just catching
ferries or just missing them.

274

At Tswwassen, the cars and trucks sped off the ferry like a full field of thoroughbreds charging for the first turn in a $100,000 handicap, and in their almost bumper-to-bumper race there is no time to stop, let alone see a weary traveler standing by her little red car. She's there, in the corner of your eye, and then you're gone.

As the last car off and dawdling along, I saw her clearly and pulled over and she met me halfway and laughed and said, "Of all mornings. Can you take me to where I can call a cab or…?"

I said, "Jump in. We'll go up to the Texaco Station and they can haul it out with their wrecker and you'll be on your way in half an hour. Okay?"

"No, that's too long. I have an important engagement. Just take me to the garage and they can haul it back to their place. But maybe, if you're going to Vancouver…?"

I said of course, and we went half a mile up the road to the station and we got out and the mechanic approached and I said, "Look, this lady's car, a red Triumph, is half in and half out of the ditch back there and she wants you to haul it out," and I turned and she added, "I don't think there is anything really wrong, but I've got to get into Vancouver, so I'll come out and get it, or send someone, this afternoon or tomorrow morning. Okay?"

The gas station owner had come up and he asked for her driver's license and jotted down her name and address and said, fine, just make sure that, if someone else comes out, they have a note from her and she said okay and we were away.

"Ahhhh," she sighed, relieved, "but I wish I knew what name was on that driver's license. In our hurry I forgot to take it back."

"What do you mean, what name? How many names have you got?"

She said it wasn't so much the name as it was how many driver's licenses she had, and I said I'd had the same license for years and most people I know probably had too.

She didn't pursue it and I asked her if she had been on the ferry since there were not many people on it at that hour and if she had been I certainly would have seen her, and if I had seen her I certainly wouldn't have forgotton her. When I was a kid on the old wild frontier she would have been described as a honey of a looker.

"Oh no. I was just driving a friend to catch the ferry. He's got to be in Victoria for a noon lunch, and trying to get a cab in this miserable weather at eight o'clock in the West End is just impossible. Everybody wants cabs. I said I'd drive him. He got there okay and coming back I skidded on this greasy stuff and zip, off I went. I stood out there for about fifteen minutes and nobody stopped, not even the highway patrol going the other way. He just waved. The bastard."

Certainly a logical explanation if ever there was one.

A lot more logical than the driver's license business.

We scooted through the Massey Tunnel in silence. Why does everybody shut up when going through a tunnel? Then the wide and puddle-spotted vegetable fields of Richmond came into view, and despite the heavy drizzle about forty Chinese women in their wide bamboo hats were weeding asparagus or celery or bok choy.

"Stoop labor. Two bucks an hour. Almost as hard as working in a wet, condemned coal mine," and she said, "I know. I did it one summer when I was a kid in Moose Jaw. I think I got two bits an hour, maybe less."

I laughed. "Maybe less. I worked in the harvest fields in Manitoba for a buck fifty for an eleven-hour day." Then I asked did she know so-and-so in Moose Jaw but added that she probably didn't because when they got back from the war, if they had any brains, they took off. The brainless are still there. "That's why it's in the shape it is now. Looks like a ghost town. Didn't it have a slogan like 'The Gateway to Golden Opportunity?' Something like that. There was a loony newspaperman on city council, I remember, and he was always thinking up big slogans and ideas to get industry in. He got a few, I think, but when an industry moved in it passed a bigger one moving out. Hah! Moose Jaw, the company town of the C.P.R. and Maple Leaf Flour Mills. Both gone now."

She laughed and said, "Still it was my home town." Then she pointed to my tape recorder. "Whazzat?"

"My tape recorder. I carry it wherever I go."

"Why? Are you a writer?"

I said I was and she suddenly was interested and asked what I had done, expecting nothing. Obviously I told her and she exclaimed, "Why, I know you. I've got several of your books. You know, my dear old mother back in Moose Jaw would slay dragons for an autographed copy of *Ten Lost Years.* I'll buy another next time I'm in Duthie's."

Traffic was not heavy up Oak Street and over the Granville Bridge and I soon drew up to the apartment she directed me to. I might have guessed it, judging from that car and her clothes and the way she talked. Twenty storeys high, luxury suites at luxury prices, indoor and outdoor swimming, saunas, jacuzzis, hot tubs, wet-bar recreational room.

She got out and thanked me and handed me a blank card, business card size, with her phone number on it and asked me to call her in about a week and come over about noon. She said she didn't function until then. We'd have a bite to eat and I could sign the books. She said books, not book.

As I drove out to Kitsilano I tried to place her. Model? Possibly, but not likely. A bit too old. Body too mature. About thirty-five. Superpersonal secretary to the president of MacMillan Bloedel? Naw. Successful business woman. Look at those clothes and that purse and that diamond ring. You don't buy those from Army and Navy. I gave up, not realizing I had probably missed the obvious, the most likely.

A week passed and the phone rang about 10:00 A.M. and a voice said, "Hi, remember me? The lady with the red Triumph in the ditch?"

I said sure and asked her how she got my telephone number. She giggled and said that was easy because my name was on the six books she had in front of her; the tough part had been picking the *B* out of the six Broadfoots in the telephone book. "C'mon over for lunch if you're free," she said, and gave me the number of the apartment.

I buzzed at noon and identified myself and pushed open the security door and got off at the fifteenth floor and knocked at 1503.

"Welcome to the Hacienda Enchilada." She grinned and took my raincoat and hung it in the closet. My trained reporter's eye noticed there were about six other raincoats there.

She said, "My friends sometimes forget they wore one," and she held out her hand and said, "My name's Melissa. Welcome. Just parade over there to the coffee table and get your writing hand in shape. I'll be right with you," and moments later she came back with a pitcher of Bloody Marys, some kind of crackers, and an avocado paste.

"Now," suddenly all business, "this one is to 'Mary's mother' and say something nice…"

"Mary? You just said your name was Melissa."

"Mary in Moose Jaw. Melissa in Vancouver. Now write."

Then there was "Charles" and "Blinkey" and "Sarah" and "Fearless Fosdick," and, handing me the last book, she said, "Okay, that's my Christmas shopping done. Now this one is for me."

"Mary or Melissa?"

"No name, just something good. Okay?"

After signing six books I had to dredge through my bag of tricks and literary skills to come up with something appropriate and I wrote, "Towards morning, even the girls from Moose Jaw get lucky."

She giggled, gathered up her books, and said she'd be back in ten minutes with food. As she muttered and purred in the kitchen I sipped my drink and looked about. Yes, this was class. Beautiful antique furniture. A fireplace ready for a match. Excellent French Impressionist prints on the walls. Rich drapes.

Over the fireplace hung an abstract, in reds and rust and dark purples and splattered with dots of yellow and greens. About two feet long by eighteen inches deep, it drew your attention and I didn't know why. I saw her looking at me from the doorway and she said, "The abstract. Look away from it for thirty seconds then look back for a minute, and then look away for another thirty seconds and then look back."

I did and the second time I looked at it, the words "Fuck You" jumped out from the swirled-up mass of clanging colors.

"I'll be damned," I said and asked where she got it and she answered "a friend did it for me. I had it here for two months before what you just read now appeared for me. You have to look at it a certain way at different times before it works. It's magic. I love it."

She went back into the kitchen and I could hear her bustling about. I looked back at the painting and the two words weren't there. Just that awful two feet by eighteen inches.

Melissa called, "C'mon, soup's on," but she pronounced it, the French way, *soupçon*, with the cedilla.

I went toward the kitchen and there was a small dining alcove I hadn't seen, hidden by the half wall of the living room. We had shrimp salad, a small grilled steak, wafers, a good cheese and tea.

"You know, I love this view." She swept her arm toward the reach of English Bay with its two lines of anchored ships, a convoy to nowhere, waiting patiently for wharfage so they could load prairie grain for the ports of the world.

"Every morning when I wake up I feel like a million bucks and when I eat breakfast and look at that view, the sea, the mountains, the big white clouds, I feel like two million bucks. So I call that my million-dollar-extra view. I'm just a prairie girl at heart."

"Look," I said, "I don't want to be rude but are you a..."

She cut me off with a snort of a laugh and and said, "Right the first time. Only you won't find me in *Roget's Thesaurus* under 'prostitute.' You have to look under 'whore.' It's got a lot of names for gals like us. The one I like most is 'daughter of joy.' Isn't that rich? Lovely. So, now you know. Just put the words 'high class' in front of it."

I told her I had no intention of doing otherwise and she continued. "That ridiculous painting—I'll bet it is the topic of many a tiddly conversation in the Timber Club, the Vancouver Club, the Union Club in Victoria, and all the nice places where the elite meet to eat, as Archie of Duffie's Tavern would say. And if you want to ask me about me and my friends, and I know you do, don't insult my intelligence about how I got into this lovely and very expensive apartment and I won't debase my opinion of you by thinking that's what you might be thinking of doing. Okay? Olay! After you drove me home last week I thought I might do a little public relations work for girls like me, daughters of joy. Want to listen?"

"Sorry I didn't bring my tape recorder," and she replied, "Bring it next time when you come to lunch. Just to lunch, you understand. This is going to be a long story. I'll start now.

"First of all, they call it the oldest profession. I'm jiggered if I know who invented that. Some writer, I guess. Maybe Dickens. Maybe Thackeray. Maybe Chaucer for all I know. He knew quite a bit about us. If lawyers and doctors are in a profession, I suppose we have a perfect right to be too," and again that snort of laughter. "Some of my best friends are..."

"Why do you call them 'friends'? Why not 'marks' or 'Johns' or even 'clients?'"

She sipped her tea and said, "Because they are my friends. This daughter of joy gives them happiness and fun, and the only difference between myself and another girl is they pay me. Well. I respect them for their success and they respect me for mine. They use crooked lawyers and crooked accountants and crooked everything every which way to get where their wives want them to be. Mr. Big, each in his own world—big company, big job, big house, big cottage in the islands, big boat, big car, big reputation. I used whatever God gave me, plus my knowledge of men and on top of that, years of hard work, rising from the bottom to the top like those funny fellows in Horatio Alger books.

"I suppose it is the oldest profession, if it can be called that. Once, I suppose, when the world was young, there was a long row of caves at the bottom of a cliff, and the one at the far end was the home of the prettiest cavegirl in caveman land. And every week or so, every one of those hairy cavemen with the underslung jaws and wearing bearskins would sneak into her cave and have his way with her, as the storybooks say, and leave a hunk of saber-tooth tiger meat or a necklace pounded out of a hunk of quartz and strung together with animal gut. As old as that. It hasn't been refined all that much, you know. The principle is still the same."

"Melissa, well put. You'd make a hell of a good public relations type for a multi-corporation."

"Right, so on with the interview. This is fun. You know, of course, that I'm going to be changing a lot of names and dates and rearranging quite a bit of landscape, but isn't that what history is? A lot of embroidering of the fact. Well, this is fact, Melissa's way."

The phone tinkled, and when she came back after a few minutes of talking she said, "A friend. He's coming over in an hour. A girl has to make a living. I've got time to throw this stuff in the washer and clean up the ashtrays and then, frolic with an alcoholic. Two in the afternoon and he's got a buzz on. A nice guy, though. So shove off, Barry, and I'll be calling you soon. I've enjoyed this. Melissa, the daughter of joy, lets her hair down in defense of her profession. Next time, lobster bisque. I'm a whiz at making lobster bisque—just the thing for businessmen with tired blood and greedy wives and who just want a few scotches, some good talk before the fire, a snack of my famous lobster bisque, and... ho hay, olay!"

On the way home I stopped at Dino's for a beer and made some furiously fast notes and put down some questions. How old? Well educated? No doubt. Just look at her bookshelves—no *Readers' Digest* condensed volumes there. The prints, the crystal, the antiques. Her taste in food. The Royal Doulton. The grandfather's clock, worth at least three grand. The manners. The hair styling, twice a week? The New York fashions, by way of Paris or Rome. That would be my guess. Her casual mention of the most prominent and prestigious men's clubs in the province. No harlot, this one. No ordinary whore. No daughter of joy. No courtesan because that type was one man's property. The dictionary didn't have a word for this one. Wrapping it all up in a little tight ball, the question begged to be asked. How much? And she sure as hell wouldn't call it a "trick." Perhaps, "an hour of pleasure" with composure, using the dictionary term for it, "serenity, calmness." Yet beneath it all there was fire. I dropped the rolled-up page of questions into the ashtray and left.

I was working on a book, laboriously transcribing tapes, and I forgot about her until the phone rang at ten one morning and I knew it was her. "Hi! The lobster bisque whiz. How about lunch today. Free?"

I said yes and she told me to drop by at noon. When she opened the door she grinned and said, "I've got four more books for you to sign. Had a hell of a time finding them. Looked all over town. I'll make you rich in spite of yourself." She pointed to the table. "Start signing. One to 'Greg,' a cousin in Toronto. Forgot him. The others to 'Monique' and 'Trish' and 'Gabrielle.' All ladies like me and I've never sent them anything before, but this I know they'll enjoy."

I though a moment and in each of the three I wrote, "May your houris be all pleasure," and she laughed and said, "I got it. They will too. Especially Trish. She knows more than the professors who taught her at McGill."

After a Bloody Mary and an excellent bisque we returned to the living room. Lighting a cigarette—she hadn't smoked before and I lifted a questioning eyebrow—she said, "I'm a little nervous. I shouldn't have been thinking of what I'm going to say. Just say it. This thing, this cigarillo, is just to keep my hand occupied, like the way those snooty British army officers in those movies about Injah always carry a swagger stick to remind them that it represents some kind of command or responsibility; but really it is just to keep them on balance because they tend to tip to port a lot."

We laughed.

"Where's the tape recorder?"

"Didn't bring it. Photographic memory. Saves a lot of hard work, transcribing."

"Okay. How much do I make? I won't tell you because I can't. A lot of money, a lot. This dress, courtesy of a nice charge account at

Madame Runge's paid up to date monthly by a friend. That lighter, diamonds and rubies galore. Worth a thousand. This ring. Insurance, a million on my life. A big bundle of stock certificates. A little guy from Howe Street toddles up here about once a month and bounces around for awhile and then has a shower and leaves, and when he goes out the door, he'll hand me another envelope and say, 'Here, kiddo, they aren't worth much now but save 'em and when I tell you to sell, you sell. You sell.' When he's gone I'll look and it will be a share certificate, to bearer, for a thousand or two thousand of this or that. Stuff I never heard of. I like him, even though he chews gum. At least he doesn't wear a bow tie. Nobody gets through that door if he's got a bow tie. I say take it off or don't come in. No man can look anything but foolish in one of those. Look at Lester Pearson, the former prime minister. He wore a bow tie. The papers said it was his trademark. Maybe so, but he'd never have got a foot inside my door with it on. Besides, what did he do for the country? Like the rest, a big fat nothingski.

"Anyway, I make a lot of money, but a lot goes out too. I write down a bunch of figures and then I cut that by 40 percent and I put down all my expenses and this apartment and my accountant says, 'Judy, you just can't bring me a bunch of meaningless figures and expect me to make sense of them and get them by the department of revenue guys.'"

I interrupted: "Judy?"

She thought for a moment. "Oh, that's the name I use with him. 'Melissa' with you. 'Mary' with my folks. A dozen other names, for a dozen different reasons. It beats all to hell sometimes trying to keep track, but it seems to work. Anyway, I say what I do is a business. Some of my friends sell oil and another is a clothier, selling made-in-Taiwan crap, and another is getting a whole lot of money by standing up before a judge and saying, 'Your Worship, my client wishes to plead guilty.' They're businessmen. I'm a businesswoman. See? My accountant say, 'Okay, Judy' and two weeks later he asks me for a check for so much and then three months later the revenue people say they want two thousand more and I send off a check and that's it for another year. It's like a stupid game, you see. Everybody knows everybody else is scoring; but if things work out 75 percent right, then everyone is happy. If I ran my business like the government does in this regard, I'd be five and tenning it down on Cordova with a crib in the Avalon Rooms.

"Back to oblivion. My father was a dirt farmer south of Moose Jaw. The Dirty Thirties—*you* know them, the book—blew his farm way off into Ontario, and the government bought his starving cows for a cent a pound on the hoof and fed the tough meat to the kids in the soup kitchens. The implement companies took back his rusted equipment and the Royal Bank of Canada took back his half-section; but the chief accountant in the bank in town tipped him off and he loaded everything he and Mother had in the house into the truck. It wasn't much, I guess. He turned the horses out into the wheat that never grew that year and I guess he only had enough gas to get into Moose Jaw because that's where they stopped. He was on relief and worked at odd jobs and they got by, somehow. God knows how. The war came along and he was probably the first guy waiting the next morning in line at the armory in Regina. He went overseas, First Division, and was there until '44, when they shipped him back with a smashed elbow and gave him a pension. With his credits he started a small welding business in a friend's garage. I was born in '46. I get all this from my mother. He died in '50. That welding machine—he was beginning to get ahead and it exploded and he was dead. My mother is alive, in Moose Jaw, happy as a clam. Daughter Mary, that's me, is a success in the business world. Mary sends her Mom two hundred and fifty dollars, two tricks, at Christmas and some flowers and two pounds of that Christmas cake they make at the little shop on Robson Street and she phones her on her birthday and writes every two months. Mom is in an old folks' home and is happy reading *The National Enquirer* and the multiple sins of Elizabeth Taylor, playing bingo three times a week, and eating herself toward two hundred pounds. Yes, she's happy as a clam. Okay, that's the first part. Okay?"

"Okay, and now I know how much you charge. Two tricks, 250 bucks. Right?"

"Used to be. Other considerations are involved now, like the rising cost of living, the falling Canadian dollar, and the price of tea in China. Don't go so fast. I knew what I was doing when I said that."

I wanted to look at that picture to see if those incredible words would leap out at me, but when I did I lost my concentration on what she was saying.

"Okay, what next? Just tell it the way you'd tell a friend."

"You are my friend. Don't I feed you my famous lobster bisque, and do you know the cost of lobster today? Fine, back on the track, Mac. I went through school in a breeze and in grade nine my teacher heard I was going to take the commercial course and she pleaded with me for half an hour to take the classics, Latin and such. But I said no.

"I breezed through ten and eleven. I was the fastest typist and the fastest at shorthand in the class, played volleyball, worked on the school annual, wrote dumb poems to a boy in class but never signed my name. Naturally. Don't give him the advantage. I wasn't asked to the graduation dance because, I found out later, every guy thought every other guy had asked me and they couldn't stand being turned down. I sat home and cried that night and my mother took my graduation dance dress out of my closet and put it in a box and said, 'Never mind, dear, things happen. Your sister can wear this two years from now. She'll grow into it by then.' I could have wrung her neck. A drink is called for after that little display of nostalgia, don't you think?"

She went to the bar in the corner and I stared at the painting but nothing happened. I lit a cigarette and took the scotch and water as she said, "Chivas Regal—nothing but the best for my friends."

Melissa said she had $275 dollars saved, a huge sum, and it had meant long hours into the night working at the town's first drive-in, babysitting in the winter, taking tickets at the hockey rink for the town's junior hockey club games, and raffling off a fur stole an uncle in Toronto set her as a Christmas present. Right out of the blue, she said. She sold three hundred tickets at two bits each on the fur and pulled down seventy-five bucks.

"Even then I had a few smarts. I thought it was an original idea but it was as old as the hills. A lot of people did it during the Depression."

A week after the graduation dance she high-tailed it forty miles down the Trans-Canada Highway to Regina and enrolled in a commercial course. She was still a virgin, but wondering.

"Maybe Moose Jaw didn't have many bright lights—Railway Street which I never set foot on, two hotels, three Chinese restaurants, and a bunch of drunks—but Regina was no better. Talk about bush. The only thing they could be proud of was a football team and the best players and the best-paid players were Americans, who were treated like kings and acted like Genghis what's-his-face."

"Khan."

"Thank you. Oh yes, there was the dammed-up glorified slough they called Wascana Lake, and on Sunday afternoon it was pure joy to walk around the lake and watch the ducks acting like what they were, dumb ducks. There wasn't a decent restaurant I could afford and my landlady in the boarding house used to hide behind the clothestree in the hall to catch the girls if they came in after eleven. Midnight on Saturday. Even if a boy had asked me out for dinner and a show on Friday night it wouldn't have been much fun because I would have been afraid of the Dragon Lady waiting in ambush."

The first job she applied for was hers, Little Miss Everything at a new and used farm implement dealership in the north end of town. The owner, an elderly man, looked her over before he looked at her credentials and references and said the pay was $150 a month and said she was getting more than he normally paid. From then on, it was the same story.

"After two weeks in that mess he called an office I had it cleaned up and humming right along. Answer the phone, write out checks, type a letter, lick the stamp, polish the handle on the big front door, do my nails, yawn, snore. Boring. Then one day the boss told me were going to Saskatoon. Wow! My longest trip. He had business there and needed me to take shorthand. It was in October, the weather was beautiful, I enjoyed the drive. We got there about three in the afternoon and the business lasted half an hour. He could have done it by phone in fifteen minutes. For half of the thirty minutes he and this other fellow talked about duck hunting. Anyway, he said it was too late to go back to Regina that night so we checked into a hotel, got rooms, and then went to dinner. I was happy. The dinner was good and he was fun, telling a lot of jokes. As you can imagine, of course, he just accidentally on purpose found a bottle of rye in his car and we had a few drinks. Then, a few for me was more than enough. So it happened. We went to bed and about midnight he moved into his room next door and that was it.

"On the drive back next morning I remember saying to myself, 'Well, you aren't a virgin, but is that really all there is to it?' Wow, but was I every dumb.

"Next week, it was the same thing, but this time it wasn't the boss but Parky, the sales manager and top salesman. There was no trip to Saskatoon and no dinner. It was to a motel. They weren't much in those days, believe me, but nice enough. This time it was better. Parky was young and had been around. This is not as ugly as it sounds.

Today, it would be nothing but then it was a different story. I enjoyed that night, and when he got home it was up to him to convince his wife he had been playing poker. This went on for quite a while. I wasn't doing it to keep my job or get a raise, although I got a thirty-dollar-a-month hike soon after. I was learning something and enjoying myself and I figured the big pash, the one true love, the man I would marry, would come later. In the meantime, I guess you could say I was practicing.

"Then I stepped over the line. That line immediately becomes a high fence and rather hard to climb back over. Parky asked if I would go out with a wealthy young farmer, from Davidson. I said fine and he was a cute guy, but still a farm boy. We had dinner, a few drinks in a motel, and then away we went. About three in the morning he got out of bed and dressed and I asked, 'What about me?' Meaning, wasn't he going to drive me home? He said, 'It's there on the dresser,' and left. I saw the envelope and there were two twenties in it. That was fantastic. It was almost as much as I was making a week answering phones, writing letters, et cetera, and boring.

"I somehow walked home and got past the Dragon Lady. I sat on my bed and looked at that envelope and said, 'Well, if you didn't know it before you know it now. You're a prostitute.' I maybe used the word 'whore,' but now I just can't bring myself to use the word. To me, there is a big difference between the two words. A whore is what you see peddling in downtown Vancouver or Calgary or Edmonton. I mean they have a whore's mentality."

I asked, "What do you mean?"

She got up and went to the window and beckoned me over and there was English Bay, the afternoon sun polishing it to the brightness of the buttons on a Dutchman's coat and there was the dark mass of the North Shore mountains and above, fluffy clouds drifting west like sheep grazing in a pasture and far to the west, the purple outline of the peaks of Vancouver Island.

"A whore wouldn't appreciate all that," she said, and as she spoke, one of the freighters blew a puff of dark diesel smoke and began to edge out of line and steam slowly toward First Narrows and Vancouver Harbor.

"Hurray!" she laughed. "Trudeau is finally getting the economy going again."

Things moved fast after the farm boy. She got herself a small but neat apartment near the downtown area and worked two days a week at the implement company, which she said was all the work that was needed. She took a modeling course, although the owner of the agency really knew nothing about modeling but a lot about other things. He introduced her to visiting businessmen and local types, and she giggled and said, "You know for two years I stayed in Regina I never got forty dollars again. That was a fluke, and the one thing that moved me along. I've often wondered: suppose that farm boy from Davidson had only left me fifteen dollars. Would I have considered it worth my while to break away?"

The end came when she was twenty-two and a local character tried to move in as her pimp. He wasn't going to take no for an answer and, thoroughly scared, she packed all her movable goods into her car and slept in a motel that night and at ten next morning she was at the bank when the doors opened and drew out $3,794 and her savings bonds and some oil stocks and by ten-thirty she was on the highway, driving west to Calgary.

"I'll tell you, I hate pimps. As far as I'm concerned I can't think of a lower form of life. I've never had a pimp and I'll quit if I have to have one. Some girls do, you know. They think of them as kind of a husband. For that matter, I won't have a colored guy come to this apartment, or an Indian or an East Indian. I don't think I'm a racist but if high-class restaurants and clubs by fair means or foul can exclude Negroes and Indians, then so can I. Why shouldn't I? I'm a businesswoman. I just won't do it, although I might make an exception for an Arabian oil sheik."

She went to Calgary because it was the most exciting place in Canada in those days, and she splurged on clothes and accessories and rented a good furnished apartment. Yes, she admitted, it was rough at times, but she survived quite nicely, thank you. She worked the two best hotels, guided by a girl from Toronto who had been in the boom town for two years and knew the ropes.

"Jeanine was very, very kind to me. She took me around to parties and introduced me to a lot of wonderful people and I played Lady Vere de Vere and after a couple of years my new apartment, a much bigger and nicer one, became a place where quite a few of those hotshot young millionaires liked to come. I'd have nice music on the hi-fi and I'd serve them a couple of drinks and a sandwich, and if they wanted to smoke a little grass, I had it there. If two fellows—say one from Calgary and one from his head office in Houston or Tulsa—wanted to come over, I'd phone Jeanine or one of the other girls. Sometimes Jeanine and I would fly up to Edmonton for the weekend. It was booming, too, but not with the wheeler-dealers and the make-a-million-in-a-hurry guys because Edmonton was more the service center for the oil industry. But there was a lot of money there, too. There's three okay hotels there and we'd rotate—it was just a case of getting to know the night manager and clerk and the head bellboys and leaving a ten-dollar tip for the maid and letting her take home any liquor we had left in the rooms. Believe me, in life it is the little things that count and they don't cost all that much money either. It is unbelievable the shallowness of human greed."

She looked at her watch and said she had an appointment in an hour and a half so we'd have to cut this visit short. "He's a funny little man. Every Friday at three o'clock for one hour. He's precisely on time and he comes in that door, says 'Good afternoon,' and goes into the bedroom and takes off his clothes down to his underwear. He puts on a bathrobe and slippers he keeps here and when he comes out I've got a scotch, three ounces of water. no ice, waiting for him and three halves of cling peaches and a plate of buttered melba toast. He eats that and drinks his scotch slowly. Little sip-sips. And I read to him…"

I interrupted, "You do *what*?"

She giggled, "I read to him. He loves Dickens. We're doing *Little Dorrit* now," and she walked over to the bookcase and took out a book and said, "You see. *Little Dorrit*." She flicked a white piece of paper, "I've got it flagged. Here is where we're at now. After fifteen minutes of reading I make another scotch, weak, and he chuckles at parts. I don't see anything funny. It really is a sad story. But he's a funny little dry stick of a man. He speaks so seldom you'd think each word was worth ten dollars. But I like him and if I told you his name you'd jump out of your skin. He's worth a great deal of money. Most Scotsmen I know are when they're up around his age."

"Kinky?"

"Good grief, Charlie Brown, no. Sometimes we don't even go into the bedroom and when we do, there is really nothing to it. Bang, like that. Amazing. Then he gets dressed and he is at that door at exactly four o'clock. I suspect he's got a chauffeur down there. And when I bolt the door there is this envelope. I put the book on the bookcase and he puts the envelope in the book. A very precise man. A dear, really. I like him a lot. And he is very, very generous. I must have read a dozen books to him."

I said, "Okay, Melissa, let's get back to Calgary."

"Yes, two, no three important things happened in those seven or eight years. This is not one of those things but I made a lot of money and I made a lot of friends and I moved to another lovely apartment and I bought a Mercedes. I keep it in a garage. The Triumph is a fun car. But the first thing, Jeanine one day asked me if I wanted to move in with her. She had a bigger apartment and she was very beautiful and successful. She must have made a least $10,000 from one big company alone and all she had to do was be hostess at their special parties for the big shots from Toronto and New York and Texas. Anyway, she asked me to move in and I told her I was happy where I was and asked her why and she said, 'I think it is time you and I became lovers.' Just like that. Lovers.

"I had been around a lot by that time and I guess I had seen everything, but somehow I had never thought of that. I really hadn't, although I had seen a lot of it around. I had actually been propositioned three or four times by some pretty rich and persnickety ladies in Calgary, but this was different. I told her no, and it took ten minutes to say it, but she just said, 'Oh, that's okay. I thought it would be a nice way to do things, seeing as we're such good friends.' Now, that was the first thing and I still don't know why it made an impression on me."

I didn't tell her, but I felt I could make an educated guess.

She said, "The second thing, I nearly got married. Shocked you, didn't I? Jim was a nice guy. That's not his name, by the way. He was just short of thirty-eight, a big, good-looking fellow. He had started off on his own in the oil business and he had made a lot of money. A *lot* of money. He was divorced and his ex was living in California. She would fly up to Calgary about three times a year and give him one hell of a hard time. He used to describe her as 'walking evil.' There was a son somewhere on the West Coast who had gone there to count his beads and do his own thing and let it all hang out, and he had messed his head up with LSD. A lawyer out there had got hold of him and was giving the old man more hard time. There was a daughter at some finishing school in France and all he would say about her was: 'Just like her mother.'

"The poor guy was a mess himself, because of these three people. He used to come to my place two or three times a week and always he brought me fresh white daisies and he said daisies meant innocence, purity, and loyalty. He wore me down and I said, 'Okay, but you know I can never enter Calgary society and he used to say, 'Calgary society? What is that? Never heard of it.'

"We were going to fly in his plane to Kelowna and get married, and then after I said yes, I thought for three whole days and I was a wreck. When he came over, with his little handful of daisies again, I told him I would say it quickly; I told him no, I couldn't marry him. He started crying and I started crying and there were tears all over the place. Then we had a couple of drinks each and went to bed and, you know, when he left, I think he was very sad but also relieved."

She got up and moved to the window and stood there for several long moments; then she snorted out that laugh and yelled, "C'mon Trudeau, get those freighters moving, eh?"

I left then and it was another two weeks before she phoned and said to come on up. After a drink and salad and a crab something-or-other I said, "Last time you said something about a third thing in Calgary, something that happened?"

"Oh yes, a couple of months after my crying jag with my oilman two big shots from Dallas called up Jeanine and said they were kicking around town on the long weekend and did she know of a friend, and the four of us would scoot out to Vancouver. They had their own executive jet. On Friday afternoon we took off and God, how that thing could move. We booked into the Bayshore here and it was drizzling and gloomy. Next morning when we got up I looked out the window and saw those mountains and the snow on them and the harbor with all the little tugs and big ships and I said, 'My God, has this been here all my life?' We had just one big wonderful and expensive weekend. The money they must have spent. Wow! On the huge suite, on the food, on us. Wheee!"

Over our Spanish coffee Melissa said that when she got back to Calgary she began preparations to move, and within two months she was in her apartment in the West End and picking up the routine again.

"I had just oodles of money. I kept it in four different banks. You know, somebody just might get suspicious. Some snoopy bank teller. I didn't need that. In fact, I haven't had any trouble, ever. Once, when I was dining alone in the International Inn in Calgary a waiter came up and gave me a note. Somebody wanted to see me in the lobby. I finished and sitting in a big chair was a big cop. I didn't know him but he asked me to go for a short walk. He was plainclothes but had cop written all over him. He said his name was Fritzy and he was on the vice squad. Like Aitch he was. He didn't mince words; he said he knew of me. I said, so what? Well, I was to pay up or else. God, how crude! I told this big Kraut I was an independent businesswoman and I had the income tax declarations to prove it, and if he made one more move, even the tiniest move, I would go straight to the chief, whom I had met at parties and I knew to be a square shooter, and I would spell it out for the chief in capital letters and if he wasn't back on a motorbike on the four-to-midnight shift next day I would be very much surprised. That's all that ever happened in that way. I mean, nothing happened.

"So, like I said, I moved to Vancouver. A couple of months getting this apartment just the way I wanted it and getting to know the superintendent and getting to know some of the *maître d*'s at the best spots and people who could help me. I did throw a lot of money around that was not tax deductible but it is all part of doing business.

"Oh, yes, I loved Vancouver from the start. A few days and you get the flavor of it, and what a flavor. Calgary was clubby and grubby in many ways. This town is high, wide and handsome. It seems so many people have sixty-footers. Three couples on a weekend cruising through the islands and up the sound. Wonderful shops and great restaurants. Ooooh, I just had this town for breakfast, lunch and dinner. Seafood. Chinese, Japanese. I nearly went off the deep end.

"I also found I had a lot of friends here. The Calgary grapevine to Vancouver was jangling away and I got established quickly. Everybody was generous. You know, I don't ask for it, like saying it costs such and such and getting it as they come through the door. After one visit they know what kind of a place I have and what I am and what they can expect. If they want it real kinky or barfy, then let them go down to Georgia and Howe at night and cruise by and stop and swing open the passenger-side door and let whatever scruff that is standing there jump in. No, not me. They know it. If they don't first treat me as a human, a person, and a lady, they've got to do it the next time or that is it," and she chopped her hand down hard on the coffee table.

"Then why that picture?"

"Bothers you, doesn't it? Oh, that's my little joke on the world."

I looked around the living room, so tastefully decorated, so feminine, so right, her home, and nodded.

"You know, I have been very brief about all this. You don't just tell everything in three or four hours. Of course, there have been bad times, and I guess there always will be. But they are mostly within myself. I can handle those times. I know I have a life that few understand. There is a girl two floors down and sometimes she comes up in the morning and we sit around and drink coffee and talk, girl talk, and she has said often, 'You know, I'll never understand you. How did you ever get into our business?' and she laughed.

"Imagine, that's what every girl expects the man, the client, to ask, and here she's asking it and she's one of us, a daughter of joy. She can't seem to get off the subject. It really bugs her.

"I said to you once it may seem to be a sordid business. Really, it isn't for me. I know that if I marry I'll probably have to move out of this town with all his money and all of mine, and I've got quite a bit. Victoria, maybe. Travel. Maybe a couple of months on Maui and down to Mexico. Maybe a little boutique I could run somewhere. The dream of so many of us, as near as I can figure out. I'm going to be losing my looks one of these days, and my body tone, but I'll tell you this—I'll never lose my class. That took a long time to acquire. From Moose Jaw to here and, in the long run, I think I'm pretty much the same person I was then as I am now. Except, one hell of a lot smarter and one hell of a lot richer.

"I suppose I'll marry. I could right now, you know. Jeanine writes and says that man in Calgary is still waiting. Yes, I think I'd like to marry. No children, thank you, and the Lord protect me from French poodles. If I marry he'll have to be rich and I'll have to like him. Not love, but like. I don't want a man who, when he gets me into his bed the first time, asks, 'Where has she been all my life?' and then when we're finished, he asks himself, 'What has she been doing all her life?' No, give me a man I like and who likes me. Love will come later."

She pushed out her arm and a small but perfect watch peeked out from the cuff of her beige cashmere sweater and said, "*Little Dorrit* time in less than an hour. He gave me this watch, by the way. I have things to do, so goodbye," and she stood up and gave me her hand, a cool and soft hand, a very calm, a very serene, beautiful lady.

At the door she said, "You've got all you want?"

I said, "I think you've told me about only a tenth, but it is enough because I know that's all you want me to know. You should write a book. I'll provide the professional editing."

That snort of laughter again. "Now *that* will be the day."

"Thanks for the nice lunches and the good talk, Melissa."

"And thank you for the ride that nasty morning," she smiled and closed the door, and I heard the bolt snick into the deadlock, as definite and final as if we had been walking down Robson Street and she suddenly turned left on Thurlow and disappeared, forever.